To
Marvin Dumon
Complements of
Curry Foundation
2/25/85

Agriculture, Stability, and Growth
Toward A Cooperative Approach

Charles E. Curry
Chairman

William Patrick Nichols
Director

Reports From A Public Policy Study of the Curry Foundation

Agriculture, Stability, and Growth

Toward A Cooperative Approach

Charles E. Curry
Chairman

William Patrick Nichols
Director

Reports From A Public Policy Study of the Curry Foundation

ASSOCIATED FACULTY PRESS / 1984
Port Washington, N.Y. • New York City • London

MANUFACTURED IN THE UNITED STATES OF AMERICA

Published by
Associated Faculty Press, Inc.
Port Washington, N.Y.

Library of Congress Cataloging in Publication Data

Main entry under title:

Agriculture, stability, and growth

Includes bibliographies.
1. Agriculture and State—United States.
2. Agriculture—Economic aspects—International cooperation. I. Curry Foundation.
HD1761.A625 1984 338.1'873 84-16858
ISBN 0-8046-9383-8

Contents

Contributors

MARTIN ABEL is president of Abel, Daft, and Early of Washington, D.C., and was deputy assistant secretary for international affairs at the U.S. Department of Agriculture during the Johnson Administration.

HAROLD BREIMYER is professor and extension economist, University of Missouri (Columbia), formerly staff economist for the Agricultural marketing Service, U.S. Department of Agriculture.

THOMAS H. CHRISTENSEN is manager for market analysis for Veliscol Chemical Corporation of Chicago, formerly project manager for the Agricultural Model at Michigan State University.

LYNN DAFT is vice president of Abel, Daft, and Early of Washington, D.C., and was associate director of the domestic policy staff, the White House, during the Carter administration.

BRUCE GARDNER is professor of agricultural and resource economics at the University of Marlaynd.

JOSEPH HAJDA is professor of political science and chairman of international trade studies at Kansas State University, formerly agriculture trade advisor to the Office of Special Representative to the President for Trade Negotiations.

HOWARD HJORT is chairman of Economic Perspectives, Inc., of Washington, D.C., and was chief economist at the U.S. Department of Agriculture during the Carter administration.

JULIUS L. KATZ is chairman of Donaldson, Lufkin, and Jenrette, ACLI Futures, Inc., of White Plains, New York, formerly assistant secretary of state for economic and business affairs.

PATRICK M. O'BRIEN is deputy associate administrator for situation and outlook, Economic Research Service, U.S. Department of Agriculture.

DON PAARLBERG is professor emeritus at Purdue University, and was chief economist at the U.S. Department of Agriculture during the Nixon and Ford administrations.

ROB PAARLBERG is associate professor of political science at Wellesley College and at the Center of International Affairs at Harvard University.

FRED H. SANDERSON is senior fellow, Resources for the Future, formerly with the Brookings Institution, and director of food policy, U.S. Department of State.

LYLE SCHERTZ is senior economist, Farm Sector Economics Branch, National Economics Division, Economic Research Service, the U.S. Department of Agriculture.

JOHN A. SCHNITTKER is president of Schnittker Associates, Inc., of Washington, D.C., and was undersecretary of agriculture during the Johnson administration.

LUTHER TWEETEN is Regents Professor, Department of Economics, at Oklahoma State University (Stillwater).

Acknowledgments

We at the Curry Foundation in assembling this volume mark a major transition in our agricultural policy project. Agriculture, Stability, and Growth: Toward a Cooperative Approach is hardly finished. Rather, it moves to a new stage.

The systematic study and analysis are completed and are embodied here. We now turn our attention to making sure that it was not all done in vain, that the fine efforts of these talented scholars and analysts are not ignored but are put to good use in clarifying issues and options available to policy makers and in shedding some light, for policymakers and disinterested viewers alike, on the forces impelling and impinging upon the policy-making process.

Yet even with much remaining to do there are already many to thank. We want, of course, to express our great gratitude to my fellow members of the Curry Foundation Board of Trustees, Carl Willard and William Curry. We also want to cite for special thanks Chacellor George Russell and the University of Missouri, Kansas City for their immense generosity in providing us with both excellent facilities and many hours of staff support in holding our National Conference on their attractive campus. We also express our thanks to Monsanto Agricultural Products Company, Mobay Chemical Corporation Agricultural Chemicals Division, First National Bank of Kansas City, the Powell Family Foundation and the Farm Foundation for their generous contributions toward the cost of holding that conference. We would add also special thanks to Dr. Bruce Bullock of the University of Missouri, Columbia for bringing to that same conference three able volunteer staff members to whom we also express appreciation, as we do to our other volunteer assistants whose names appear on the following pages.

However, our final and particular appreciation goes to those people who were so very indispensible to the conduct of the ASG study. Those are the members of the Advisory Committtee, the writers and reviewers of the fifteen ASG papers, and the conference speakers, panellists and moderators who gave such generous portions of their time and provided such valuable insights and analyses to our study of these challenging issues. Their names, too, are listed on the following pages and it is to them that we are most indebted.

Charles E. Curry
Chairman
Curry Foundation

ASG Advisory Committee Membership

Martin E. Abel . . . . Abel, Daft, and Early
Governor John Carlin . . . . State of Kansas
Lynn M. Daft . . . . Abel, Daft, and Early
John C. Datt . . . . American Farm Bureau Federation
W.W. Graber . . . . Kansas grain farmer
Dr. Don Hadwiger . . . . Iowa State University
Dr. Clifford Hardin . . . . Center for the Study of American Business
Dr. Dale E. Hathaway . . . . The Consultants International Group, Inc.
Robbin S. Johnson . . . . Cargill, Inc.
Wayne Rasmussen . . . . United States Department of Agriculture
Dr. Fred H. Sanderson . . . . Resources for the Future
Thomas N. Urban . . . . Pioneer Hi-Bred International, Inc.

ASG Staff

Wm. Patrick Nichols . . . . Project director
Suzanne Brooke . . . . Personal assistant to the chairman
Thomas J. Carrier . . . . Office manager
Melinda Cohen . . . . Staff assistant

ASG Writers and Reviewers

Pat O'Brien . . . . United States Department of Agriculture
Dr. Fred Sanderson . . . . Resources for the Future
Dr. Tom Christensen . . . . Michigan State University
John Schnittker . . . . Schnittker Associates
Joseph Hajda . . . . Kansas State University
Julius L. Katz . . . . ACLI International, Inc.
Bruce Gardner . . . . University of Maryland
Harold Breimyer . . . . University of Missouri (Columbia)
Luther Tweeten . . . . Oklahoma State University
Rob Paarlberg . . . . Wellesley College
Vern Ruttan . . . . University of Minnesota
Lyle Schertz . . . . United States Department of Agriculture
Howard Hjort . . . . Economic Perspectives, Inc.
Don Paarlberg . . . . Purdue University
Lynn Daft . . . . Abel, Daft, and Early
Martin Abel . . . . Abel, Daft, and Early

Special acknowledgments to Monsanto Agricultural Products Co., Mobay Chemical Corporation Agricultural Chemicals Division, First National Bank of Kansas City, the Powell Family Foundation, and Farm Foundation, for assisting ASG through their contributions.

Speakers For The National Conference

Hon. Ike Skelton . . . . U.S. Congress, 4th District, Missouri
Hon. Pat Roberts . . . . U.S. Congress, 1st District, Kansas
Dr. Michael L. Cook . . . . President, Farmland World Trade

Panelists For The National Conference

U.S. Economic Policy and the Condition of American Agriculture

Fred Sanderson . . . . Resources for the Future
Robert Z. Lawrence . . . . Brookings Institution
Michael Boehlje . . . . Iowa State University
Julius L. Katz . . . . Donaldson, Lufkin & Jenrette ACLI Futures Inc.

U.S. Agricultural Policy: Farm Policy Options, Our Markets, Our Competitors and the Developing World

Robbin Johnson . . . . Cargill, Inc.
Howard Hjort . . . . Economic Perspectives, Inc.
Don Paarlberg . . . . Purdue University
John Schnittker . . . . Schnittker Associates
Harold Breimyer . . . . University of Missouri (Columbia)
Rob Paarlberg . . . . Wellesley College
Pat O'Brien . . . . U.S. Department of Agriculture
Luther Tweeten . . . . Oklahoma State University

Influencing Agricultural Policy: Who Plays the Game and How is it Changing?

Howard Hjort . . . . Economic Perspectives, Inc.
John G. Peters . . . . University of Nebraska (Lincoln)
Carl Schwensen . . . . Wheat Growers
John Gordley . . . . Office of Senator Robert Dole (R, KS)
Cy Carpenter . . . . Minnesota Farmers Union
Jim Riley . . . . National Cattlemen's Association
Rodney Leonard . . . . Community Nutrition Institute

Can Washington Produce a Change?
Constraints on Congress and the Executive Branch

Don Paarlberg . . . . Purdue University
Clifford Hardin . . . . Center for the Study of American Business
Don Hadwiger . . . . Iowa State University
Gene Moos . . . . House Agriculture Committee
Wayne Rasmussen . . . . U.S. Department of Agriculture
Walter W. Graber . . . . Kansas grain farmer
Lauren Soth . . . . Des Moines Register

Volunteers

Laura Gabel . . . . University of Missouri (Columbia)
Cathy Hulbrendt . . . . University of Missouri (Columbia)
Paul Harte . . . . University of Missouri (Columbia)
Audrey C. Nichols . . . . Bethany, Missouri
Janet Curry . . . . Williams College

Preface

by Wm. Patrick Nichols, Director, Curry Foundation

Martin Abel and Lynn Daft, in writing the final chapter of this volume have also created the final report and culminating analysis of a year-and-a-half long study from which this volume takes its name, "Agriculture, Stability, and Growth: Toward a Cooperative Approach."

Their charge was to draw into a coherent perspective the previous components of this detailed examination of the relationship between "farm policy" and certain central and closely related issues of trade and foreign policy. This they have done in an interesting and challenging way which should shine a clarifying light on the way we view the options for and the process toward the 1985 farm bill.

In the ASG final report, "Future Directions for U.S. Agricultural Policy," Abel and Daft have done, principally, three things. They have outlined a framework for viewing and analyzing developments pertinent to the formulation of U.S. agricultural policy, specifically over the next year but with insights relevant to the understanding of agricultural policymaking in general. They have also summarized key components of the current policysetting, drawing upon insights offered and widely held by the participants in the ASG study and placing particular emphasis on those factors which distinguish the 1984-85 setting from previous circumstances. They, thus, provide a backdrop against which the framework mentioned above may be placed for most perspicuous viewing.

Finally, the authors have prescribed a group of general policy orientations which are also widely held among the distinguished scholars and analysts involved in ASG and which help the reader and viewer provide a normative content to the understanding which should be enhanced by the other two enterprises.

Abel and Daft create their framework by drawing a "best case" and "worst case" scenario for the circumstances surrounding agriculture and the policy making process. Though what they are concerned with ultimately is policy outcomes the reader should be careful to note that "best case" and "worst case" are not best and worst for the prospects of generating good policy but rather best and worst for American agriculture at the moment in which they apply. In fact, it would appear that the general policy orientation on which so many of the ASG participants find accord would fare better under a worst case than a best case scenario. In the best case prices, incomes and exports are up; interest and dollar exchange rates and budgetary costs are down and the world is looking a good bit rosier for the agricultural sector than it does at this writing. In the worst case all of the variables mentioned above are as bad as or worse than they are at present.

Under a best case scenario the authors speculate that policy discussions will revolve around adjustments and repairs which might be applied to current policy. They mention, as likely topics for consideration, retaining loan programs but altering them to increase market flexibility; retaining deficiency payment programs (target prices) but increasing flexibility here too, and, perhaps, targeting the benefits to some smaller category of farmers; and altering diversion programs to make them more cost effective for supply control purposes and more enduringly effective for soil conservation purposes.

If a worst case scenario were to prevail the writers foresee a highly "contintious and divisive" farm bill debate. This set of circumstances would increase the possibility of enacting some of the changes listed for consideration under a best case scenario. However, policy makers would also, Abel and Daft believe, face a series of difficult dilemmas. They would be expecteds to provide farm income support yet grapple more effectively with budget costs. They would need to support U.S. prices while allowing U.S. agricultural competitiveness in the world market. They would search for ways to allow farm assets and values to seek an equilibrium (almost certainly by falling further) while not disrupting farm credit markets in a critical way. They would need to determine how to restrain government payments to farmers while keeping some kind of carrot to induce participation in voluntary supply controls. And, they would need to determine how far they can and should allow administrative discretion over farm policy, which would require more restraint in using their own authority to mandate policy decisions in advance.

All of this, according to Daft and Abel, could shake out in a variety of policy directions. However, they warn of two, specific, major developments which loom as significant possibilities. First, the budget crunch could win out over other considerations leaving agriculture with a set of farm programs which are on the books but which there is no money to finance. And, agricultural interests could be "bludgeoned into accepting major reforms" with each group forced to merely make do with what minimal assistance it can get.

However, they do hold out the possibility that this same worst case could engender some genuine policy creativity and that "some new and workable approaches to farm programs might result." In this instance, then, a further deterioration of the present, rather dire circumstances, might create the incentive for a set of policies correctly geared to producing a better set of circumstances for the American agricultural economy in the future.

But in order to assess what those policies might be, what the chances are of arriving at them and what role each potential participant might play in the process it is necessary to formulate a clear understanding as to where we stand at present.

What, then, is the case at present as Abel and Daft see it?

We are in the fifth year of the decade in which the raging bull market of the seventies has made a Protean transformation into a surly and seemingly intractable bear. To blame? "A deep and prolonged world recession, an appreciating dollar, serious international financial problems . . . and inflated U.S. price supports."

The bear is nourished by the expectation that surplus capacity will prevail and that stocks of key commodities will grow again as they did earlier in the decade. The needed dramatic growth in exports seems highly unlikely, the authors suggest, though they do contend that policies can play a significant role in promoting something better than worst case circumstances in stocks and exports.

Further sustenance is afforded the bear, Abel and Daft believe, by the growth in budget deficits which they confidently contend do have a great deal to do with current high interest rates and the inflated value of the dollar. (See, also, comments by Robert Z. Lawrence to ASG National Conference, appendix number one.)

They analyze the agricultural component of U.S. deficit spending in terms of entitlement and non-entitlement spending and cite entitlement spending as the chief culprit, amounting to 85 percent of the $22.3 billion farm program budget for Fiscal Year 1984 (these figures do not include costs of Payment-In-Kind which were and are a temporary entitlement and which some contend could prove to have cost $10 billion for 1983 alone). The authors go on to explain that farm program costs grew much faster in 1982 and 1983 than costs in any other budget category and raise the possibility that budgetary considerations alone could be the determining factor in the 1985 farm bill, perhaps with Congress leaving high support price entitlements on the books but not appropriating the money to fund them.

Further, these writers offer as another important background consideration the increasingly widely recognized trifurcation by gross income levels of the farm sector. The lowest income group (grossing less than $20,000 a year and producing less than 10 percent of the nation's farm product while constituting 60 percent of farm numbers) they contend don't often participate in or need commodity programs. The highest income group (the 5 percent of farmers grossing $200,000 or more and producing 45 percent of the product) they state flatly are the chief beneficiaries of programs they don't need. The portion in the income belt between (35 percent of farmers, 44 percent of product), say Abel and Daft, are the group most in need of help.

Another key consideration on which the authors dwell at considerable length is the financial bind in which many farmers find themselves. (See, too, comments by Michael D. Boehlje to ASG National Conference, appendix number two.) Here, too, the plight of various groups of farmers vary dramatically and Abel and Daft provide some intriguing details as to the manifestations of that problem: increased debt to income ratios, illiquidity, higher interest rates with shorter loan maturities, etc. And the solution to these problems, they insist, does not lie in price and income programs.

Those, then, are some of the key components the authors cite in delineating the economic circumstances to which they framework is to be applied. However, they also cite some important, and less tangible circumstances—political, psychological and philosophical. For instance, there is a growing sentiment in the agricultural community that farm programs are actually a secondary consideration in improving the plight of agriculture. Pre-eminent, according to this line of thought, is the macroeconomic situation. Agriculture is merely a part of a broader economy, these people reason, and many of the factors which have worked greatly to its detriment fall well outside of its traditional policy perimeters. Much of the anguish now being suffered by this particular sector is the result of a questionable use of fiscal and monetary policies and these must be changed before action in the realm of farm policy can provide much relief, this argument continues. This sort of sentiment is manifest in Abel and Daft when they fault high deficits, and high exchange and interest rates as fundamental to the problem, and propose macroeconomic remedies.

They also cite approvingly the pervasive dissatisfaction with the mechanisms and performance of farm policy in dealing with the traditional problems of agriculture. They are even more specific in their disapproval of those same mechanisms to handle new difficulties which they cite (e.g., the financial stress problems mentioned above).

Another intangible factor likely to have a major impact on the 1985 farm bill deliberations, according to Abel and Daft, is the widened circle of participation. More groups and people than ever before are likely to involve themselves in the 1984-85 deliberations. Most of these identified by the authors are people with direct links to the agricultural sector but who have simply not weighed heavily into the policy frays of the past. Economic hardships and the policy responses to them seem likely to propel several such new participants into the process largely, perhaps, in self-defense. (Many farm suppliers, for instance, felt a major detrimental impact from the PIK set-asides which prompted farmers to buy fewer supplies from them than anticipated.) These new kids on the block will bring with them new interests and perspectives and may well prove to be a significant factor in increasing or limiting potential policy options.

It also seems to the authors quite possible that the relative harmony which has traditionally prevailed among commodity groups might become discordant if economic, political and budgetary difficulties continue. They cite some of the different objectives which commodity groups might adopt and suggest that the diversity of problems facing different subsectors of agriculture could combine with general economic adversity to cause these groups to do battle over shares of a shrinking pie.

The red meat industry, not traditionally a major player in agricultural policy, may have presaged both of these last two possibilities by doing battle with the dairy industry over the latter's efforts to restrain dairy production by getting government to provide cash inducements to farmers who would cull their herds. The meat people, of course, feared that the culled cattle would glut the beef market to the detriment of both beef and pork producers.

Finally, the writers cite a philosophical intangible as having the potential to effect the developing debate. That intangible is the growing concern with equity. More people, they believe, are going to say, simply, "That's not fair," upon realizing the huge advantages derived by a few large farmers from policies designed principally with smaller farmers in mind.

The last major function Chapter 7 serves is to provide a set of prescriptions for general policy orientation. It seems safe to say that these prescriptions, and most of the debate in the process of ASG was based on a shared goal of making U.S. agricultural policy more responsive to an international market economy. Though positions on the particulars of policy often varied considerably most participants share two general objectives with Abel and Daft: They want the U.S. to be competitive in agricultural production and they want policy to play a role.

Instrumental in this, the authors are in the majority in believing, is the importance of getting America's macro-economic house in order. In pursuit of this goal Abel and Daft make an explicit appeal for an "installment plan" not a mere down-payment, to reduce the federal budget deficit.

They also call for agriculture to take its licks in the cost cutting which they see as being imperative in pursuit of that goal. Here, again, they place particular emphasis on reducing the cost of entitlement programs such as price supports. In dealing more specifically with agricultural policy and agriculture related trade policy they call for a tighter link between the two to ensure that "they are consistent and mutually supportive." They call for farm policy to be made with full cognizance of the need to offset certain macro-economic effects.

They call for the U.S. to take the lead in improving the world's trade climate, contending that such improvement is in this nation's interest. And, they abjure cartels and agreements to organize trade or nations' agricultural policies.

They also share a disapproval widespread among ASG participants of policies to achieve "deep and sustianed" production cuts. The concern here is that such policies insure that others will take developing markets and that the protection of prices through controlled production causes the U.S. to set a price floor under which its competitors will consistently creep to the detriment of American competiveness.

Though they make no explicit call for the targetting of benefits they do raise this as a possibility and repeatedly point to the perils in handling agriculture's diverse problems with broad based commodity price supports.

Finally, they stress unequivocally the need to support Third World economic development and, specifically, agricultural economic development. This, Abel and Daft join others in arguing, makes sense not just for humanitarian reasons but, ironically, for agricultural-economic reasons. Such policies actually help to generate new markets for American agricultural products in those very countries experiencing agriculture based growth.

This, then, is a summary of what Martin Abel and Lynn Daft, say much more fully and much more persuasively in their paper, the final report of the ASG study. They've done a fine job of making sense of a long and multi-faceted project which has provided a wide variety of insights and suggestions about a troublesome field.

When in the spring of 1984 Chairman Charles E. Curry instructed us at the Curry Foundation to begin a study of agricultural issues it had already occurred to him and us that there were several nexus areas between what has traditionally been called farm policy (commodity price supports, farm loan programs, conservation policies and the like) and U.S. foreign and trade policies which have had a dramatic impact upon American and world agriculture and which were inadequately understood. That inadequacy of understanding seemed to be exacerbated by a number of key paradoxes which surround American agriculture. The ASG study has both provided clarifying insights as to some of these and raised some others.

These ostensible contradictions we realized, sometimes induce pessimism and gloom. There is, for instance, the commonly noted anomoly of a world with one quarter of its population either teetering on the brink of hunger or plunged fully into its grasp while that same world already produces roughly enough calories to sustain its entire population and while the United States and other exporting nations complain of markets overburdened with surplus foodstuffs. There is also the oddity of a farm sector in which many producers feel threatened with bankruptcy while the aggregate figures for farm sector wealth and income paint a rather promising picture, while the debt to equity ratio is remarkably strong by comparison with that of other sectors of the economy and while the actual bankruptcy rate is low by comparison with that of other businesses.

A further paradox is that many argue that the traditional response to over production and low prices is now obsolete. When American farmers were producing for a "closed" domestic market alone surpluses could be reduced and prices increased by effective production controls or disincentives at little budgetary cost. Though PIK has made it quite clear that production restriction policies can still reduce surpluses it has also provided evidence that such policies may be very expensive not only to the consumer but to the federal government and taxpayer. And, it has raised the possibility that in restricting production we invite others to increase production correspondingly so that little is gained with regard to medium or long term world prices while badly needed foreign markets are lost to our competitors.

To all of these disadvantages, too, it may be appropriate to add the damage done to other sectors of the U.S. agricultural community: Those other producers who must buy higher priced raw goods, those agribusiness people who must sell to farmers who are reducing production and thus curtailing their purchases, and those who make their livings processing and selling raw products, for instance.

It also now appears quite plausible that programs designed for stability in agriculture have actually led to instability through erratic swings in policy and in prices. It seems clear, for example, that a commodity loan/stockpile program designed to restrict commodity price swings led to a stock build-up which actually depressed prices for some grains by "overhanging the market" and thus prompted the PIK program. PIK, coupled with a summer drought, led in its turn to dramatic increases in prices which only weeks before had been unsatisfactorily low.

Finally, it may be that decades of farm programs designed unfailingly with the small to medium sized family farm in mind have actually served to undermine those farms, at least in some segments of the farm economy. For instance, farm and tax policy may have created misleading signals and unwise investment incentives in the 1970s which induced efficient operators and capable managers to make investment decisions which then seemed quite rational and which now jeopardize their operations and their livelihoods.

Those are some of the paradoxes we saw facing U.S. agriculture and they are disturbing. However, there are also some rather more promising paradoxes in the agricultural sector, some of which we had identified at the outset of the ASG study and some of which have come to light during the course of it. For instance, as mentioned above, the potential widespread development of Third World agriculture and basic agribusiness which has long seemed to constitute a major threat to U.S. markets may actually hold the promise of benfitting them greatly. Many experts, including most of ASG's principle writers, believe that no matter how quickly Third World agricultural production grows the odds are extremely good that the increased wealth it brings will create an even faster growth in the demand for agricultural imports so that the faster Third World agriculture grows the faster U.S. food export markets grow.

Another promising puzzle is the possibility that the decline of certain segments of U.S. agriculture may be of rather prompt benefit to the farm sector generally. The most commonly noted example here is sugar which many argue is unable to compete with foreign sugar but much of which is planted on land adaptable to more competitive uses.

Also odd at first glance is the fact that though the number of farms in the U.S. continues to decline the general deterioration of rural America seems to have been reversed. Many small towns are showing renewed signs of strength.

Finally, there may even be promising developments hidden behind the alarming real decline in American agricultural exports. Though these have been declining both in real dollars and in gross volume for the last three years and though this trend is certainly in part attributable to the staggeringly heavy price and exports subsidies established by the European Economic Community (as well as to the recession, the inflated value of the dollar, the grain embargo and other factors) the very cost of that kind of agricultural policy already seems to be causing our European competitors to think more seriously than ever before about the virtues of accepting the discipline of a competitive market place. And if the decline in export sales is followed by several years of fluctuating markets but general, gradual growth (as predicted by another of ASG's key writers) the result may ultimately be beneficial to the farm sector and agribusiness as they take more seriously such long-term considerations as conservation, risk management, optimal resource allocation and, finally and most relevantly to our purposes here, the options for a coherent, long-term agricultural policy.

The Curry Foundation set out some 18 months ago to make a contribution to this last goal by commissioning, with the help of our distinguished advisory committee members, a battery of four basic papers and two reviews of each as the first step in the ASG process. These papers and the attendant reviews constitute the first four chapters of this volume.

In the first of these, Dr. Pat O'Brien provides a number of important insights in his analysis of potential growth in markets for U.S. agricultural products. His general conclusions include a warning that though U.S. agricultural markets are likely to grow as a matter of general trend, that growth is likely to be slow and with wide fluctuations from year to year. He also contends that such growth could be slowed further by mistaken policy initiatives or overreaction to the fluctuations. O'Brien's paper is critiqued by Dr. Fred Sanderson and Dr. Tom Christianson who added independent insights and interpretations to O'Brien's material but expressed general accord with his principle contentions.

John Schnittker writes chapter 2, the ASG paper on prospects for integrating the agricultural strategies of exporting nations. He and his reviewers, Dr. Joe Hajda and Dr. Julius Katz, agree on the improbability of any real integration but also counsel communication and restraint in unilateral trade initiatives.

Dr. Bruce Gardner of the University of Maryland lays out with care in Chapter 3 the various options available to U.S. farm policy. He articulates wide-randing options while expressing doubts that the 1985 farm bill is likely to embody any major new departures.

Gardner himself comes down on the side of a policy gradually moving in the direction of greater reliance on the marekt. His reviewers, Drs. Luther Tweeten, and Harold Breimyer, articulate still other policy options and are, in other writings, outspoken defenders of quite different perspectives on the role of farm policy.

In Chapter 4, Dr. Robert Paarlberg, composes what might be read as the most encouraging paper of the four in examining the relationship between U.S. agricultural policy and Third World agricultural development. He receives a generally sympathetic review from Lyle Schertz when he suggests that superficial harmonies and disharmonies of interest are often misleading and that there is considerable potential for U.S. agricultural exports in agriculture based development in the Third World. Paarlberg also notes, however, that these options are often specific to certain products. He displays particular optimism for the prospects for feed grain sales.

Dr. Vern Ruttan, who wrote the second critique of Paarlberg's paper, was in such thoroughgoing accord with Paarlberg that he thought it redundant to include his coments here. They are, thus, omitted.

These papers were the subject of consideration by some 60 of the nation's leading agricultural experts in a Washington conference held in February 1984. At this conference, as at the later National Conference, certain key ideas were injected and key trends identified which helped to shape the remainder of the study.

Former Secretary of Agriculture Clifford M. Hardin, for instance, piqued the interest of those attending both conferences with his thoughtful and insistent contention that nothing of consequence can be done to reform U.S. agricultural policy until something is done to reform the committee system in Congress. He contends that the decentralization of influence brought about by the Congressional reform movement of the 1970s has transferred power essential for effective policy making from committee chairmen, who can assess and weigh a broad range of interests against one another, to highly specialized subcommittee chairmen who often fall in the thrall of narrow constituencies. They, he suggests, will not allow the reform needed in agricultural policy until they are reformed into diminished influence.

The papers and discussions of the February conference supply the raw material for Chapters 5 and 6 in which two former chief economists for USDA provide overview analyses which constituted the principle discussion materials for the May 1984 National Conference on the campus of the University of Missouri, Kansas City. These writers, Don Paarlberg and Howard Hjort, discuss how the ideas offered in the preliminary papers relate to one another and what implications they and the February discussions may have for a 1985 revision of U.S. farm and agricultural policy.

Among the areas of importance they and other participants cite are the pre-eminent importance of macro-economic consideratins mentioned above. They also point to the wide differences in type and degree of farm problems among different geographical, economic, and commodity sectors. Some farmers suffer deep rooted, structural problems while others face merely cyclical or cash flow difficulties or no major difficulties at all. These writers, relatedly, cite the possibility of better targetting specific aid to specific sectors. Another often stressed theme is the importance of reducing the interference of farm programs with the marketplace and market signals which are seen as essential not only to U.S. national competitiveness but to the good management, and ultimately the survival, of the individual American farmer.

Paarlberg has written a chapter which largely summarizes the foregoing written arguments and those made in February and identifies a surprising convergence of participant opinion on fundamental goals and policy orientations. Though he acknowledges that there was general agreement on only a few policy prescriptions (he does cite, for instance, near consensus on the importance of avoiding deep and sustained production cuts and on encouraging Third World agricultural development) he finds very widespread agreement on the objective of better accommodating U.S. agriculture policy to the market place. In fact, most of the more specific areas of agreement he cites seem to be linked by this common goal.

Hjort recognizes the same areas of convergence, but then boldly argues that they are in considerable measure mistaken. He clearly believes that policy decisions were crucial in precipitating the current, lamentable state of affairs and believes that wiser policy interventions in the future can and should play the principle role in improving the circumstances of U.S. agriculture.

Hjort places far more emphasis on the links between market stability and economic growth than do the other participants and he sets out precise prescriptions for policies which he believes would enhance both. For instance, he defies the clear trend of thought among ASG participants by contending that loan prices have not consequentially undermined U.S. market competitiveness and should be increased as a stabilizing measure. Target prices, on the other hand, he urges we eliminate.

The National Conference in Kansas City which discussed these papers added several noteworthy components to thc ASG study. One was the injection of vigorous dissent by many practicing farmers to the general agreement on free market policies. These farmers vigorously stressed the severity of the plight which they and their colleagues face and often argued for guaranteed commodity prices set at a high percentage of parity combined with mandatory production controls. Some even hinted that they felt experience has proven export based salvation a chimera and that America might be well advised to seal off her markets and produce, again, for a closed economy.

A second challenging development was the introduction of Michael Boehlje's analysis of the nature of the farm finance problem (see appendix #2). Citing his colleague at Iowa State, Neil Harl, Boehlje contended that the problem for many U.S. farmers is not income per se, but debt service and debt to income ratios and that price and income policies may be particularly ill-adapted to addressing such problems.

All of which brings us back to Daft and Abel and the ASG Final Report, Chapter 7 of this volume. This paper concludes the Curry Foundation study by weaving together most of the many strands of thought which have contributed to and been generated by the project. It tells the reader and the policy participant where most of a large group of diverse but uniformly thoughtful analysts stand on the key questions now likely to surround the 1985 farm bill debate. It explains not only the shared perspectives as to where we stand and how we got here but it gives a variety of very important suggestions as to where we should go.

However, it does more than that. It also suggests to those who would watch with intelligent care the emerging 1985 farm bill debate, or who would participate in it, what key factors to monitor as the debate takes place and the policies emerge. It details the principle factors likely to effect the tone and direction of the deliberations and thus gives us a better idea as to how each participant and policy itself may respond to the events of the ensuing days. It sketches a framework for public understanding as well as important policy ideas for economic growth and stability in the sector, under the assumption that understanding is absolutely essential to cooperation.

It, thus, seems a fitting conclusion to a policy study project designated from the beginning, "Agriculture, Stability, and Growth: Toward a Cooperative Approach."

Chapter 1

World Market Trends and Prospects: Implications for U.S. Agricultural Policy

Patrick M. O'Brien

The purpose of this paper, as commissioned by the Foundation, is to assess prospects for the world market for farm products through the late 1980s and comment on their implications for U.S. agricultural policy. The assessment is part of a broader effort to support improved public policy making in the upcoming farm bill debate.

The Foundation's effort is a timely one. The 1985-88 farm bill cycle is already underway well in advance of previous cycles. Moreover, there is growing agreement among interested parties, far stronger than at the start of the past cycles, that significant changes in agricultural policy are needed. This interest in policy change is based in part on reaction outside the farm sector to sharply higher 1982 and 1983 public expenditures in support of agriculture and the questions they raise regarding the appropriate role for government in agriculture. There is also considerable interest in policy change within the sector, however, related to concern that agriculture may ultimately be poorly served by policies that weaken its capacity to adjust to changes in market conditions and compete effectively here and abroad.

The farm sector's experience with trade so far in the 1980s has also generated interest in policy change. On several occasions over the last thirty years, growth in exports promised to ease agriculture's problems with excess productive capacity and lagging prices and incomes. That prospect was more real than ever in the 1970s. However, the export reversals the United States has suffered since 1980 have raised serious questions about the costs and benefits of participating in an increasingly volatile world market.

In this environment an assessment of prospects for the world market for the next several years becomes critical. However, basing agricultural policy on expectations of where the world market will be even a few years ahead can be dangerous. The trends shaping world and U.S. agriculture are complex, often conflicting, and subject to dramatic interruptions. For example, the bullish outlook common at the start of the 1980s shaped key provisions of the 1981 farm bill. With the unexpected shifts in the market experienced over the last three years, the essentially market-oriented but inflexible farm bill passed in 1981 became the basis for unprecedented government intervention in the sector in 1982 and 1983.

With this notion of the risks and potential payoffs involved, this paper reviews with basic trends that shaped the world market over the last several decades, prospects for these trends continuing over the remainder of the 1980s, and what their continuation or interruption would mean for U.S. farm policy.

BASIC TRENDS

World Agricultural Supply and Demand Trends

Postwar changes in world agricultural supply and demand combined to increase the importance of the United States in the world market for farm products and the importance of the world market to the United States dramatically. While subject to interruption, the underlying trends in question were strong enough to generate the unprecedented growth in world and U.S. agriculture summarized in table 1. While these trends will undoubtedly continue to be subject to interruption, they are deeply rooted enough to insure their importance in shaping the market ahead. An assessment of the most important of these supply and demand trends follows.

Supply Trends—At least three basic supply trends have been at work since 1950 in varying degrees across all the regions of the world. The most fundamental has been a trend toward increased pressure on agriculture's natural resource base as initially more of the land and water well-suited and readily available for use were committed to producing farm products. This increased pressure has, subsequently, been reflected in: (1) declining growth in cropland and increased reliance on more-intensive cultivation; (2) increasing reliance on non-renewable, particularly energy-based inputs; and (3) growing dependence on a shrinking circle of countries, dominated by the United States, with underutilized agricultural resources.

TABLE 1

World Agricultural Production, Consumption, and Trade Growth Rates

Item	Compound Annual Growth Rate		
	1950-82	1950-72	1972-82
World			
Production	2.70	2.85	2.35
Consumption	2.70	2.85	2.35
Trade	5.30	4.95	6.25
Per capita production	.85	.95	.50
Per capita consumption	.85	.95	.50
United States			
Production	2.15	2.05	2.80
Consumption	1.70	1.90	1.20
Trade	6.40	5.50	8.90
Per capita production	.85	.55	2.00
Per capita consumption	.45	.45	.40
Foreign			
Production	2.75	2.90	2.30
Consumption	2.85	3.00	2.55
Trade	4.95	4.70	5.65
Per capita production	.80	.95	.45
Per capita consumption	.95	1.05	.70

Source: USDA/ERS World Agricultural Production and Trade Indices, and FAO Agricultural Production and Trade Indices.

Agricultural land use around the world expanded less than .5 percent per year from 1950 to 1980. Moreover, growth was concentrated in the 1950s and 1960s despite stronger market incentives to expand area during the second half of the period. Growth from 1965 to 1980 actually slowed to .3 percent (table 2). This growth pattern contrasts sharply with fragmentary information suggesting that acreage expanded .6 to .9 percent per year during much of the first half of the century.

Table 3 translates this increasing pressure on natural resources into per capita terms. Per capita arable area has tended to decline in all twenty-one of the countries/regions shown and was 25 percent smaller at the world level in 1980 than in 1955. Equally important, differences in per capita arable area across countries widened significantly with two distinct groups of land-rich and land-poor countries emerging. For example, per capita land area in the East Asian countries with almost a third of the world's population dropped to less than .1 hectare. Per capita area in countries such as Canada, Australia, Argentina, and the United States with less than a twelfth of the world's population declined somewhat but remained many times larger than in the land-poor countries. An even more disproportionate share of the world's reserves of potentially arable area is also concentrated in this second group of countries.

What would otherwise have bee downward pressure on agricultural production and upward pressure on commodity prices was successfully countered in the land-tight as well as the more richly endowed countries by a trend toward intensifying resource use and accelerating growth in productivity. Tables 4 and 5 provide an indication of the strength of these intensification and productivity trends that forestalled a more Malthusian outcome.

As table 4 shows, irrigation grew seven times faster around the world than expansion in arable area, while the portion of cropland irrigated increased by more than one-half.. The use of fertilizer, a key input in the technology package used to raise crop yields, grew from less than 20 to 80 kilograms per hectare at the world level from 1950 to 1980. As table 5 shows, the strongest growth in fertilizer took place from 1965 in tandem with slowed growth in arable area.

Variations in these trends across regions and between countries within regions were pronounced. But growth in output related to intensifying resource use and natural resources augmented with manmade, often pretroleum-based, inputs such as fertilizer generally accounted for over three-fourths of growth in supply since 1950.

These trends in combination supported postwar growth in world food supplies at an unprecedented 2.5 to 3 percent per year, more than twice the

TABLE 2

World Cropland, Selected Years

	1965	1970	1975	1980	1980/1965 Compound Annual Growth Rate (%)
	Million Hectares				
World	1,381	1,418	1,437	1,454	+
Developed Countries					
United States	176	190	188	191	– .1
Canada	42	42	43	44	+ .5
Western Europe	93	91	88	87	– .4
Japan	6	6	5	5	–1.1
Oceania	40	42	42	44	+ .8
Centrally Planned Countries					
Eastern Europe	55	54	54	54	– .2
Soviet Union	229	233	232	232	+ .1
P.R. China	104	102	101	99	– .3
Developing Countries					
Central America	38	40	42	42	+ .7
South America	105	111	120	125	+1.3
Brazil	52	54	59	62	+1.4
Argentina	30	33	35	36	+1.0
North Africa/Middle East	82	84	86	87	+ .5
Subsaharan Africa	140	146	151	156	+ .8
South Asia	203	206	210	211	+ .3
India	163	165	168	169	+ .3
Southeast Asia	69	71	75	77	+ .7
East Asia	11	11	10	10	– .4

Source: USDA/ERS World Agricultural Production and Trade Indices, and FAO Agricultural Production and Trade Indices.

TABLE 3

Per Capita Cropland, Selected Years

	1955	1960	1965	1970	1975	1980
			Hectares			
World	.434	.432	.411	.379	.349	.323
Developed Countries						
United States	1.131	1.021	.952	.930	.884	.857
Canada	2.500	2.256	2.125	1.999	1.900	1.853
Western Europe	.316	.303	.283	.263	.255	.248
Japan	.061	.065	.050	.053	.045	.042
Oceania	2.533	2.856	3.234	3.302	3.079	3.037
Centrally Planned Countries						
Eastern Europe	.500	.481	.459	.436	.418	.398
Soviet Union	1.138	1.034	.993	.958	.914	.882
P.R. China	.164	.151	.142	.121	.106	.097
Developing Countries						
Central America	.690	.633	.546	.463	.393	.344
South America	.534	.519	.616	.584	.555	.521
Brazil	.387	.556	.619	.562	.544	.508
Argentina	1.395	1.295	1.321	1.383	1.325	1.260
North Africa/Middle East	.625	.591	.531	.505	.428	.393
Subsaharan Africa	.578	.535	.553	.515	.460	.446
South Asia	.342	.321	.291	.263	.252	.222
India	.382	.361	.328	.298	.272	.244
Southeast Asia	.253	.260	2.73	.260	.216	.200
East Asia	.085	.082	.075	.067	.062	.056

Source: USDA/ERS World Agricultural Production and Trade Indices, and FAO Agricultural Production and Trade Indices.

TABLE 4

Measures of Land Use Intensity: Irrigation

	1965 (Million Hectares)	1980 (Million Hectares)	1965-80 Compound Annual Growth Rate (%)	Share of 1980 Agricultural Land Irrigated (%)
World	156	212	+2.2	15
Developed Countries				
United States	15	21	+2.3	11
Canada	—	1	+2.0	1
Western Europe	6	10	+2.1	11
Japan	3	3	—	67
Oceania	1	2	+1.1	4
Centrally Planned Countries				
Eastern Europe	2	5	+5.2	9
Soviet Union	10	18	+4.6	8
P.R. China	39	46	+1.2	46
Developing Countries				
Central America	4	7	+4.0	13
South America	6	8	+4.7	5
North Africa/Middle East	10	13	+1.2	15
Subsaharan Africa	2	3	+3.2	2
South Asia	42	59	+2.4	28
India	27	39	+2.7	23
Southeast Asia	4	5	+3.1	12
East Asia	1	1	+1.8	52

Source: FAO *Production Yearbooks,* various issues 1976-82.

TABLE 5

Fertilizer Use per Hectare of Arable Land

	1965	1980	1965-80 Compound Annual Growth Rate (%)
	Kilograms per Hectare		
World	32.4	79.9	6.2
Developed Countries	76.6	115.8	2.8
United States	63.0	111.6	3.9
Canada	16.3	43.2	6.7
Western Europe	129.5	218.4	3.5
Japan	332.2	372.1	0.8
Oceania	40.7	37.7	-0.5
Centrally Planned Countries	31.4	116.8	9.2
Eastern Europe	12.0	24.1	4.7
Soviet Union	24.8	80.9	8.2
P.R. China	18.1	154.6	15.5
Developing Countries			
Central America	6.5	49.1	14.4
South America	12.2	46.0	9.3
North Africa/Middle East	8.1	33.8	10.5
Subsaharan Africa	1.9	9.7	11.5
South Asia	*6.7	*37.6	*12.2
India	4.7	30.9	13.4
Southeast Asia	*	*	*
East Asia	*	*	*

*Data incomplete.

Source: FAO *Production Yearbooks,* various issues 1976-82.

pace of the first half of the century. World food supplies at the start of the 1980s were more than 120 percent greater than at the start of the 1950s. Moreover, these gains were made despite generally declining real prices for farm products on the world market and in most of the countries of the world. Productivity gains were strong enough to combine with falling real prices for key inputs to keep net producer returns in most countries constant or rising even while product prices fell. Prices for wheat and the other grains traded internationally, for example, declined from 1950 to 1983 at a trend rate of 1 percent per year (chart 1). If measured relative to the prices of the manufactured products traded internationally, the prices of agricultural products fell even faster—more than 1.5 percent per year.

However, the agriculture posting these unprecedented supply gains underwent considerable structural change. Agriculture in the developed and in many of the developing countries became increasingly dependent, albeit at varying rates across regions, on non-renewable petroleum-based inputs purchased outside the sector. While agriculture tended to become more dependent on productivity growth over the last three decades, productivity growth became dependent on increasing energy use (chart 2). This reality of an increasingly non-renewable agriculture dependent on a petroleum-based technology contrasts sharply with the classical image of agriculture as a renewable activity largely dependent on land, labor, and farm-produced inputs.

A less pronounced but potentially as important development was the trend toward more variable agricultural production in much of the world (table 6). Variability at the world level appears to have changed little, with ups and downs in one country offsetting change elsewhere. But increased year-to-year variations in many individual countries have been marked. And many of the countries with the most pronounced increases in volatility tend to be key trading countries with a disproportionally large impact on the world market. While difficult to measure precisely, this increase in year-to-year swings in farm output appears to relate in some cases to agriculture's expansion into marginal area more sensitive to swings in weather or possibly to increased weather variability or a more fundamental change in climate. In more than a few countries increasingly unstable agricultural production was related to changes in government policies affecting production via support pricing, input subsidization, procurement, and marketing.

These supply trends gradually changed the United States' position in the world market to that of the dominant supplier of bulk farm products. The resource and productivity trends noted above resulted in the concentration of un- or underutilized capacity in a shrinking circle of countries and the emergency of a growing circle of countries producing at or near what in

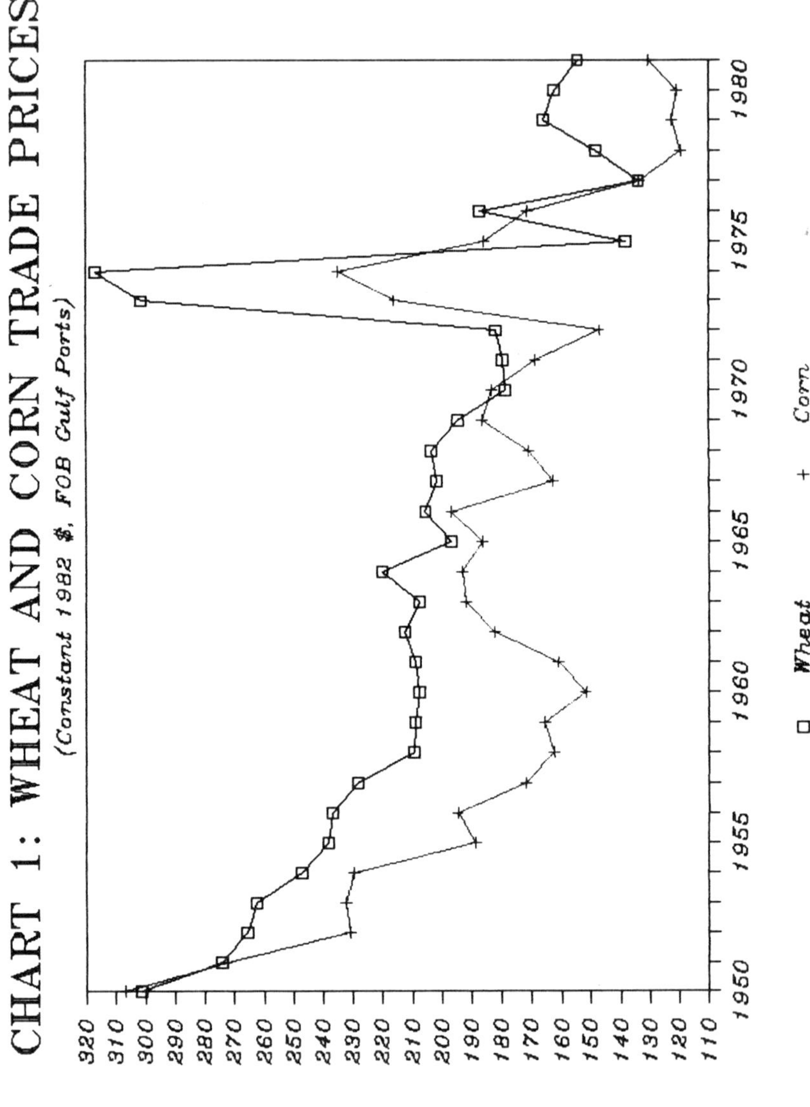
CHART 1: WHEAT AND CORN TRADE PRICES
(Constant 1982 $, FOB Gulf Ports)
Dollars Per Ton
320
310
300
290
280
270
260
250
240
230
220
210
200
190
180
170
160
150
140
130
120
110
1950
1955
1960
1965
1970
1975
1980
Wheat
Corn

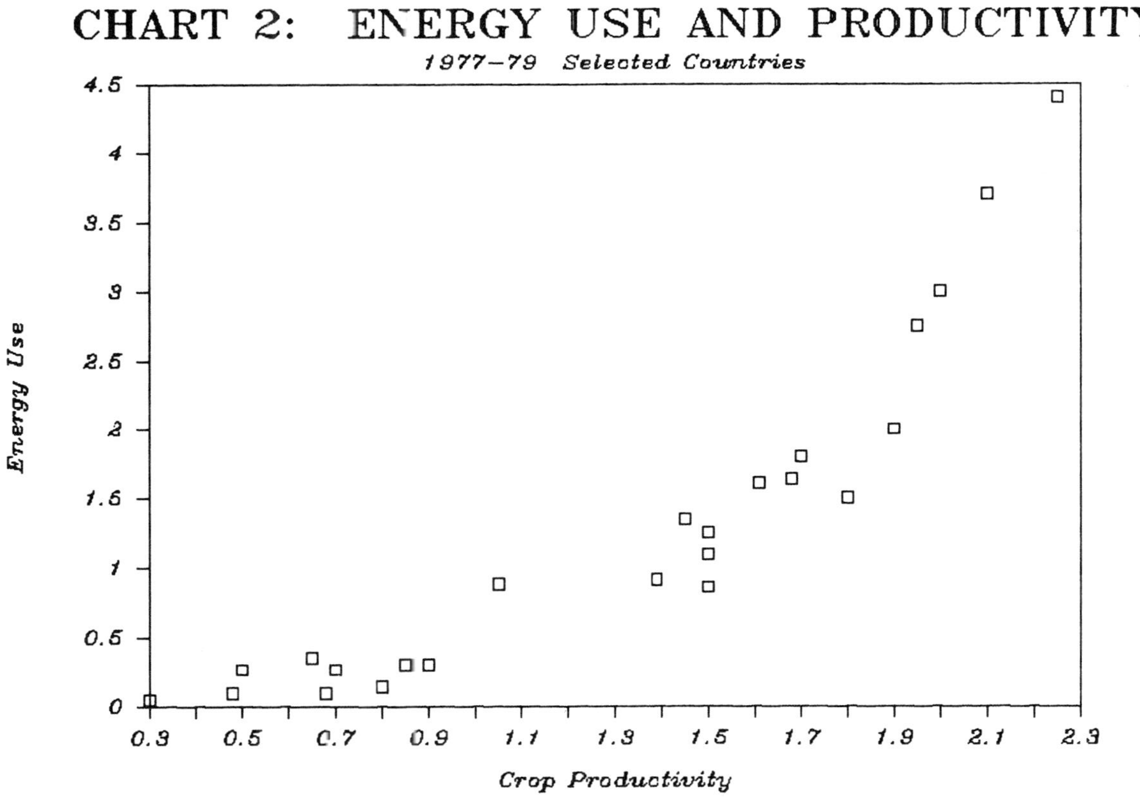
CHART 2: ENERGY USE AND PRODUCTIVITY
1977–79 Selected Countries
Energy Use
4.5
4
3.5
3
2.5
2
1.5
1
0.5
0
Crop Productivity
0.3
0.5
0.7
0.9
1.1
1.3
1.5
1.7
1.9
2.1
2.3

TABLE 6

Variability in Agricultural Production, Selected Countries/Regions*

Item	1961-72	1972-83
	Percent	
Production Variability		
United States	1.6	3.5
EEC-10	2.1	3.2
Australia	4.1	5.5
USSR	5.0	6.1
Middle America	1.1	3.0
North Africa/Middle East	2.9	3.9
East Asia	4.4	7.1
World	1.5	1.6

*Measured as the coefficient of variation from best-fit linear or curvilinear time trends.

the short term was full capacity. Growth in per capita production slowed or actually declined in many of the countries in this second group. But if this trend toward concentration put the United States in a far stronger market position, it left the United States far more dependent on growth in exports to support continued growth in production at the end of the period than at the start.

Demand Trends—Trends in population, income, and government policies affecting agriculture combined to generate equally unprecedented growth in demand for farm products since 1950.

World-wide population growth over the last three decades added 2 billion people; this 80 percent increase in the number of people to be fed clearly accounts for much of the postwar growth in demand (table 7). However, the importance of population growth can be overstated. Per capita food intake levels actually declined in many of the developing countries that accounted for much of the world's population growth. After accounting for per capita intake declines in parts of Asia, Africa, and Latin America, the increase in global food demand associated with population growth since 1950 was probably less than 60 percent—half of the total increase in demand and two-thirds of the increase in the number of people to be fed.

On the other hand, it is difficult to undervalue the contribution post war growth in per capita incomes and resulting affluence have made in changing the level and composition of demand for farm products (table 8). In most of the world growing affluence led first to increased consumption of starchy foodstuffs until minimum caloric intake levels were reached, but then toward stronger demand for livestock products to upgrade and diversify diets. In the affluent countries further growth in income allowed consumers to increase the proportion of their diets made up of livestock products from 10-20 percent in 1950 to 30 percent or more by 1980.

As table 9 and chart 3 demonstrate, an increasingly large proportion of the world's population made the dietary transition in the 1960s, and 1970s toward the meat-oriented diets pioneered by the affluent countries before and immediately after the war. While less than 300 million people enjoyed diets with a quarter or more of their calories from livestock products in the early 1950s, more than 800 million had made the transition by 1980. An added 300 to 500 million consumers in the middle income countries were poised to make the transition at the start of the 1981 world recession.

What is critical about this dietary transition is not the absolute increase in caloric consumption involved but the fact that production of a single livestock calorie generally requires use of 4 to 6 calories of feed input. Given

TABLE 7

World Population by Country and Regions, Selected Years (Thousands)

Region/Country	1950	1955	1960	1965	1970	1975	1980
World	2,525,304	2,762,386	3,028,656	3,331,787	3,693,896	4,064,387	4,437,998
Developed Countries	547,741	581,145	616,091	652,490	683,185	714,412	739,349
United States	152,271	165,931	180,671	194,303	205,052	215,973	227,658
Canada	13,737	15,736	17,909	19,678	21,324	22,725	24,012
Western Europe	285,891	296,072	308,189	322,646	333,686	343,627	348,731
Japan	83,771	89,815	94,092	98,883	104,345	111,566	116,782
Oceania	12,071	13,591	15,230	16,980	18,778	20,521	22,166
Centrally Planned Countries	829,143	916,730	994,865	1,076,944	1,197,660	1,303,210	1,382,715
Eastern Europe	106,062	111,753	116,536	121,108	125,503	130,017	134,575
Soviet Union	180,075	196,159	214,329	236,936	242,757	254,393	265,540
P.R. China	543,006	608,818	664,000	724,900	829,400	918,800	982,600
Developing Countries	1,148,420	1,264,511	1,417,700	1,602,353	1,813,051	2,046,765	2,315,934
Central America	51,742	59,062	68,145	79,056	91,710	105,950	122,157
South America	113,259	128,645	147,498	168,791	191,694	214,868	240,217
North Africa/Middle East and West Asia	59,724	67,903	78,039	89,116	102,208	117,599	136,326
Subsaharan Africa	218,462	243,444	273,576	310,704	355,797	407,759	469,147
South Asia	102,595	115,342	132,796	151,879	173,095	196,143	223,446
India	381,912	407,741	444,367	493,270	548,520	613,010	684,458
Southeast and East Asia	220,726	242,374	273,279	309,537	350,027	391,436	440,183

Source: Bureau of the Census, U.S. Department of Commerce.

TABLE 8

Real per Capita Income Growth Rates

Country/Region	Compound Annual Growth Rates 1950-80 (%)	1960-70 (%)	1970-80 (%)	1977-80 Per Capita Income ($)
Developed Countries				
United States	2.6	2.8	2.0	9,700
Canada	3.3	3.4	2.8	9,200
Western Europe	3.8	4.2	2.6	5,900
Japan	7.5	9.1	3.5	7,300
South Africa	2.4	3.2	.8	1,500
Oceania	2.7	3.2	1.4	7,350
Centrally Planned Countries				
Eastern Europe	4.1	3.8	4.2	3,250
Soviet Union	3.4	3.5	3.0	3,700
P.R. China	4.8	5.2	3.8	500
Developing Countries				
Latin America	3.3	3.2	3.0	1,200
North Africa/Middle East	N.A.	N.A.	4.5	1,250
Subsaharan Africa	N.A.	N.A.	1.6	375
Developing Asia	2.4	2.3	2.1	300

Source: ERS/USDA; World Bank.

TABLE 9

Countries in Dietary Transition, 1977-79 and 1990

Country/Class	1977-79 Per Capita Income (Dollars)	1977-79 Daily Livestock Calorie Intake (Calories)	1977-79 Population (Millions)	1990 Per Capita Income (Dollars)	1990 Daily Livestock Calorie Intake (Calories)	1990 Population (Millions)
Class 1[a]						
(transition completed)						
Switzerland	12,990	1,305	6.3	13,850	1,150-1,400	6.6
Denmark	10,580	1,415	5.1	13,550	1,150-1,400	5.2
Sweden	10,540	1,250	8.2	12,025	1,150-1,400	8.2
United States	9,770	1,450	218.5	12,100	1,150-1,400	233.6
France	8,880	1,235	53.3	11,525	1,150-1,400	55.4
United Kingdom	5,720	1,200	55.8	6,850	1,150-1,400	56.9
Poland	3,650	1,200	35.8	4,900	1,150-1,400	39.0
Hungry	3,480	1,270	10.8	4,675	1,150-1,400	11.0
Class 1 Total	—	—	554.5	—	—	586.0
Class 2						
(transition in progress, early and late stage),						
Group A[b]						
Italy	4,600	835	56.4	5,500	900-1,100	58.6
Japan	7,700	600	114.9	13,050	800,1000	123.9
USSR	3,710	925	261.0	5,100	1,000-1,200	291.2
Greece	3,450	760	9.1	4,925	850-1,050	9.7
Hong Kong	3,340	700	4.6	5,050	800-1,000	5.4
Venezuela	2,850	525	14.0	3,850	600-800	19.4
Yugoslavia	2,100	800	22.0	3,000	850-950	24.0
Romania	1,650	810	21.9	2,500	850-950	24.0
Costa Rica	1,610	455	2.2	2,175	600-800	2.7
Group A Total	—	—	610.3	—	—	674.0

TABLE 9
(Continued)

Countries in Dietary Transition, 1977-79 and 1990

Country/Class	1977-79 Per Capita Income (Dollars)	1977-79 Daily Livestock Calorie Intake (Calories)	1977-79 Population (Millions)	1990 Per Capita Income (Dollars)	1990 Daily Livestock Calorie Intake (Calories)	1990 Population (Millions)
Group B[c]						
Saudi Arabia	6,590	390	8.2	9,950	550-750	10.9
Brazil	1,510	395	119.5	2,425	500-650	162.3
Mexico	1,400	375	65.4	1,900	500-650	91.7
South Korea	1,310	170	36.6	1,975	250-350	43.2
Turkey	1,250	290	43.1	1,675	375-475	53.9
Malaysia	1,150	235	13.3	1,650	350-450	17.0
Tunisia	990	225	6.1	1,575	350-450	7.7
Nigeria	600	80	80.6	950	250-350	121.0
Philippines	530	150	45.6	775	250-350	61.4
Thailand	530	110	44.5	850	200-300	57.7
Indonesia	350	30	136.0	600	100-200	173.9
Group B Total	—	—	823.7	—	—	1,101.0
Class 2 Total	—	—	1,434.0	—	—	1,775.0
Class 3[d]						
(pre-transition)						
Zambia	510	110	5.3	575	150-200	7.8
Haiti	240	144	4.8	290	175-225	6.7
Pakistan	240	240	76.1	280	250-300	108.4
Ethiopa	110	150	31.0	120	150-200	41.6
India	180	85	643.9	215	100-125	820.9
Bangladesh	90	50	84.7	95	50-75	115.0
Class 3 Total	—	—	2,050.9	—	—	2,513.0

TABLE 9
(Continued)

Countries in Dietary Transition, 1977-79 and 1990

[a]Class 1 includes countries plus West Germany, Belgium-Luxembourg, Norway, Netherlands, Canada, Australia, Austria, Finland, East Germany, New Zealand, Czechoslovakia, Ireland, Israel, and Argentina. Countries are characterized by per capita incomes of $4,000 or more and intake of 1,150 calories of livestock products or more per person per day. Adjustments have been made for several countries such as Italy, Poland, Japan, and Hungry because of currency conversion difficulties or differences in dietary patterns related to natural resource endowment.

[b]Group A of Class 2 includes countries listed plus Libya, Spain, Singapore, Bulgaria, Trinidad, Tobago, Portugal, Iraq, South Africa, and Nicaragua. These countries are characterized by per capita income of $1,500 to $5,000 and intake of 450 to 1,150 calories of livestock products per person per day.

[c]Group B of Class 2 includes countries listed plus Libya, Chile, Algeria, Panama, Jamaica, Jordan, North Korea, Syria, Ecuador, Ivory Coast, Guatemala, Colombia, Dominican Republic, Morocco, Peru, El Salvador, the Congo, Bolivia, Cameroon, Honduras, Zimbabwe, Liberia, and Egypt. These countries are characterized by per capita incomes of $400 to $1,500 and intake of 200 to 450 calories of livestock products per person per day.

[d]Class 3 includes listed plus Ghana, Senegal, Kenya, Sudan, Togo, Lesotho, Uganda, Central African Republic, Mauritania, Guinea, Madagascar, Mozambique, Niger, Tanzania, Zaire, China, Sierra Leone, Benin, Sri Lanka, Rwanda, Malawi, Afghanistan, Burundi, Upper Volta, Chad, Burma, Mali, Nepal, and Bhutan. These countries are characterized by per capita incomes of up to $400 and intake of up to 250 calories of livestock products per person per day.

Sources: FAO *Production Yearbook* 1980, World Bank *1980 World Bank Atlas,* and World Bank *Population Projections, 1975-2000* prepared in 1980.

CHART 3. Dietary Transitions: Grain and Meat Consumption Patterns

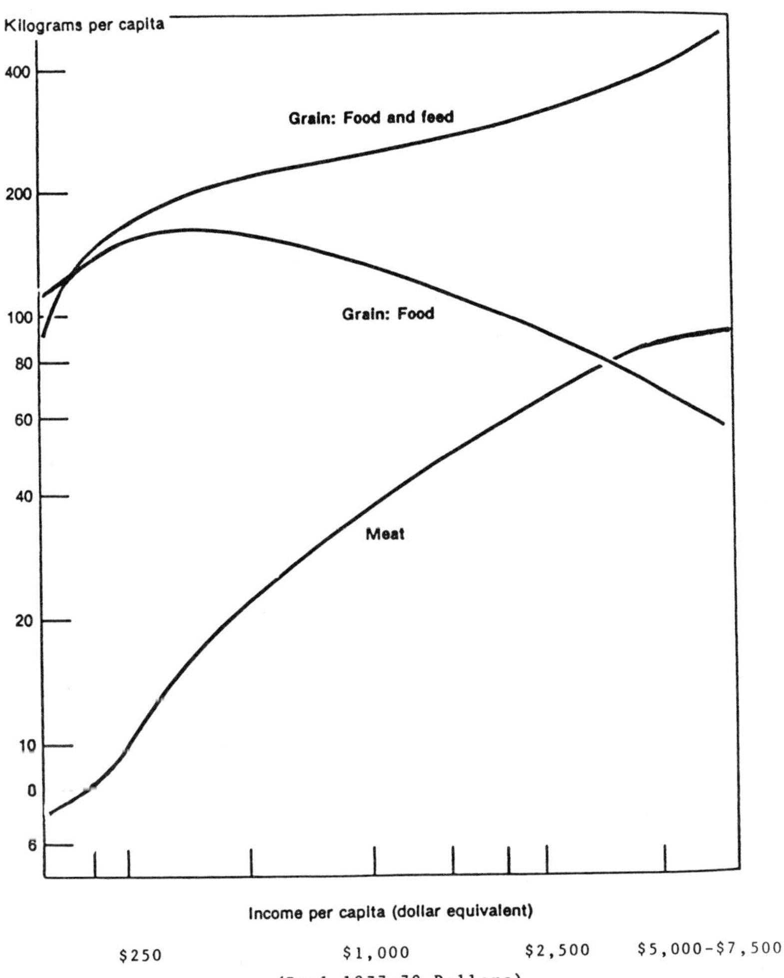

this "inefficient" calorie conversion process, even slow growth in demand for livestock products can generate strong growth in feed demand. As chart 4 shows, the transition can result in shifting up to 50 percent of a country's crop output, including items such as forages, from direct human consumption to indirect consumption via meat, milk, and eggs.

Trade and agricultural policies in many of the largest countries of the world reinforced, in some cases accelerated, growth in demand for farm products. As already noted, the prices of farm products moving on the world market fell over most of the period. This was due in large part to a tendency for the exporters to overproduce and to use the world market to dump surpluses rather than allow excess resources to leave their agricultural sectors. Given the aid and credit programs used by the exporters to dispose of the generally large surpluses that resulted, the effective cost of importing food was undoubtedly even lower than implied in chart 1.

Many importing countries adopted domestic food policies early in the postwar period designed to keep food prices low for their urban populations. The cheap-food policies in question often focused initially on government food subsidies and/or procurement and marketing restrictions that kept the prices their farmers received low. Over the late 1960s and 1970s in particular, interest in demand-enhancing policies increased substantially, and many of the more affluent developing countries and lower-income developed countries put new or expanded food subsidy programs into place to accelerate diet improvement. Many also eased food import restrictions that had heretofore worked to tie local growth in consumption to lagging growth in local production.

As in the case of supply, growth in demand varied widely across countries and regions. Much of the world gain was concentrated in diet improvements in the low-income developed countries and high-income developing countries. Gains in the lowest-income countries were far more modest, leaving many people eating at or below recommended nutritional minimums. Table 10 puts the more limited gains of low-income developing countries into perspective.

But in general terms, the end result of these different demand trends and the supply trends at the start of the 1980s was a world—with significant exceptions across and within countries—eating better than at any other time in history despite thirty years of unprecedented growth in population. Moreover, this improvement came at a decreasing real cost as the world spent porportionately less and less of its resources on meeting food needs. Clearly, agriculture was able to deal with increasingly serious resource constraints and still contribute to improving the world's standard of living.

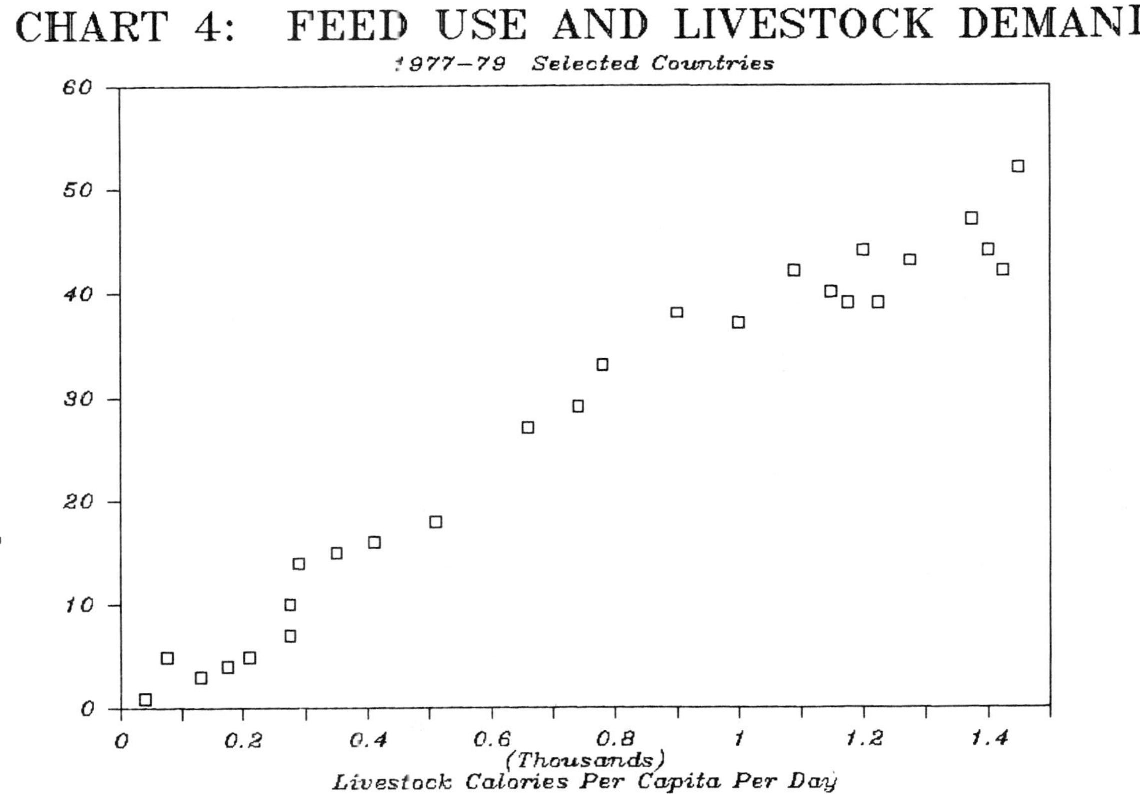
CHART 4: FEED USE AND LIVESTOCK DEMAND
1977–79 Selected Countries
% Crop Production Used As Feed
60
50
40
30
20
10
0
0
0.2
0.4
0.6
0.8
1
1.2
1.4
(Thousands)
Livestock Calories Per Capita Per Day

TABLE 10

Per Capita Caloric Intake Levels in Selected Regions

	Calories Per Capita Per Day						
Years	North America	West Europe	Soviet Union, East Europe	Far East, China	Near East	Subsaharan Africa	Latin America
1934-38	3260	2880	2850	2090	2295	N.A.	2160
1948-52	3180	2750	2780	1890	2220	N.A.	2315
1957-59	3210	2910	3080	2060	2470	N.A.	2510
1961-63	3320	3150	3240	1980	2290	2070	2400
1964-66	3360	3230	3270	2010	2340	2100	2470
1966-68	3385	3255	3300	2020	2415	2135	2510
1969-71	3470	3335	3380	2150	2430	2195	2530
1972-74	3495	3390	3415	2190	2500	2175	2520
1975-77	3520	3380	3465	2250	2657	2210	2555
1978-80	3545	3420	3410	2265	2550	2230	2560

Note: Data after 1960 are more reliable than earlier data.

Source: 1934-59 data are from FAO *Third World Food Survey,* Rome, 1963.
1961-66 data are from FAO *Fourth World Food Survey,* Rome, 1977.
1966-77 data are from FAO *Monthly Bulletin of Statistics,* November 1979.
1978-80 data are from FAO *State of Food and Agriculture,* Rome, August 1983.

An Emerging World Market for Agricultural Products

The supply and demand trends of the last thirty years were in part the source of and in part the result of the evolution of a world market to facilitate the open and regular exchange of farm products between producers and consumers in different countries. Few of the importing countries could have supported the significant consumption gains made since 1950 without access to the world market to augment local production. Nor could many of the exporting countries, particularly the United States, have expanded output nearly so quickly without the world market as an outlet.

The world market that emerged has a number of characteristics common to all markets but several that are uniquely agricultural. Markets, particularly world markets, work to balance the interests of participating producers and consumers only; they operate with little or no concern about the interests of non-participants. Hence, hundreds of millions of hungry non-participants could exist alongside cumbersome surpluses and low and declining prices for the foodstuffs moving between participants. Participation ultimately depends, on the demand side, on the ability to buy and, on the supply side, on the ability to deliver reasonably priced products of acceptable quality.

A less obvious but no less critical characteristic of the world market is the inelasticity of import demand and the relative elasticity of export supply. Importers tend to be relatively unresponsive to price changes in making purchasing decisions. Low prices generate only limited increases in demand while high prices generate only limited decreases in demand. It is a matter of policy as well as economics in many of even the largest importing countries that food imports, while necessary and growing, are made only to supplement locally produced supplies. Hence, many factors other than trade prices affect buying decisions.

Export supply, on the other hand, is relatively elastic; a price increase generates large increases in production due at least in part to the considerable un- or underutilized agricultural resources available in the exporting countries. Price declines, however, often do not result in proportional production cutbacks because of the high cost of idling agricultural resources with only limited alternative uses. These import and export characteristics in combination made the world market unusually volatile. Swings in a weighted index of the real prices of farm products moving on the world market have been as wide as ± 20 to 30 percent in less than a year (e.g., 1972/73, 1974/75, and 1977/78) and have set record real highs and lows in less than two years. Individual product prices are even more volatile (table 11).

The Postwar Groundwork for a World Market—While there was considerable trade in selected farm products for extended periods before World War 2, there was effectively no world market to facilitate the regular, large-scale exchange of farm products. For long periods of time, particularly during the interwar period, many countries closed themselves off more or less completely from agricultural trade.

Two developments associated with the war made possible the emergency of a world market for farm products. Experience with transporting war materials between countries demonstrated that large-scale trade was possible. The physical infrastructure was in place, particularly after peace slowed the movement of armaments, to support a world market. Improvements in communication also made possible the timely exchange of information needed to support a global market.

The postwar political settlement also put in place the international institutional infrastructure needed to support a world food market. The collapse of the international trading system and the economic depression of the 1930s, followed by World War 2, destroyed past political and economic relationships and created a vacuum. The international institutions put in place in the late 1940s were particularly well suited to encouraging the emergence of world markets. The General Agreement on Trade and Tariffs (GATT) established a framework for trade and a commitment to its gradual liberalization.

The International Monetary Fund (IMF) and its provisions for a system of fixed, convertible exchange rates provided the initial impetus for the evolution of the financial component of the market. A complex global financial system evolved to support world markets with banking and credit services. The accumulation abroad of the dollars used to offset U.S. trade deficits and ultimately the appearance of the Eurodollar market insured enough world liquidity to support a world market.

The development of the world market after 1950 can be traced by using several measures. The volume of farm products traded increased 5 to 6 percent per year, almost twice the pace of growth in food production (table 1). Trade volume doubled from 1934-38 levels by the early 1960s and tripled by the early 1970s (table 12). Even more striking was growth in the number of countries willing to depend on the world market, either as a regular outlet for their production or as a source of supply. The number of countries regularly importing or expecting more than 1 million tons of food increased from 6-7 during the interwar period to over 20 in 1965 and over

TABLE 11

Real International Agricultural Prices*

Year	Real Agricultural Export Prices	Year	Real Agricultural Export Prices
	Index 1977-70 = 100		
1950	154	1965	97
1951	152	1966	95
1952	128	1967	95
1953	125	1968	101
1954	139	1969	107
1955	129	1970	102
1956	128	1971	91
1957	123	1972	92
1958	105	1973	118
1959	109	1974	138
1960	106	1975	96
1961	99	1976	104
1962	99	1977	119
1963	111	1978	93
1964	109	1979	92
Interannual variability in selected international commodity prices		1980	98
		1981	85
		1982	74

*Index of export prices for agricultural products expressed in terms of trade prices for a basket of manufactured, industrial, and primary products.

TABLE 12

World Food Production and Trade (1934-38 = 100)

Years	Food Production	Food Trade	Year	Food Production	Food Trade
1934-38	100	100	1965	171	226
			1966	176	239
1946	108	76	1967	184	239
1947	108	95	1968	190	247
1948	110	103	1969	190	247
1949	112	105			
			1970	196	266
1950	116	100	1971	202	276
1951	118	121	1972	202	295
1952	120	116	1973	214	318
1953	125	113	1974	216	305
1954	129	113			
			1975	220	313
1955	135	124	1976	225	337
1956	141	150	1977	229	339
1957	141	153	1978	241	336
1958	149	153	1979	243	387
1959	149	163			
			1980	241	405
1960	151	174	1981	249	413
1961	153	189	1982	255	418
1962	157	197	1983	260	413
1963	161	208			
1964	169	218			

Source: ERS/USDA "Indices of World Food and Agricultural Production," June, 1983.

40 in 1980. This growth in trade worked to allow growth in consumption in importing countries despite lagging growth in supply in those countries. In exporting countries it allowed growth in production despite lagging growth in consumption.

Food consumption in the fastest-growing importing countries expanded a third or more faster than food production as the importers grew from depending on trade for 5-10 percent to over 20 percent of their supplies (chart 5). In many cases this growth in imports was the result of the supply problems cited earlier. But growth in food imports was also symptomatic of economic success. In the middle-income countries in particular strong economic performance resulted in a veritable explosion in food demand. Their agricultures, while often performing well by historical standards, could not keep pace with growth in demand. But while their food imports were on the rise, these generally claimed a declining share of these countries' foreign exchange earnings. The reverse was unfortunately true, however, in many of the low-income countries that also grew more dependent on trade. Exporters also became more dependent on trade as foreign demand grew to account for 35 to 40 percent of their agricultural production, compared to less than 10 percent before the war and less than 20 percent in the 1960s. Production in the major exporting countries—such as the United States-grew as much as 25 percent faster than domestic use.

Strong economic growth during most of the 1970s put this growth in trade in an unusually positive light. In the importing countries strong growth in domestic economic activity and export earnings outside agriculture kept the cost of increased dependence on imports—i.e., rising food import bills and displacement of uncompetitive domestic producers—low enough to be palatable. Linkage to the rapidly growing world market also allowed exporters to use otherwise excess capacity and minimize costly government support for commodity prices and farmer incomes.

The U.S. Role in the Evolution of the World Market—The United States played a critical role in the evolution and operation of this world market. U.S. policy makers helped engineer the postwar financial and trading order. More importantly, however, U.S. willingness to tie its domestic market directly to the world market provided the adjustment base needed to allow the market to function during periods of shifting world supply or demand with a minimum of price disruption. For a number of reasons, many related to domestic farm policy goals, the United States held the sizeable stocks necessary to stabilize the market and offset potentially disruptive yield- and/or demand-related swings. With this U.S. underwriting, the costs of increased dependence on the volatile world market could be

CHART 5.

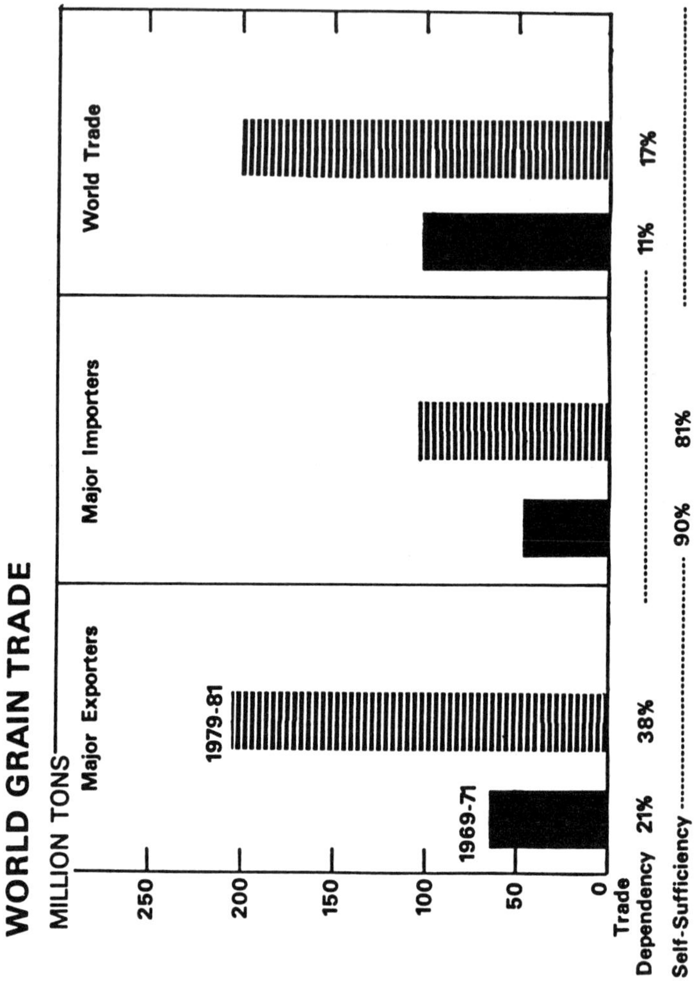

WORLD GRAIN TRADE

MILLION TONS

250
200
150
100
50
0

Major Exporters
Major Importers
World Trade

1969-71
1979-81

Trade Dependency 21% 38% 11% 17%

Self-Sufficiency 90% 81%

kept to a minimum ands growth in trade pushed to the maximum. In this environment the United States grew over the 1950-80 period from one of many exporters supplying less than 15 percent of the products traded to being the major exporter supplying over 40 percent of the trade.

The Growing Importance of Farm Trade to the United States

The trends in world supply, demand, and trade outlined above were partly the source of and partly the result of dramatic postwar changes in U.S. agriculture. In short, the growing importance of the United States in the world market paralleled equally dramatic growth in the importance of the world market to U.S. agriculture. Exports grew steadily from 1950 to 1981 and so much more rapdily than domestic demand that the portion of farm production shipped overseas almost ripled by 1981. By 1981 the output from more than two out of every five acres was being exported (table 13).

This growth in the export market was critical in shoring up a sector troubled with excess capacity, lagging commodity prices, and eroding incomes. The farm sector's resource base and growth in agricultural productivity were such over most of the post-war period that only 60 to 70 percent of its capacity to produce was needed to meet domestic demand. Without export outlets and with few alternative uses for the sector's resources, as much as 30 to 40 percent of its capacity would have been left idle—quite likely at considerable government expense, given the farm programs in place.

Moreover, given the economies of scale possible with the sector producing nearer full capacity to meet export demand, unit costs were undoubtedly lower over most of the period, and the cost of government intervention in the sector to support socially acceptable farm incomes considerably lower. Farm exports also lent considerable support over the postwar period to the value of the dollar. Agriculture's positive trade balance helped to offset the pressure that a negative non-agricultural trade balance would otherwise have brought on the dollar in exchange markets.

Residual Supplier Advantages and Disadvantages—The growing importance of exports in shaping U.S. agriculture related not only to the volume of products traded but also to the volatility of the world market and the U.S. role as residual supplier. While excess capacity made exports an increasingly attractive outlet, export volatility raised the cost of participating in the world market. During the 1970s the "costs" of being the residual

TABLE 13

U.S. Crop Acreage Harvested, Total and for Export, Averages 1950-80 and Annual 1971-82

Calendar Years	For Export: Food Grains	Feed Grains[a]	Oilcrops	Cotton	Other Crops	Total	Total Harvested[b]	Acreage Diverted[c]
	Millions of Acres							
1950	23	11	4	8	4	50	345	0
1951-55	19	9	4	6	4	42	345	0
1956-60	23	13	9	7	3	55	324	24
1961-65	31	21	13	4	3	72	313	57
1966-70	25	14	18	4	4	65	297	54
1971-75	35	20	26	5	4	90	317	24
1976-80	41	28	34	7	7	117	344	0
1971	20	15	21	4	2	62	305	37
1972	38	18	27	5	3	91	294	63
1973	38	21	27	6	4	96	321	19
1974	39	21	28	4	7	99	328	0
1975	39	25	26	4	6	100	336	0
1976	32	26	28	5	6	97	337	0
1977	42	26	32	6	6	112	344	0
1978	40	25	35	7	7	114	337	0
1979	42	29	38	8	8	125	349	0
1980	50	34	37	7	9	137	352	0
1981	51	23	40	6	9	129	366	0
1982	43	23	38	4	9	117	365	0

[a] Includes feed required to produce livestock products exported.

[b] Area in 59 principal crops harvested, as statistics reported, Econ. and Stat. Serv., USDA, plus acreages in fruits, tree nuts, and farm gardens.

[c] Total diverted or set aside under various programs, Agr. Stab. and Conserv. Serv., USDA, including limited acreage devoted to substitute crops.

supplier in a volatile market were generally positive. The United States expanded output sharply and captured over two-thirds of the unusually large increases in world trade.

The slowdown in growth in world trade and the dropoff in U.S. exports experienced since 1981 indicated, however, that there were also serious disadvantages involved in being the world's residual supplier and in being increasingly dependent on exports. While growth in world agricultural trade slowed, U.S. exports *declined* from $44 billion in 1980/81 to $34 billion in 1982/83—nearly 25 percent. The shock was severe enough to throw agriculture into recession and contribute to the development of a $20 to 30 billion complex of government programs to bail out a sector with net incomes normally in the $20 to 25 billion range.

The 1981-83 dropoff in exports also emphasizes the limited extent to which the U.S. government, let alone the U.S. farmer, can control or even forecast year-to-year movements in agricultural exports. By 1980 U.S. farm exports had come to depend not only on agricultural developments here but virtually anywhere in the world and on a host of national and international macroeconomic, financial, and foreign policy considerations traditionally related only tangentially to agriculture.

Increasingly Complex Policy Trade-offs—This growing sensitivity of U.S. agricultural exports to broader macroeconomic policy developments was demonstrated geographically over the 1970s and early 1980s with changes in U.S. monetary policy and the international value of the dollar. U.S. monetary policy had been relatively stable over most of the 1950s and 1960s while the changes in policy that did take place tended to have little impact on agriculture.

Both these conditions changed dramaticaly in the 1970s. Monetary policy became a great deal more volatile as the Federal Reserve actively intervened to accelerate or slow down economic activity and inflation through its controls on growth in the money supply and interest rates. Moreover, agriculture's increasing dependence on exports combined with the emergence of a well-integrated international capital market and the shift to a system of flexible exchange rates to make the sector far more sensitive to these fluctuations in monetary policy than at any time in the past.

In 1981 and 1982, for example, the Federal Reserve slowed the economy by restricting growth in the money supply. This slowed growth, combined with large federal deficits, increased U.S. interest rates sharply and attracted significant amounts of capital from abroad. The resulting rise in the value of the dollar in foreign exchange markets as foreign financiers moved to invest in the United States choked off exports while lowering the price of imports. In a world of flexible exchange rates and large-scale international capital flows, it was the export sectors of the economy—such as agriculture—and sectors competing with imports—such as the automobile and steel industries—that bore a disproportionate share of the adjustment generated by changes in monetary policy.

The situation was reversed during the dollar depreciation of the 1970s and could shift again later in the 1980s with faster growth in the money supply. Interest rates would decline, capital would flow out of the country, the value of the dollar would weaken, and exports would expand while imports contracted. In either case a disproportionate share of the burden of adjustment—positive or negative—is borne by the trade-sensitive sectors of the economy such as agriculture, steel, and autos.

In short, policies adopted to serve the broader needs of the economy may not serve the interests of the agricultural sector. Conversely, the economic policies that serve agriculture's interests best may not serve the needs of the general economy. Equally important, agricultural policy makers and possibly even national policy makers are finding themselves with less and less control over trade flows that are more and more critical to the health of the farm sector and economic growth elsewhere in the general economy.

PROSPECTS

The supply, demand, and trade trends identified above are fundamental enough that they will quite likely continue to shape world and U.S. agriculture over the next several decades. At issue, however, in assessing prospects for the next 4 to 5 years is the extent to which shorter-run developments will strengthen or weaken longer-run trends. The dramatic shifts in the market experienced from the late 1970s through the early 1980s point out both the extent to which short-run disruptions can overshadow longer-run trends and several sources of potential disruption. Prospects for the continuation and/or interruption of the trends identified above are treated in the materials that follow.

Slowed Growth in Foreign Supply and Demand

Foreign Demand Growth Likely to Weaken—Analysts studying foreign agriculture are in general agreement that the demographic, economic, and policy factors that shaped agricultural demand over the last thirty years will continue. But the after effects of the economic and financial reversals experienced since 1980 should work to keep growth in demand below trend over most of the life of the 1985 farm bill.

Demographers are in general agreement that the 1980s will be a period of gradually slowing population growth rates (table 14). Annual increases in the number of people to be fed could drop off to possibly 1.7 percent per year by 1988 compared with over 2 percent during the peak growth of the early 1960s and 1.8 percent at the end of the 1970s.

It is far more uncertain, however, if and how lower population growth rates will affect demand for farm products. The absolute number of people to be fed will continue to increase at an unprecedented pace. The world will add another 80 million people in 1984 and more than 300 million people over the life of the 1985 farm bill. Feeding this addition at even minimum intake levels would require an increase in food production abroad roughly equivalent to 70 million tons of wheat—about the equivalent of the record 1983 U.S. wheat crop.

Moreover, with population growth rates slowing, age structures in the developing countries experiencing the sharpest slowdowns in population growth will shift, with more and more people moving into the 15 to 45 year age category with the highest per capita nutritional needs. If provision is made for changing age structure in developing countries and its impact on demand, the added food production necessary to balance population growth jumps to 80 million tons, and the impact of slowing growth rates is essentially canceled out.

As over the last thirty years, however, the full impact of this increase in the number of people to be fed is not likely to be reflected in effective demand for food. The mid-1980s are likely to be characterized by the same patchwork pattern of increases and decreases in per capita food intake that will work to convert the 8 percent increase in population prospective over the life of the 1985 farm bill into possibly a 5 to 6 percent increase in demand for agricultural products.

While specific projections vary, macroeconomic forecasters generally agree that economic growth during the mid-1980s is likely to be less favorable than over most of the 1960s and 1970s (table 15).

Prospects for the industrialized countries have received the most attention. The early 1980s were marked by the worst postwar slowdown in their histories, and the recovery forecast to begin in earnest outside the United States in 1984 and 1985 is likely to be weak in comparison to cyclical upturns following earlier recoveries. Moreover, the recovery forecast for 1984 and early 1985 is dependent on U.S. recovery proving strong enough to spark export-led growth in the other industrialized economies. Recovery is also dependent on the United States reducing its federal deficits sharply in

TABLE 14

World Population, Selected Countries and Regions 1982-90*

Country/Region	1982	1983	1984	1985	1986	1987	1988	1989	1990
					Millions				
Developed Countries	773.9	780.1	786.1	792.5	798.7	805.0	811.3	817.6	823.8
United States	229.8	232.1	234.3	236.5	238.7	241.0	243.2	245.4	247.6
Canada	24.7	25.0	25.4	25.7	26.1	26.4	26.7	27.1	27.4
EEC-10	271.6	272.4	273.2	274.0	274.8	275.7	276.5	277.3	278.2
Other Western Europe	79.9	80.4	80.8	81.3	81.8	82.3	82.8	83.2	83.6
South Africa	30.0	30.7	31.4	32.3	33.0	33.8	34.6	35.4	36.2
Japan	119.6	120.9	122.2	123.6	125.0	126.3	127.7	129.1	130.5
Oceania	18.3	18.6	18.8	19.1	19.3	19.5	19.8	20.1	20.3
Australia	14.9	15.1	15.2	15.4	15.6	15.8	16.0	16.1	16.3
New Zealand	3.2	3.2	3.2	3.2	3.3	3.3	3.3	3.3	3.3
Centrally Planned Countries	1,414.0	1,430.0	1,446.2	1,462.4	1,478.3	1,494.4	1,510.0	1,526.0	1,541.4
Eastern Europe	136.3	137.1	138.0	138.8	139.6	140.5	141.3	142.2	143.0
USSR	270.7	273.2	275.6	278.1	280.6	283.1	285.6	288.2	2909.8
P.R. China	1,007.0	1,019.7	1,032.6	1,045.5	1,058.1	1,070.8	1,083.1	1,095.6	1,107.6
Developing Countries	2,336.9	2,394.0	2,451.8	2,510.3	2,569.9	2,631.4	2,694.3	2,758.5	2,824.4
Latin America	362.9	371.3	380.0	388.7	397.2	406.1	415.1	424.2	433.6
Mexico	71.3	73.2	75.1	77.0	78.9	80.9	82.9	84.9	86.9
Brazil	127.1	129.9	132.7	135.7	138.5	141.4	144.4	147.4	150.5
Argentina	28.7	29.1	29.6	30.0	30.3	30.7	31.0	31.4	31.8
Other Latin America	135.8	139.1	142.6	146.0	149.5	153.1	156.8	160.5	164.4

TABLE 14
(Continued)

World Population, Selected Countries and Regions 1982-90*

Country/Region	1982	1983	1984	1985	1986	1987	1988	1989	1990
					Millions				
North Africa/Middle East	259.5	257.3	275.4	283.7	292.3	301.2	310.3	319.6	329.3
High-Income	104.2	107.5	111.0	114.5	118.2	122.0	125.9	129.9	134.1
Low-Income	155.3	159.8	164.4	169.2	174.1	179.2	184.4	189.7	195.2
Central Africa	246.3	252.2	259.0	265.6	272.2	279.0	286.0	293.2	300.5
East Africa	80.9	83.3	85.8	88.3	90.8	93.5	96.2	98.9	101.8
South Asia	953.3	975.2	997.6	1,020.5	1,044.0	1,068.0	1,092.5	1,117.6	1,143.3
India	723.4	739.3	755.6	772.2	789.2	806.6	824.3	842.4	861.0
Other South Asia	229.9	235.9	242.0	248.3	254.8	261.4	268.2	275.2	282.3
Southeast Asia	152.4	156.0	159.7	163.3	167.1	170.8	174.7	178.7	182.7
Thailand	48.7	49.8	50.9	51.9	53.0	54.0	55.1	56.2	57.3
Other Southeast Asia	103.7	106.2	108.8	111.4	114.1	116.8	119.6	122.5	125.4
East Asia	281.6	288.4	294.3	300.2	306.3	312.8	319.5	326.3	333.2
Indonesia	149.4	152.1	155.5	158.6	161.7	164.9	168.2	171.5	174.9
High-Income	65.8	67.2	68.7	70.0	71.3	72.7	74.1	75.5	76.9
Low-Income	67.4	69.1	70.1	71.6	73.3	75.2	77.2	79.3	81.4
Rest of World	32.2	33.0	33.7	34.5	35.2	36.0	36.7	37.5	38.2
World Total	4,557.0	4,637.1	4,717.8	4,799.7	4,882.1	4,966.8	5,052.3	5,139.6	5,227.8

*Data are midyear, except for China, where they are endyear.

Source: Bureau of the Census, U.S. Department of Commerce, unpublished as of printing.

TABLE 15

Changes in Real Gross National Products, Selected Countries and Regions*

Country/Region	1982	1983	1984	1985	1986	1987	1988	1989	1990
	Annual Percent Change								
World	.50	2.00	3.24	3.03	3.16	3.51	3.51	3.28	3.51
Developed Countries	– .27	2.01	3.46	2.91	2.91	3.41	3.42	3.07	3.42
United States	–1.90	3.10	5.10	2.40	2.20	3.70	3.50	2.50	3.20
Canada	–4.80	2.00	3.00	2.50	2.50	3.30	3.20	2.50	2.70
EEC-10	.00	1.00	2.00	3.00	3.00	3.00	3.00	3.00	3.30
Other Western Europe	1.00	1.00	2.00	2.80	2.70	2.80	3.00	3.50	3.30
South Africa	2.00	2.00	3.50	3.50	4.00	4.00	3.50	3.00	4.00
Japan	2.50	3.00	4.00	4.00	4.50	4.50	4.50	4.50	4.50
Oceania	2.80	2.00	2.00	3.00	3.00	3.00	3.00	3.00	3.00
Centrally Planned Countries	2.50	2.37	2.50	2.71	2.71	2.71	2.71	2.71	2.71
Eastern Europe	1.50	1.00	1.50	1.50	2.00	2.00	2.00	2.00	2.00
USSR	2.50	2.50	2.50	2.50	2.50	2.50	2.50	2.50	2.50
P.R. China	4.00	4.00	4.00	4.00	4.50	4.50	4.50	4.50	4.50
Developing Countries	1.61	1.59	3.34	4.48	5.15	5.26	5.21	5.24	5.20
Developing America	– .67	–2.51	.36	3.78	4.73	4.82	4.73	4.79	4.73
Middle America	.82	–2.38	.48	2.00	5.42	5.80	5.42	5.65	5.42
Mexico	1.00	–2.50	0	2.00	6.50	7.00	6.50	6.80	6.50
Other Middle America	.24	–2.01	2.00	2.00	2.00	2.00	2.00	2.00	2.00
Brazil	0	–5.00	0	5.50	5.60	5.60	5.60	5.60	5.60
Argentina	–5.70	0.00	1.00	3.50	4.00	4.00	4.00	4.00	4.00
Other South America	–1.00	.15	.50	3.00	3.00	3.00	3.00	3.00	3.00

TABLE 15
(Continued)

Changes in Real Gross National Products, Selected Countries and Regions*

Country/Region	1982	1983	1984	1985	1986	1987	1988	1989	1990
	Annual Percent Change								
Developing Africa and Middle East	2.63	3.03	4.50	4.09	4.83	4.78	4.73	4.76	4.71
Subsarahan Africa	2.00	2.00	3.00	3.00	3.00	3.00	3.00	3.00	3.00
N.A. & Mid. East	2.85	3.40	5.02	4.47	5.48	5.41	5.34	5.38	5.31
High-Income	1.50	2.00	4.00	5.00	6.50	6.40	6.30	6.30	6.20
Low-Income	5.60	6.23	7.10	3.40	3.40	3.40	3.40	3.50	3.50
Developing Asia	3.21	4.94	5.66	5.83	6.04	6.37	6.37	6.37	6.37
South Asia	.98	4.24	4.29	4.24	4.24	4.96	4.96	4.96	4.96
India	0	4.00	4.00	4.00	4.00	4.00	4.00	4.00	4.00
Other South Asia	4.09	5.02	5.19	5.00	5.00	8.00	8.00	8.00	8.00
Southeast Asia	6.53	6.45	6.45	6.75	6.75	6.75	6.75	6.75	6.75
Thailand	6.70	6.60	6.60	7.00	7.00	7.00	7.00	7.00	7.00
Other Southeast Asia	6.00	6.00	6.00	6.00	6.00	6.00	6.00	6.00	6.00
East Asia	4.15	5.14	6.72	7.13	7.63	7.75	7.75	7.75	7.75
High-Income	4.88	6.07	7.63	7.50	8.00	8.00	8.00	8.00	8.00
Low-Income	1.95	2.33	4.00	6.00	6.50	7.00	7.00	7.00	7.00
Indonesia	5.00	5.50	6.00	6.00	6.00	6.00	6.00	6.00	6.00

*Data are for calendar year.

Source: Statistical Reporting Service/USDA "Agricultural Statistics 1983."

order to minimize the squeezing out of investment abroad possible if high U.S. interest rates continue to siphon off foreign capital.

By mid-decade, however, economic activity should have expanded sufficiently in Western Europe and Japan to boost growth well above depressed 1981-85 levels. Overdue structural adjustments, as well as changes in technology and energy use, are expected to be well underway by 1986. However, even post-recovery growth over the 1985-88 period should lag below rates during comparable stages of previous recoveries. Growth for the developed countries for the decade as a whole is likely to average in the 3 percent range, compared with 5 percent over the two previous decades.

Economic growth in the centrally planned countries is also forecast to be slow by historical standards. In China cutbacks in investment, slowed growth in agricultural output, and structural adjustments in the industrial sector are expected to keep growth rates below the postwar average. The Soviet Union's current Five Year Plan also suggests slower economic growth and lagging growth in the labor force. Similar problems appear likely for most of the Eastern European countries.

Growth in the developing countries as a group is forecast to recover from the 1981-83 recession more slowly than in the developed countries. The one to two year lag involved reflects both the severity of the developing countries' own energy and productivity problems and the impact of the recession on their sales of primary products abroad and their ability to arrange commercial and concessional financing for development. Economic growth should accelerate somewhat in 1986 and beyond, as export opportunities improve and as internal structural adjustments ease energy and productivity problems.

Prospects for a relatively small group of low-income developed and to high-income developing countries with a combined population of 400 to 500 million—the middle income countries—stand out in contrast to an otherwise weak global economic outlook. Their brighter economic prospects depend on one or a combination of factors including strong export postions in items such as minerals or petroleum, well-planned and administered development programs, and sufficient development momentum built up over the 1970s to overcome the general problems outlined above.

As in the case of population, there is considerably less certainty about how sharply the generally slower economic growth through the late 1980s will curtail growth in agricultural demand. The recession experienced to date in the 1980s has had less impact on demand than many forecasters expected. Changes in economic activity across countries and the absolute levels of income enjoyed in much of the world helped to minimize sthe negative impact of slower economic growth on demand for farm products.

In most developed countries the lackluster recovery forecast for 1984 and 1985 will translate into relatively weak increases, but increases nonetheless, in per capita incomes, consumer buying power, and demand for meat and feedstuffs. Demand growth in 1986-88 could strengthen further, albeit not to historical rates, with economic recovery. Income-related shifts in diets toward more livestock products are likely to continue and may actually accelerate in the middle income countries in 1985 and beyond. While two to three year prospects for demand growth are very poor for countries such as Poland, Mexico, and Brazil, demand for farm products could pick up noticeably in these countries in 1986 and beyond after their current financial problems ease. Thus, while weak by the historical standards set during previous recoveries, demand for farm products abroad could expand 2.3 to 2.5 percent during the life of the 1985 farm bill. This compares with growth of 2.5 to 3 percent from 1950 to 1982 (table 1).

Mixed Foreign Supply Prospects—While the consensus is less pronounced than in the demand area, analysts studying foreign food production prospects suggest that the trends toward increased pressure on agriculture's natural resource base and increasing reliance on productivity growth will continue to slow growth in production. However, the increased investments made in expanding agricultural capacity and the changes in farm policy, including rising producer prices in many developing countries during the food scares of the 1970s, should be coming on line over the next several years and will work to prevent any sharp decline in growth rates.

The global natural resource inventories done over the last decade in response to concern with what was commonly seen as agriculture's shrinking resource base suggest that sufficient potentially arable area is available to double the world's cropland. However, the inventories in question focused almost exclusively on physical potential and tended to ignore the agronomic, environmental, and economic problems involved in any large-scale conversion to cropping.

From a purely economic perspective, the limited data available on the cost of converting potentially arable area to cropland suggest that the highest payoff opportunities for land development have been taken advantage of. Much of the acreage left is marginal land subject to one or more serious limitations that rule out conversion unless producer incentives improve substantially. In some cases large capital investments in clearing, drainage, etc., would have to be made. In many cases, given the inputs needed on a more or less regular basis to augment limited soil fertility and to ease problems of erosion, pests, and disease, operational costs after the land is converted to cropping would also be high.

Moreover, lower yields and greater interannual variability in production can also be expected from much of the land converted in marginal areas. With these limitations, growth in the land committed to agriculture could well contribute even less to expanding agricultural production over the decade ahead than over the postwar period to date.

While far fewer in number and more limited in scope, the agricultural technology inventories done over the last decade point to a significant backlog of productivity-enhancing know how available for adoption in the 1980s. But accelerating technology adoption and productivity growth is likely to be difficult. The high cost and in some cases limited availability of petroleum has already shifted concern with productivity in many countries, including the United States, toward increasing input efficiency and developing alternative energy technologies and production techniques rather than maximizing output.

While the development of alternative technologies will take a number of years, changes in production techniques are already underway. Minimum tillage, drip irrigation, and integrated pest management may be used more intensively to slow growth in the use of costly inputs. Given reactions to higher energy costs to date, total energy use per unit of output is likely to decline or at least stabilize in the agricultural sectors of most of the developed countries. This may be less the case in developing countries where petroleum-based technologies are likely to continue to be adopted, although at a somewhat slower rate, if only because of their ready availability and greater pressure to increase output.

Critical from a broader supply perspective is the impact this changing productivity emphasis will have on the pace of growth in output. Chart 2 suggests that, at least initially, growth in productivity should slow expansion in output, particularly if the land added to agriculture's resource base is of more marginal quality. If this is the case, slowed growth in the natural resources committed to agriculture could combine with slower growth inproductivity to slow growth in output abroad from the postwar 2.3-2.9 percent to less than the 2.3-2.5 percent growth in demand identified above as likely ahead (table 1).

Balancing Foreign Supply and Demand: Demand for U.S. Farm Products

This imbalance between trend growth in supply and demand abroad would normally work to increase the rest of the world's dependence on the

United States with its considerable un- or underutilized capacity as a source of supply. The imbalance in prospect for the next several years is significantly narrower than the imbalance of the 1970s, approximately the same as the imbalance over the postwar period to date, and well within the United States' capacity to fill.

What remains uncertain, however, is how much of this imbalance will be converted into effective demand for U.S. exports. The declining value of the dollar over the 1970s worked in two ways to facilitate the conversion of unmet foreign demand into U.S. exports (chart 6). With most of the trade prices for farm products denominated in dollars, a weaker dollar worked to lower the cost of importing substantially. With other key imports such as petroleum and items such as debt service also denominated in dollars, a cheaper dollar also worked to increase countries' overall international buying power. These price and income effects were most pronounced in the middle-income countries, major actors in the 1970s explosion in import demand.

The far stronger and more precipitous appreciation of the dollar experienced so far in the 1980s worked in reverse through these price and income relationships to weaken the conversion of unmet local demand into U.S. exports. With little change in the tight monetary policy and federal deficits underlying the dollar's appreciation, demand for U.S. farm exports could continue to be weaker than the imbalance likely between foreign demand and supply would suggest.

Forecasters are in general agreement that this is the more likely outcome for the first half of the 1985 farm bill cycle. There is less agreement, however, about the second half of the cycle. Smaller deficits and faster growth in the money supply could result in a marked weakening of the dollar, reflecting the United States' large and growing trade deficits. In this kind of an environment the outlook for growth in trade and U.S. exports would improve substantially.

Policy Prospects: A Critical Unknown

As the experience of the last decade demonstrated graphically, farm, food, and agricultural trade policy developments over the next 4 to 5 years could modify longer-term supply and demand trends substantially. A return to the 1970s expansionist demand policies could accelerate growth in demand significantly. Conversely, continued retrenchment aimed at minimizing import bills and good subsidy expendsitures in many of the heretofore fastest-growing middle-income countries could slow growth in demand toward 2 percent.

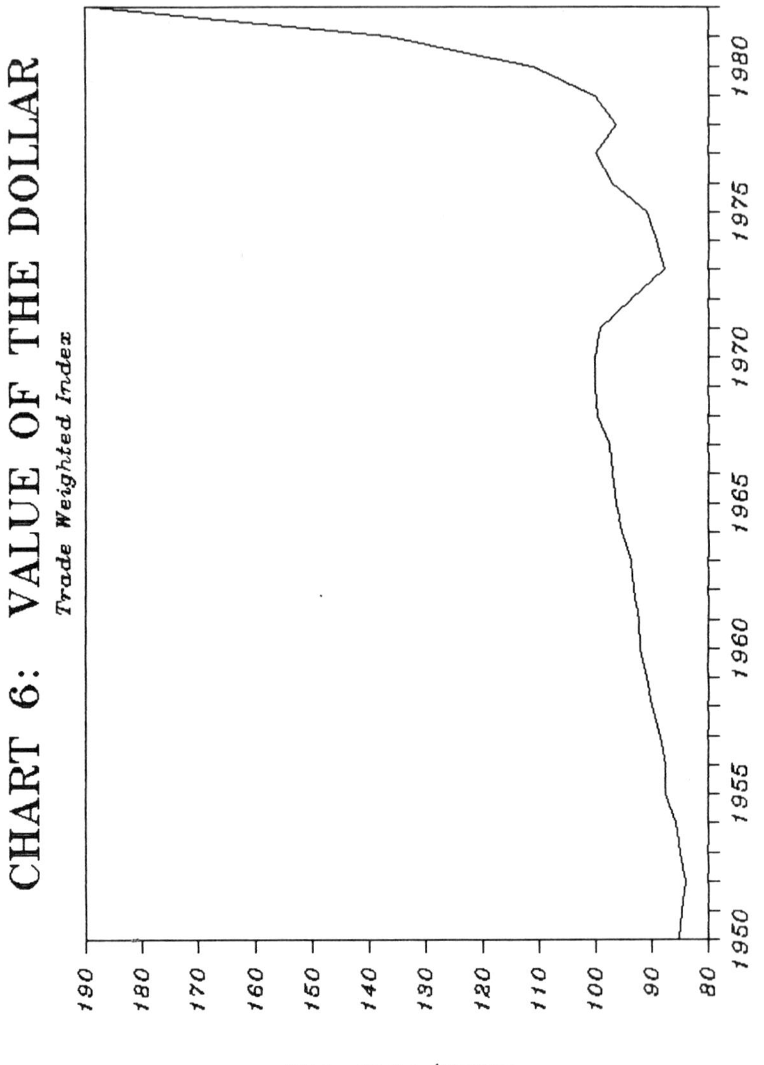
CHART 6: VALUE OF THE DOLLAR
Trade Weighted Index
Index, 1970=100
190
180
170
160
150
140
130
120
110
100
90
80
1950
1955
1960
1965
1970
1975
1980

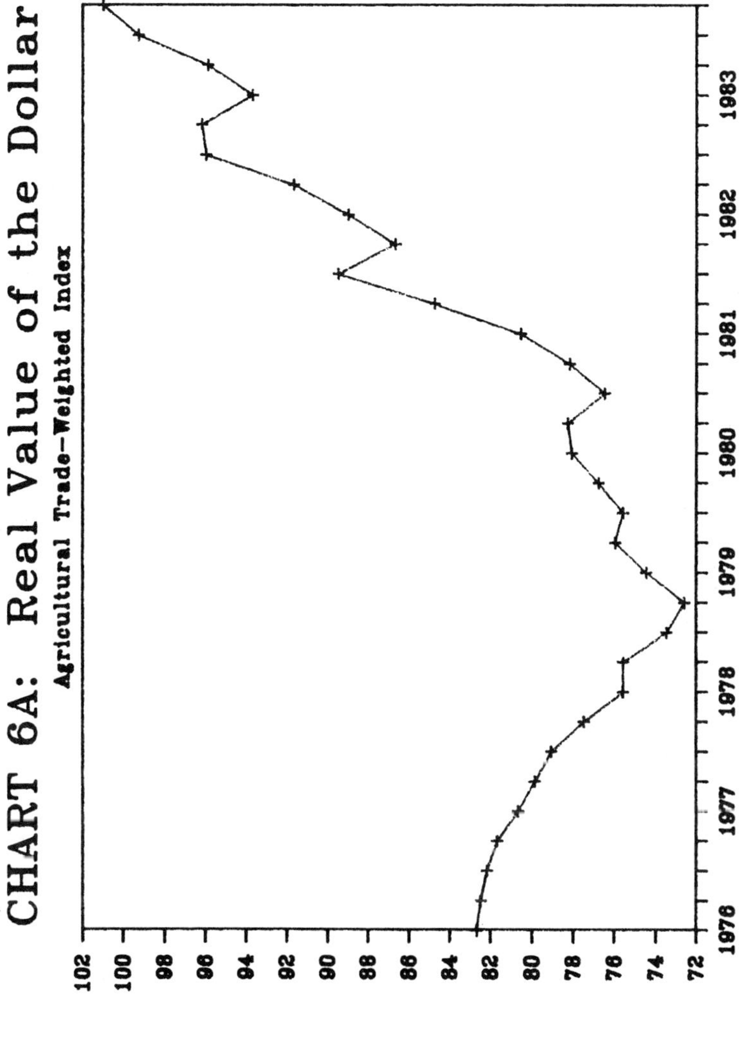
CHART 6A: Real Value of the Dollar
Agricultural Trade-Weighted Index
April, 1971=100
102
100
98
96
94
92
90
88
86
84
82
80
78
76
74
72
1976
1977
1978
1979
1980
1981
1982
1983

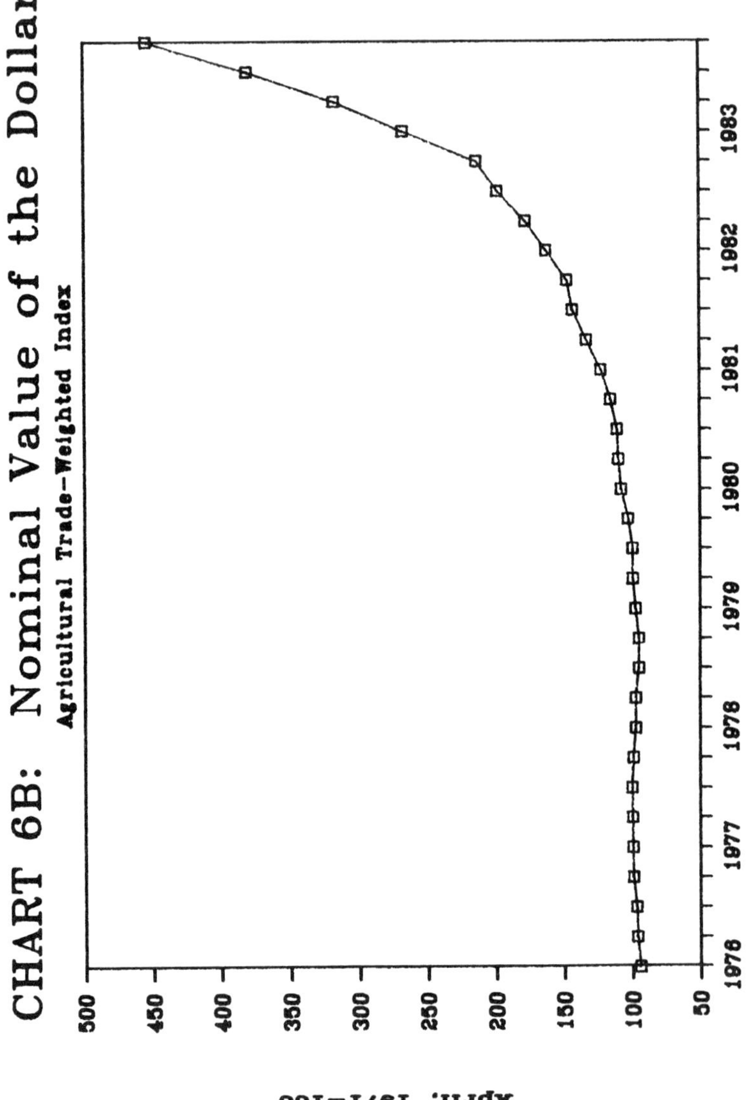
CHART 6B: Nominal Value of the Dollar
Agricultural Trade-Weighted Index
500
450
400
350
300
250
200
150
100
50
April, 1971=100
1976
1977
1978
1979
1980
1981
1982
1983

Prospects for the demand-oriented policies in question for the life of the 1985 farm bill are mixed. For at least the next 1 to 3 years, concern with import bills and subsidy program costs are likely to overshadow concern with dietary improvements and pent-up consumer demand. But with faster economic growth in 1986 and beyond, demand-dampening policies will become increasingly difficult to continue, and policy could shift toward having a more neutral or even positive impact on demand growth.

Policy prospects in the supply area are mixed. Emphasis on expanding domestic output increased significantly in the late 1970s and the early 1980s. Producer prices were raised in many countries while procurement and marketing programs were modified in an effort to expand local output. This emphasis reflected concern not only with rising food import bills but also with deteriorating farm incomes and commodity prices and the prospect of resource dislocation in agriculture.

However, the programs put in place have proved more costly and in many cases less effective than anticipated. As a result, support for these policies could wane later in the 1980s as costs, measured both in terms of higher consumer prices and government support expenditures, mount and economic recovery increases the opportunities for transferring excess resources out of agriculture. Hence, growth in supply in the importing countries could prove somewhat faster in the early years of the 1985 farm bill cycle but slower from possibly 1986 on.

An Uncertain World Market

Should the supply and demand prospects outlined above materialize, agricultural trade will continue to expand but at possibly two-thirds the postwar pace. Even with the pace of growth slowing, however, volume increases will be quite large, and both importing and exporting countries will likely find themselves increasingly dependent on trade (chart 7). At issue, however, is whether the world market will be strong enough over the next 4 to 5 years to facilitate trade to the same extent as over the 1950-80 period.

A number of forces that emerged over the late 1970s and early 1980s raise serious questions about the future operation of the market. Interannual fluctuations in supply and demand increased dramatically. Year-to-year swings in yields and production in many of the largest importing and exporting countries increased dramatically, at least in part because of increased use of marginal resources, more variable weather, and possibly even more fundamental climate changes. Year-to-year changes in demand due to macroeconomic developments and shifts in food and trade policies

CHART 7.

WORLD GRAIN TRADE
MILLION TONS
Major Exporters
Major Importers
World Trade
1969-71
1979-81
1990
250
200
150
100
50
0
Trade Dependency
21%
38%
43%
11%
17%
18%
Self-Sufficiency
90%
81%
79%

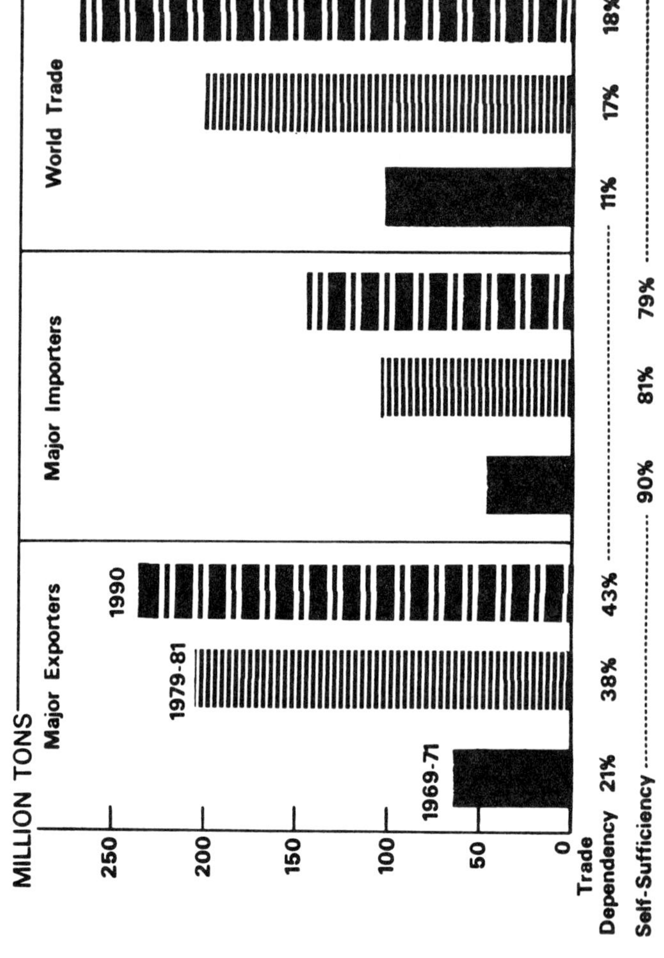

have also become more pronounced. The majority of the countries faced with these widening fluctuations adjusted imports or exports to stabilize their domestic markets.

As a result, the year-to-year changes in trade prices and quantities necessary to keep the world market in balance have increased sharply. But while the world market's adjustment burden has been expanding, its adjustment base—countries willing to adjust their production, use, and prices to fluctuate in response to world market signals—has tended to shrink. More and more countries have strengthened existing or put new protectionist trade policies in place to shield them from adjustments in response to changes in market conditions.

This volatility problem could worsen over the next several years if demand becomes increasingly price-inelastic and unpredictable and if producers in exporting countries continue under unusually severe financial pressures that encourage them to overproduce, and more and more countries withdraw from the adjustment process. Equally important, should the tendency toward adopting/strengthening protectionist trade policies continue, the world market's adjustment base could continue to shrink and exacerbate the volatility problem even further.

The Trade Policy Confrontation

As potentially serious as it may be, however, this volatility problem tends to be overshadowed by the trade policy pressures currently being brought to bear on the world market. After several decades of working compromise, the allocation of the costs and benefits associated with trade has emerged as a serious point of contention among the major trading countries.

Tracking the development of the world market over the last three decades emphasizes the close relationship between trade policy and economic growth. During periods of rapid economic growth, barriers to trade weakened in most of the importing countries, at least in part because the structural adjustments involved in shifting uncompetitive resources out of agriculture were made more easily and pressures to increase imports to meet domestic demand were greater. The exporters' concern with winning market access and expanding market shares, even at the cost of adopting unfair trade practices such as export subsidization, gave way during the strong economic growth of the 1970s in particular to expanding output fast enough to meet strong growth in world import demand.

In short, a rapidly expanding world market distracted attention from the restrictive, protectionist trade policies at work to limit imports and protect domestic farmers in countries such as Japan and allowed the United States and the EEC to follow otherwise conflicting policies of expanding exports as an outlet for their growing agricultural surpluses.

The macroeconomic reversals of the 1980s changed this trade policy environment dramatically. Moreover, events within agriculture worked to reinforce the change. Since 1979 the internal farm problems facing virtually all the major trading countries have worsened. Importers and exporters alike face serious pressure on commodity prices, farm incomes, and government farm expenditures as a result of the recession's weakening of demand and the effect of generally good weather and growth in productivity on supply.

The importers also face growing balance of payments problems in part because of agricultural imports but also because of difficulty in selling their non-agricultural products abroad—often in the food exporting countries seeking greater access to their agricultural markets. As a result, they have become far more sensitive to the cost of importing farm products—not only in terms of foreign exchange but in terms of the employment and GNP transferred to exporters. The exporters face a somewhat different but equally pressing set of problems. Given their inability or unwillingness to adjust output to slowed growth in import demand, the exporters have accumulated large enough surpluses to push real commodity prices to a twenty-year low.

Many countries have reacted to these macroeconomic and farm problems by intensifying efforts to increase exports or restrict imports and to isolate their farmers from "foreign" disruptions. The resulting head-to-head confrontation between exporters for market shares and between exporters and importers for market access had disrupted the operation of the world market.

Market Impacts

By far the most serious trade policy confrontation to date has been between the United States and the EEC, but relations among Brazil, Japan, Canada, Australia, and Argentina have also worsened. This widening confrontation is currently threatening to undermine the operation of the market—particularly its ability to balance changes in supply and demand with a minimum of price disruptions and to move the market away from a viable, stable equilibrium.

The protectionist/expansionist trade programs put in place or strengthened in many countries substitute the output of local, higher-cost producers in importing countries, or in exporting countries subsidizing sales abroad, for the output of lower-cost producers in the relatively free trading exporting countries. The welfare of all participants is adversely affected. Export subsidy programs tend to encourage consumption in the short term by making prices artificially low temporarily—particularly in relation to the prices likely after efficient producers are forced out—while discouraging investment in productive capacity in the low-cost producing countries being squeezed out of the market.

Equally important, these trade programs and the rhetoric used to defend them have also tended to raise the cost of the trade dependency noted earlier via their impact on market stability while increasing the attractiveness of self-sufficiency policies. An increasingly volatile world market could well generate as strong a move away from trade dependence as the relatively stable market during much of the postwar period generated in favor of trade. An increasingly inequitable sharing of the costs and benefits of participating in the world market would tend to have the same effect.

The Participation Crisis

The economic forces at play in the early 1980s have also tended to undercut the world market in another key area—participation. As already noted, the number of countries importing and exporting on a regular basis increased steadily from 1950 through 1980. The economic growth of the 1970s, combined with easy credit and a weakening dollar, allowed many of the developing and less affluent developed countries to buy into the world market and accelerated this participation trend.

But economic setbacks so far in the 1980s have ruled out continued participation for many of the 1970s new participants and entry for many potential participants. In many cases recession has weakened growth in demands for farm products and reduced these countries' import needs measured in terms of effective market demand. Moreover, changes in the value of the dollar and the resulting rise in the cost of farm products purchased with dollars have also reduced their capacity to import. The dollars needed to purchase farm products internationally cost 25 to 100 percent more in local currencies in 1983 than in 1981. This effectively raised the prices of all dollar-denominated imports, both agricultural and non-agricultural, and eroded many developing countries' international buying power significantly. Faced with worsening exchange constraints, many food-short countries have been forced to put farm imports low on their priority lists. The tightening in credit available from private and public sources as well as from the exporters themselves has also tended to rule out an expedient used widely toward the end of the 1970s.

While less dramatic than the trade policy confrontation and the rhetoric it has generated, the participation crisis is potentially as serious. If the bearish economic and financial developments of the last three years are seen as temporary deviations from trend, then future participation in the world market is not an issue. A return to more normal economic growth, a stable international financial regime, and a cheaper dollar will reaccelerate participation. In this environment the problem of effective versus ineffective import demand for farm products should lessen over time. Differences in per capita food consumption levels and rates of growth in food consumption should continue to narrow as more developing countries become fully integrated into the world market.

But should the economic and financial problems currently troubling the world prove to be more lasting, the world market could face a serious loss of momentum. The loss in welfare likely with a slowing or reversal in participation would affect not only the countries locked out of the market but countries participating in the market itself as well. From a single-country perspective, participation in the world market has improved welfare in several ways. The countries that have participated most in the world market—measured in terms of trade as an outlet for production or as a source of supply—are characterized by more stable food supplies as well as higher per capita consumption levels, lower food prices, and/or higher farm incomes than they would otherwise have enjoyed. From a broader perspective, increased participation has also tended to fill out an otherwise thin, potentially unstable market to the benefit of all participants.

Successfully weathered, these trade policy and participation pressures could result in a stronger world market serving both importer and exporter needs better. Unresolved, however, these pressures could result in a weakening of the world market and bring with it dramatically slower growth in world agricultural production, consumption, and trade and quite likely generally higher food, feed, and fiber prices.

IMPLICATIONS FOR U.S. AGRICULTURAL POLICY

The world market trends and prospects outlined above have a number of critical, in some areas conflicting, implications for U.S. agricultural policy.

In the most general terms, they suggest that the rest of the world will continue to become increasingly dependent on a small circle of exporters, particularly the United States, as a source of supply (chart 7). The pace, however, should slacken off from the 1970s. Growth in foreign demand for U.S. farm products in particular could slow dramatically from the pace set in the 1970s but should recover enough from the reversals of the early 1980s to leve the rest of the world dependent on the United States for more than 10 percent of its food supplies by 1990.

Commodity supply-demand balances generated using the resource, productivity, population, income, and policy assumptions outlined above in parts 2 and 3 imply that growth in U.S. exports shold expand 3 to 4 percent per year from 1985 through 1990, or at about the pace of the 1960s but only a third the pace of the 1970s (table 16). "Normal" year-to-year fluctuations in production or use abroad, changes in the value of the dollar, or policy developments abroad and resulting changes in import demand, could raise or lower U.S. export growth in any one year sharply—possibly to as high as 10 percent or as low as the 4 to 5 percent drop experienced in 1982.

In a similar vein, the United States is also likely to become increasingly dependent on the world market as an outlet for its farm product despite slower growth in exports. This increasing U.S. dependence on exports relates as much to domestic considerations as to world market developments. Foreign demand is fast becoming the only significant source of growth in demand for the burgeoning supplies of farm products likely to be available in the United States over the next several years.

If the 1950-80 trend continues, the U.S. farm sector's capacity to produce will expand 2 percent or more per year through 1988 on the basis of productivity gains alone. This productivity growth, combined with fuller use of the sector's land base, will put the farm sector in a position to expand output 3 to 4 percent per year, or roughly 15 to 20 percent by 1988. Moreover, past productivity growth and land use patterns have been such that an increase in output of 2 percent or more could be compatible with the slowly rising nominal prices and declining real farm prices implied earlier. The unprecedented capacity gains of the 1950s and 1960s were actually made during a prolonged period of declining real prices. Capacity could well expand at an even faster pace with constant or rising real commodity prices.

Prospects for growth in domestic demand for farm products is considerably less favorable. Demand weakened over the last 2 to 3 years with economic downturn. Equally important but less visible, per capita consumption of many farm products is fast approaching saturation levels, and conventional sources of demand may not increase significantly even with economic recovery. Even with a return to stronger macroeconomic growth later in the 1980s, growth in domestic demand for farm products could lag at as little as three-fourths the pace of growth in productivity.

TABLE 16

U.S. Agricultural Trade Balance (Fiscal Years)

Item	1981	1982	1983	1984	1985	1986	1987	1988	1989
	Billions of Dollars								
Exports	43.8	39.1	35.5	39.0	42.7	46.1	50.0	54.2	58.1
Imports	17.2	15.4	15.8	17.0	18.5	20.0	21.5	23.0	24.5
Trade Balance	25.6	23.7	19.7	22.0	24.2	26.1	28.5	31.2	33.6
	Millions of Tons								
Export Volume	162.3	158.1	149.0	154.2	159.4	165.1	171.8	177.4	182.9

Source: ERS/USDA (implied in tables 1-15, previously unpublished calculations).

The trends and prospects summarized above also suggest that the world market will continue to be an extremely competitive market and possibly an increasingly volatile market. While growth in world trade should pick up from the depressed levels of the early 1980s, the pace is not likely to be fast enough through the late 1980s to ease the exporters' excess capacity problems and use of questionable trade practices to expand export market shares. Competition will consequently continue to be intense, and the current trade policy confrontation among exporters and between importers and exporters could well continue, possibly worsen.

Market volatility is also likely to continue to be a problem. The dramatic change in trade prospects since 1981 points out how sharply the world agricultural outlook can change in a short period of time. Foreign and U.S. crop yields both seem to be becoming increasingly variable. This could be due to a combination of increasingly variable weather and the use of resources which are more sensitive to normal weather fluctuations. Macroeconomic conditions and agricultural trade policy changes abroad have also become considerably less stable and are a growing source of uncertainty for the world market and an export-oriented U.S. agriculture. Swings in supply and demand as pronounced as the shifts experienced over the 1978-80 and 1983-83 period could well become commonplace.

These problems of intensified competition and increased market volatility could raise serious questions about the advantages of U.S. participation in the world market despite the lack of an alternative outlet for the farm sector's product.

Agricultural Policy Implications

Operationally, what do these broad generalizations mean for U.S. agricultural policy?

They suggest at first glance a return to the problems and policy remedies of the 1950s and 1960s—i.e., slowing growth in agricultural output to meet lagging growth in demand in the domestic and export markets through a set of essentially inward-focused farm programs. Given the internationalization of American agriculture that has taken place since 1970, however, the farm policies of the 1950s and 1960s would be ill-suited for the 1980s. Continuing the ill-matched domestic and trade policies of the 1970s could prove equally unattractive. Their continuation would leave the United States vulnerable to increasingly wide and disruptive swings in world supply, demand, and prices. Maximizing the return on the increased reliance on trade necessary to keep the sector functioning effectively in the 1980s will ultimately depend on:

1. Replacing the maze of trade and trade-related programs put in place over the last thirty years with a comprehensive agricultural trade policy
2. Strengthening the linkages between domestic farm programs and agricultural trade programs
3. At least recognizing the impact macroeconomic and foreign policy considerations far removed from the farm sector or agricultural trade can have on agriculture

Developing a Comprehensive Agricultural Trade Policy

A critical first step will be developing a comprehensive agricultural trade policy that identifies the United States' changing interests in the world market and furthers those interests in the extremely competitive environment more effectively than existing programs.

The major trade and trade-related programs currently in place were developed primarily in the 1950s and 1960s to advance narrowly conceived U.S. interests in surplus disposal. The commercial and concessional trade and aid programs developed focused heavily on using what was seen as a very limited world market for bulk food, feed, and fiber as an outlet for a relatively small share of the United States' excess supply of these products. Provisions were actually included in PL 480 and the export credit programs to highlight surplus disposal; for example, commodities exported under these programs had to be judged by the secretary of agriculture to be in excess supply.

The notion of exports as a dynamic marketing opportunity for any significant portion of the farm sector's output was weak at best. For example, the export promotion programs put in place were and continue to be small compared to the value of trade involved and promotion programs in the other exporting countries. Moreover, relatively little effort was put into identifying broader U.S. interests in agricultural trade as a source of foreign exchange earnings or economic activity and employment outside the farm sector.

The experience of the 1970s demonstrated that this perception of U.S. trade interests was no longer valid. The world market was far more dynamic than policy makers had recognized, and U.S. interests in farm exports grew to extend well beyond surplus disposal. The $44 billion in farm products exported in 1981 accounted for almost a third of the sector's output. In products such as wheat, cotton, soybeans, and feed grains, the export market had become the primary market. Moreover, national accounts data suggest that, despite its concentration in bulk products receiving little if any processing beyond the farm gate, the $44 billion in farm products exported in 1981 generated over $100 billion in economic activity and 2.5 to 3 million jobs elsewhere in the economy.

As the United States' experience so far in the 1980s has also demonstrated, programs designed to further narrowly conceived surplus disposal interests often do not well serve the U.S.'s widening interests in trade. For example, the residual supplier role the United States assumed early in the postwar period to facilitate moving excess supplies abroad worked to concentrate a disporportionally large share of the trade slow down of the 1980s in the United States.

The first step in developing a broader international agricultural policy involves defining, possibly redefining, U.S. interests in trade more clearly. It is clearly in the United States' interest to expand exports of farm products. Expanding exports utilize otherwise under- or unutilized capacity in the farm sector with few if any alternative uses and in the process raise farm income, reduce government expenditures in support of agriculture, and possibly lower the unit cost as a result of economies of scale.

The basket of farm products exported, however, is of increasing importance. Expanding exports of the bulk prodsucts that currently dominate U.S. sales abroad limit benefits outside the sector severely while exporting a more balanced basket including processed products will expand the payoff elsewhere in the economy significantly. Equally important, expanding exports at the cost of increasing year-to-year export variability could well be counterproductive. The benefits from exporting more "on average" can be more than offset by the costs incurred as a result of more volatile commodity prices, farm incomes, and government support payments.

Program-wise, these interests could well be furthered by a mix of new and existing trade programs. Existing export promotion programs could be expanded substantially and focused on promoting a more balanced basket of farm products. Export credit programs could also be expanded to support more aggressive U.S. export marketing and to reinforce the United States' temporarily weakened competitive position due to dollar exchange rates currently above long-run equilibrium levels. Aid programs could also be more effectively linked to trade and to improving the U.S.'s position in developing-country markets. Improved market information and analysis could also help U.S. exporters identify and capture trade opportunities. The EEC's experience since the mid-1970s points out how productive cooperative public sector-private sector efforts to expand exports can be, and, by contrast, the limited U.S. success in this area.

While the EEC's aggressive export promotion programs include many marketing elements worthy of inclusion in a more aggressive U.S. program, large-scale export subsidization is not among them. Export subsidies of the type used widely by the EEC have a superficial appeal: they appear to offer a way of expanding market share and disposing of unwanted surpluses at the cost of only a few cents on the dollar. Any large-scale subsidization by the United States in the current environment, however, would likely touch off competitor reaction and lead to a subsidy war that would leave all the exporting countries worse off. As noted above, they would also work in the longer term to weaken the operation of the world market and ultimately damage U.S. interests. It is concern with the possibility of a generalized subsidy war that is currently moderating the United States' response to the EEC's program and limiting use of export subsidies to tactical response to counter violations of GATT subsidy rules by others.

The program options available to minimize the volatility problem center on two initiatives: (1) improving the operation of the world market so as to dampen year-to-year swings in trade prices and quantities, and (2) shifting the United States' position in the market away from being a residual supplier toward being a preferred supplier.

A key element of an integrated U.S. agricultural trade policy is the recognition that a strong, efficient world market works to the U.S.'s advantage both by promoting trade and by easing volatility. In the short term, resolving the trade policy conflict with the European Community is in the United States' interest even if it involves compromises that pull the United States temporarily away from the pursuit of a freer trade environment. Any further weakening of the world market could undermine its ability to function and damage all the participants' interests. In a more cooperative environment, progress might also be made toward developing a coordinated stockholding policy among exporters designed to further their common market stabilization goals.

Over the longer term liberalizing world trade to encourage future growth and to facilitate market adjustment becomes critical. Efforts in this area could well be directed initially toward reform of the General Agreement on Trade and Tariffs (GATT). GATT's success in the industrial trade area is noticeably lacking in the agricultural area. Trade in farm products was largely excluded from the benefits of the GATT when it was originally created. That, combined with the reluctance to discuss domestic commodity programs in later multilateral negotiating sessions, has kept agriculture from sharing in the general trade liberalization that has occurred since.

It is also important that GATT expand its membership. GATT was originally created in large part to serve the interests of the industrialized countries of the West. The centrally planned economies and less developed countries were not signatory to the agreement in the beginning. Although membership in the agreement has grown over the years, the centrally planned and less developed countries are still largely outside the reach of the agreement. But it has been largely those countries that have expanded their farm trade most rapidly. As a result, GATT has become less and less effective in dealing with trade problems.

As the world economy recovers, the United States should make a serious attempt to renegotiate the GATT or to establish a comparable new organization in its place. High priority shold be given to including agriculture in these negotiations, to including as many countries as possible, to expanding treatment of unfair trading practices such as export subsidies, and to establishing rules for distortions in foreign exchange markets as well as in product markets.

U.S. and world interests in trade in agricultural as well as non-agricultural products could also be furthered by the development of a more stable international financial regime. Better coordination of monetary policy in the largest countries is also critical. What is unclear, however, is whether a more supportive international financial underpinning for trade can be put into place through informal cooperation sponsored by existing institutions such as the IMF or whether a new international monetary organization, possibly a world central bank, with powers comparable to the GATT in trade matters, is needed.

Linking Agricultural Trade and Domestic Farm Policies

Shifting the United States' position in the world market from a residual to a preferred supplier and in the process reducing year-to-year fluctuations in foreign demand depends heavily on strengthening the United States' market position. As a matter of policy, the critical concern here is insuring that the domestic agricultural programs put in place do not undermine U.S. standing as a competitively priced, reliable supplier of high-quality products. Recurrent attempts to support farm prices above long-term market clearing levels and alternatively subsidizing our farmers to produce more and paying them in addition to restrict production are at the core of the problem.

The farm policies put in place as recently as 1981 and several of the program decisions made since have worked to impair the United States' competitive position and reinforce the United States' role as a residual supplier. In an increasingly volatile and competitive trade environment, it is clear that U.S. domestic farm programs have to be flexible and responsive to unpredictable market developments. The loan and target support levels put in place clearly assumed the continuation of the 1970s bull export market and high inflation rates. With the slowed inflation and weakened export demand that actually materialized, high loan and target support levels priced U.S. products well above the other exporters. In this environment importers tend to view the United States increasingly as the high-priced supplier of last resort.

Furthermore, high U.S. support levels combined with the appreciation of the dollar to provide the other exporters (with depreciating currencies) with both the incentive to expand production and the competitive edge to capture market share. The PIK program put in place in 1983 to bring world and U.S. agricultural supply and demand into closer balance did so by cutting back unilaterally on U.S. production and stocks. The entire process worked to raise questions about the reliability of the United States as a supplier and to improve the competitive position of other suppliers.

Being a dependable supplier at competitive prices over the longer run also means that U.S. farm programs should encourage our most efficient producers without unduly sheltering the high-cost, inefficient producers. This will assure that the United States' competitive position is based on an industry of low-cost producers who can withstand periods of low prices. Providing price guarantees that get capitalized into higher asset values, and ultimately production costs, undermines competitiveness. This goal might be secured without abandoning any provision for a safety net for producers in years of unusually large supplies or weak demand by keeping price support programs in place but setting support levels low enough to allow the market to work. Revenue insurance programs and income stabilization programs could also be explored as a means of protecting farmers from undue short-term market pressure while keeping our products competitively priced and our reputation as a reliable supplier intact.

This concern with domestic program-trade program linkages is two-way. Given the extent to which U.S. agriculture has been internationalized, the solutions to many heretofore domestic farm problems may well be found in the international area. Domestic farm adjustment programs that concentrate entirely on supply adjustment and support payments that require large-scale government expenditures may well be far less efficient than a mix of domestic programs and trade expansion programs.

Linkages Outside Agriculture

It is also critical that the linkage between domestic policies outside agriculture and agricultural trade be recognized. Policy decisions regarding growth in the money supply and interest rates, for example, can have far more effect on farm production costs and exports and in turn on the economic well-being of the sector than farm policy. In this environment it is critical that policy makers outside agriculture at least realize the full impact of their decisions.

CONCLUSION

If the trends of the last several decades continue over the next several years, the world will become increasingly dependent on the United States as a source of supply while the United States becomes more dependent on the world market as an outlet for its farm products. While economic and policy forces in the United States and abroad are likely to slow growth in this interdependence from the breakneck pace of the 1970s, the pace should pick up considerably from the reversals experienced so far in the 1980s.

TABLE 17

World Agricultural Production, Consumption and Implied U.S. Trade Levels, Selected Countries

Year/Region	Area	Yield	Production	Utilization			Net Trade
				Feed	Non-feed	Total	
	Mil. Ha.	Tons/Ha.	Million Metric Tons				
Wheat							
1979-81							
Developed countries (less U.S.)	40.9	2.35	98.2			70.0	+30.2
Developing countries	67.1	1.39	94.0			131.0	–37.2
Centrally Planned countries	97.7	1.83	179.5			216.6	–31.7
World (less U.S.)	205.7	1.80	371.7			417.6	–38.7
1988-89							
Developed countries (less U.S.)	45.7	2.62	117.1			73.8	+43.3
Developing countries	72.2	1.71	123.7			185.5	–61.8
World (less U.S.)	94.2	2.44	229.9			256.9	–27.0
Rice							
1979-81							
Developed countries (less U.S.)	2.8	4.07	11.4			12.0	+ 0.5
Developing countries	105.2	1.42	150.7			153.9	– 2.1
Centrally Planned countries	34.4	2.86	98.7			99.2	– 0.5
1988-89							
Developed countries (less U.S.)	2.4	4.54	10.9			11.1	– 0.2
Developing countries	111.8	1.70	189.7			192.2	– 2.5
Centrally Planned countries	34.0	3.32	112.8			113.1	– 0.3
World (less U.S.)	148.2	2.11	313.4			316.4	– 3.0

TABLE 17
(Continued)

World Agricultural Production, Consumption and Implied U.S. Trade Levels, Selected Countries

Year/Region	Area	Yield	Production	Utilization: Feed	Utilization: Non-feed	Utilization: Total	Net Trade
Wheat	Mil. Ha.	Tons/Ha.	Million Metric Tons				
Feed Grains							
1979-81							
Developed countries (less U.S.)	43.4	3.06	132.8	123.8	33.9	157.7	–23.7
Developing countries	145.5	1.09	158.6	64.6	105.0	169.6	–12.1
Centrally Planned countries	111.1	2.00	222.8	124.0	129.5	253.5	–29.8
World (less U.S.)	300.0	1.71	514.2	312.3	268.6	580.9	–65.6
1988-89							
Developed countries (less U.S.)	45.2	3.43	155.0	140.3	38.1	178.4	–24.0
Developing countries	146.8	1.28	188.0	97.8	121.4	219.2	–31.2
Centrally Planned countries	111.3	2.57	285.6	157.7	147.7	305.4	–19.8
World (less U.S.)	303.3	2.07	628.0	393.8	307.2	701.0	–75.0
Oilseeds							
1979-81							
Developed countries (less U.S.)	—	—	5.2			31.7	–26.5
Developing countries	—	—	25.2			16.4	+ 8.8
Centrally Planned countries	—	—	12.1			19.8	– 7.7
World (less U.S.)	—	—	42.5			67.9	–25.3
1988/89							
Developed countries (less U.S.)	—	—	5.9			37.3	–31.4
Developing countries	—	—	35.7			27.0	+ 8.7
Centrally Planned countries	—	—	17.2			27.0	– 9.8
World (less U.S.)	—	—	58.8			91.3	–32.5

TABLE 18

U.S. Agricultural Exports, Fiscal Years

Commodity	1982	1983	1984	1985	1986	1987	1988	1989
	U.S. Farm Export Volume (Million Metric Tons)							
Wheat & prods.	45.5	39.5	38.0	40.0	41.0	42.5	44.0	45.5
Feed grains	58.2	55.9	61.0	63.0	66.0	69.0	72.0	75.0
Rice	2.9	2.2	2.5	2.6	2.8	2.8	2.9	3.0
Soybeans	25.5	25.3	25.3	26.1	26.0	27.5	27.8	28.6
Soybean meal	6.3	7.3	7.1	6.8	7.0	7.2	8.0	8.4
Cotton	1.6	1.2	1.3	1.4	1.4	1.5	1.5	1.5
Subtotal	140.0	131.4	136.2	139.1	144.2	150.5	156.2	162.0
Other	18.1	17.6	18.0	18.5	19.0	19.3	19.7	20.0
Total	158.1	149.0	154.2	157.6	163.2	169.8	175.9	182.0

REVIEW OF
*"World Market Trends and Prospects: Implications for U.S. Agricultural Policy"**
Fred H. Sanderson

Dr. Sanderson's review was based on an earlier draft of Mr. O'Brien's paper.

I have recently had occasion to review several long-term projections of world food demand and supply, including the FAO's "Agriculture toward 2000," Patrick O'Brien's contribution to "Global 2000," and a projection of "Global Demand for Food and Fiber through 2000," just completed by Economic Perspectives, Inc., in cooperation with Resources for the Future. I was struck by the similarity of the broad numerical results (although there are significant differences concerning particular regions and commodities). Yet we find contrasts in tone and interpretation that do not necessarily follow from the analyses. "AT-2000" expressed alarm over the production trends in the developing countries (which seemed to have leveled off in the mid-seventies) and the burden the projected food deficits would impose on their balance of payments. "Global 2000" is remembered for its emphasis on higher energy prices and other resource constraints and for its prediction that real costs of production would double by the end of the century. The EPI/RFF report points to moderate improvements in per capital food consumption in all regions of the world except sub-Saharan Africa, though generally at somewhat slower rates than in the 1970s. It also projects increased dependence on trade but significantly reduced pressure on resources, in terms of rates of growth, compared with the last decade. It implies that there will be no reversal of the long-term downwards trend in real food prices. It does not address explicitly the balance of payments aspects which, in truth, are beyond the scope of all three projections. On the whole, the EPI/RFF report takes a calmer view of the prevailing trends than the other two.

To place O'Brien's paper for the Curry Foundation in this spectrum, one has to remember that his projections stop in 1988/89. Long-rund trends are discussed only in qualitative terms, and that discussion reflects some of his earlier concerns with resource constraints. However, his medium-term projections point to much slower growth of foreign demand for U.S. exports and, hence, reduced pressure on U.S. resources and stable or even falling real prices, at least for the 1980s. I get the impression from his paper that he views this prospect as a temporary drop from the long-term trend and that he would probably agree that the 1970s were a deviation in the opposite direction.

BASIC TRENDS

In his discussion of basic trends O'Brien starts out with the traditional Malthusian theme of resource constraints, of which he cites three manifestations:

1. The declining rate of growth of crop acreage and the increased reliance on more-intensive cultivation
2. Increasing reliance on non-renewable, especially energy-related, inputs
3. The world's growing dependence on a "shrinking circle of countries, dominated by the United States, that still have underutilized agricultural resources

I submit that this picture is not only overdrawn but misleading. The fact that most production growth now comes from increased yields (as well as double cropping) does not necessarily mean that the world is "running out of suitable land"; in general, it merely means that recent technological developments are making it more economic to use already cultivated land more intensively. Nor is the increasing dependence on non-renewable inputs particularly ominous if one considers the limited demands agriculture is making on the rather ample reserves of materials needed for the production of fuels, fertilizer, and pesticides.

Neither are increased grain imports necessarily an indication that the importing countries are pressing against the limits of their production potential. In most developing countries there is a vast unexploited potential for increasing yields per hectare and substantial possibilities of increasing the cultivated area. There are several reasons other than resource constraints that explain the increasing reliance on trade. First, we need to remind ourselves that there is such a thing as comparative advantage. Second, food imports may be the result of a temporary supply-demand imbalance. Much of the growth in imports occurred in developing countries experiencing rapid economic growth at a stage in their development when a large proportion of the rising incomes were spent on upgrading their diet. Their agriculture, though generally performing rather satisfactorily, could not keep up with the grapid growth of demand. Third, increased foreign exchange earnings and the easy availability of foreign credits also favored food imports. While food imports were increasing, they claimed a declining share of the importing countries' foreign exchange resources. In this group of countries rising food imports were a symptom of economic success—or of good fortune, as in the case of the oil-exporting countries—but only in a few instances a reflection of their limited production potential.

Paradoxically, many low-income countries performed well by the self-sufficiency standard; these countries as a group did not increase their food imports significantly. Nevertheless, it is the low-income countries that should be cause for continuing concern because balance could be achieved only at very low levels of food consumption. But the lack of progress cannot be blamed on the lack of natural resources. For these countries the problem is to break out of the vicious circle of low productivity and low purchasing power.

This brings us to the demand side of the equation. Despite the usual emphasis on supply constraints, most long-term projections recognize effective economic demand as the primary force in the expansion of the global food system. O'Brien is right in drawing attention to the unprecedented postwar growth in per capita incomes and its impact on the demand for farm products. What we are seeing is a dietary transition superimposed, with a lag, on the demographic transition. Unfortunately, the dietary transition, as manifested in changing income elasticities, is even more difficult to predict than the demographic transition.

Another source of uncertainty in projecting both supply and demand is the distortions introduced by government interventions. The distortions affect the supply-demand balance in individual countries, but around the world it is likely that they largely offset each other.

Contrary to the fears voiced in the 1970s, real world prices of basic foods and feedstuffs continue on their long-term downward trend, as noted by O'Brien. The basic reason for this is that agricultural technology has overcome the effects of higher energy costs and of diminishing returns to inputs, and agricultural productivity has risen faster than productivity in most other economic sectors.

But price instability has reemerged as a major problem. O'Brien offers several explanations, including some that I believe are questionable or of minor importance. In the economic sphere, I doubt that it can fairly be blamed on the growth of the world market, on the integration of capital markets, or on floating exchange rates. As Gale Johnson has shown, unrestricted world trade would spread the burden of adjustment to fluctuations in world supply and demand and provide a high degree of stability. The principal problem is that most importing countries and the European Community have insulated themselves from fluctuations in the world market, thus throwing the entire burden of adjustment on the United

States and a few other exporting countries. Another reason is that the United States, while attempting to act as a balance wheel in the world grain market, has not been willing or able to pursue policies adequate to offset the destabilizing policies of its trading partners. In some instances U.S. policies have contributed to the instability.

PROSPECTS FOR THE 1980s

O'Brien's projections are difficult to assess because the results of his analysis are shown only for three broad (and rather heterogeneous) categories of countries and because so little is revealed about the underlying estimates of demand and supply for commodities other than grains and oilseeds. All that can be done in the circumstances is to compare his results with the historical trends and with medium-term interpolations of the long-term projections mentioned earlier.

O'Brine's assumptions concerning population growth are consistent with those used elsewhere. His economic growth projections are on the low side. The average growth rate of world GNP is projected at only 2.8 percent for 1982-89, as compared with about 4 percent in the 1970s. The economic growth for the developing countries is projected at 4 percent, as compared with 5 percent in the 1970s. An even sharper drop is projected for the centrally planned economies (including China), from 6.4 percent in the 1970s to 2.6 percent. The developed market economies, whose economic growth had already slowed down considerably in the 1970s, are projected to grow at 2.8 percent, a slight drop from 3.2 percent in the 1970s. Compared with the World Bank projections (which are generally followed in the EPI/RFF study), O'Brien is more optimistic for the developing world (except Latin America) but more pessimistic for the developed market economies, the USSR, and Eastern Europe.

One would expect that the economic slowdown should be reflected in an acceleration of the long-term downward trend in the rate of growth of the demand for food. According to FAO, world food consumption (production) increased by 2.7 percent in the 1960s and 2.3 percent in the 1970s. Yet O'Brien projects world demand for farm products at 2 to 2.5 percent annually through 1985 and 2.5 to 3 percent in 1986-88. For grains, he projects the world demand (excluding the United States) to grow by 2.4 percent a year between 1979-81 and 1988/99—only a slight drop from the 2.6 percent rate of the 1970s. This would imply a very strong recovery in the next six years since world grain consumption has been virtually flat since 1978/79.

Table 1 compares O'Brien's annual growth rates of grain production and consumption, 1979-81 to 1988/89, for the world less the United States and separately for developed, centrally planned, and developing countries, with the historical growth rates during the 1970s and corresponding growth rates for 1978-80 to 1990 taken from the EPI/RFF projections. As can be seen, EPI/RFF projects significantly slower growth of total demand around the wrold, for the developing countries and the centrally planned economies, than O'Brien, but a higher rate of demand growth for the developed market economies. The same is true of oilseeds (table 2). This may be explained in part by the difference in income growth assumptions and probably by different income elasticities as well. EPI/RFF's grain production estimates are also distinctly lower than O'Brien's except for the developed countries (other than the U.S.). For oilseeds they are about the same around the world, lower for the developing countries but substantially higher for both the developed and centrally planned countries.

Despite these differences, the projected changes in trade flows are fairly close (table 3). Both O'Brien and EPI/RFF project increases in the rest of the world's grain and oilseed deficits, though at a slower rate than in the 1970s. (The increases projected by EPI/RFF are larger, partly because they cover a longer period.) The only difference in signs concerns grain imports by the centrally planned economies, where O'Brien anticipates a 15 million ton reduction in the deficit, whereas EPI/RFF projects a 19 million ton increase (only 8 million tons of this difference is explained by the use of different base periods).

Table 4 shows projected U.S. exports of grains, soybeans and meal, and cotton to 1988/89 (the EPI/RFF figures are interpolations). Both O'Brien and EPI/RFF project further export growth for grains and oilseeds though at a much slower pace than in the 1970s. Cotton exports are flat in O'Brien's projection, up slightly in that of EPI/RFF. Both imply lower U.S. market shares than in the 1970s.[1] The consensus on trade is remarkable, considering the differences in the underlying projections of demand and production.

The projected slowdown in U.S. export growth—from 10 percent annually in the 1970s to 2.2 percent for grains, from 7.3 percent to 2.3 percent for soybeans[2]—implies greatly reduced pressure on the capacity of the United States to meet market demand; and with increased foreign competition, it also points to continuing downward pressure on real prices.

TABLE 1

Historical and Projected Annual Rates of Growth of Grain Production and Consumption (Percent)

	Developed (Less U.S.)	Centrally Planned	Developing	World (Less U.S.)
Grain Production				
1970s[a]	2.1	2.0	2.4	2.2
O'Brien[b]	2.0	2.8	2.7	2.6
EPI/RFF[c]	2.3	1.5	2.3	2.0
Grain Consumption				
1970s[a]	1.5	3.0	3.2	2.6
O'Brien[b]	1.2	2.2	3.4	2.4
EPI/RFF[c]	1.9	1.6	2.6	2.1

[a] 1969/70 to 1970/71 to 1980/81. *Source:* USDA, World Ag. Situation, Dec. 1980.

[b] 1979-81 to 1988/89. From table 17 of O'Brien paper.

[c] 1978-80 to 1990. From table 17 of EPI/RFF projections.

TABLE 2

Projected Annual Rates of Growth of Oilseed Production and Consumption (Percent)

	Developed (Less U.S.)	Centrally Planned	Developing	World (Less U.S.)
Oilseed Production				
O'Brien[a]	1.5	2.3	3.2	2.4
EPI/RFF[b]	5.4	3.2	1.7	2.6
Oilseed Consumption				
O'Brien[a]	1.7	2.8	4.8	3.7
EPI/RFF[b]	2.6	2.6	3.2	2.8

[a] O'Brien: 1979-81 to 1988-89 (from table 17).

[b] EPI/RFF: 1978-80 to 1990 (from table 18).

TABLE 3

Projected Changes in Trade of Cereals and Oilseeds in the 1980s[a] (Million MT)

Country Category	O'Brien[b] 1979-81 to 1988/89		EPI/RFF[c] 1978-80 to 1990	
	Cereals	Oilseeds	Cereals	Oilseeds
Developed (Less U.S.)	+12	–5	+11	–10
Centrally Planned	+15	–5	–19	0
Developing	–44	0	–30	–4
World (Less U.S.)	–17	–7	–38	–14

[a]+ denotes improvement in trade balance (increase in surplus or reduction of deficit), – denotes deterioration (increase in deficit or reduction of surplus).

[b]"World Market Trends and Projects," table 17.

[c]"Global Demand for Food and Fiber Through 2000," tables 22 and 23. (Centrally planned include Taiwan.)

TABLE 4

U.S. Agricultural Exports (Million MT)

Commodity	Actual		O'Brien (1983)[a]			EPI/RFF[b]	O'Brien (1980)[c]	
	1969/70 to 1971/72	1981/82	1981/82	1985/86	1988/89	1988/89	1981/82	1988/89
Grains	3.9	110.0	106.6	109.8	123.5	135.0	122.6	139.6
Soybeans[d]	15.4	33.3	33.4	34.8	39.1	42.0	30.7	34.7
Cotton	0.7	1.5	1.6	1.4	1.5	1.8	1.5	1.4

[a] "World Market Trends and Prospects," table 18.

[b] "Global Demand for Food and Fiber Through 2000," interpolateds from linear trend 1979-81 to 2000.

[c] "Global Prospects for Agriculture," table. USDA/ESS, Agricultural-Food Policy Review: Perspectives for the 1980s, April 1981.

[d] Soybeans and meal, in soybean equivalent.

AGRICULTURAL POLICY IMPLICATIONS

This prospect may seem to suggest a return to the problems and remedies of the 1960s. That conclusion does not follow, however, because of the transformation of American agriculture which has occurred in the meantime. As O'Brien points out, American agriculture now depends on exports for almost one-third of its output. Moreover, with the near-saturation of the domestic demand, exports have become virtually the only source of market growth. The output mix has shifted toward export crops in which the United States enjoys a distinct and fairly secure comparative advantage. Structural changes have strengthened the capacity of U.S. agriculture to compete successfully in the world market. Turning our backs on the world market is, therefore, not a viable option. Whatever policies we adopt must take account of our dependence on the world market.

O'Brien has some suggestions to this end on which I shall not comment here in detail because the subject will be taken up at length in connection with the other papers. I certainly agree that we need to take a hard look at those of our policies that impair our competitive position in the world market. These include our recurrent attempts to support farm prices in excess of long-term market-clearing levels, and the related supply controls that one hopes have reached their apogee in last year's PIK program. They also include macroeconomic policies that drive up the value of the dollar above its long-term equilibrium level. Market stabilization remains a desirable goal, but the responsibility should be shared with other exporting countries, preferably through a coordinated stockholding policy. The GATT rules need to be clarified and strengthened to prevent the escalation of export subsidies and the impairment of trade concessions. But we need to keep in mind that the United States, and the American farmer in particular, have an enormous stake in upholding the agreement negotiated after the war, which on the whole, has served us well. There can be little doubt that any attempt to "renegotiate" the GATT would leave us worse off than we are now.

O'Brien finds merit in certain types of export promotion, such as cutrate export credits ands the blending of commercial exports with aid programs, which are thinly disguised export subsidies. Others would have us adopt dual price systems, as applies to sugar and dairy products in the European Community, in which domestic producers and consumers, in effect, subsidize agricultural exports. Export subsidies have a superficial appeal because at first sight they seem to offer an inexpensive way of disposing of unwanted surpluses—all one has to do is to undercut the competitor by a few cents a bushel. The trouble is that competitors will react; and before we know it we shall find ourselves caught in a subsidy contest that could become extremely costly for all exporting countries. Clearly, this is not the way to go.

There are several policy options that would enable us to compete more effectively in the world market without systematic resort to export subsidies.[3] A great deal would be accomplished if we could see our way to abandon the schizophrenic policy of, first, subsidizing our farmers to produce too much and, then, paying them some more to restrict production. We could move, instead, to a safety net of loan rates, at 70 to 80 percent of a moving average of market prices, similar to the program already in effect for soybeans. Other possibliities would be revenue insurance, which would extend the principles of federal crop insurance to farmers' gross receipts, or a farm income stabilization fund that would be partly financed by farmers' contributions. All these options could be combined with a more cost-effective farmer-owned grain reserve aimed exclusively at reducing year-to-year fluctuations and protecting our reputation as a reliable supplier. These options would avoid the rigidities and market distortions that characterize our present programs, and they would also cost a lot less.

NOTES

1. O'Brien suggests two major reasons for this: (1) U.S. domestic policies that tend to make the United States the residual supplier; (2) overvaluation of the dollar, which he assumes will persist through the 1980s. However, to my knowledge, there are no reliable estimates of their effects on U.S. exports.
2. The EPI/RFF projections are somewhat higher, but this may be due to the fact that they are linear interpolations from a long-term trend, whereas O'Brien's presumably take account of the current downward deviation from trend.
3. This does not exclude the occasional tactical use of export subsidies to counter violations of the GATT export subsidy rules by others.

REVIEW OF
*"World Market Trends and Prospects: Implications for U.S. Agricultural Policy"**
Thomas H. Christensen

Professor Christensen's review was based on an earlier draft of Mr. O'Brien's paper.

The purpose of this review is to recapitulate the major points put forth in Patrick O'Brien's paper and to make additional comments and observations based on this author's own perspectives. The policy recommendations which are eventually presented in this paper are developed from a historical perspective of the basic trends in world agriculture, on how short-term economic events and policies are likely to modify the impact of these trends on world trade, and the probable effects of agricultural policies on world trade and U.S. agriculture over the life of the 1985 farm bill. This review will follow the same format as the original paper, presenting first the basic trends which have influenced world trade historically, then the factors which are expected to determine trade levels in the next five years, and finally a review of agricultural policies around the world with recommendations for U.S. policies.

BASIC TRENDS

An important distinction was made between long-term trends in world agriculture and how short-term events modify or even interrupt the effect of the fundamental long-term trends. Many analyses of world agriculture fail to distinguish between the basic market forces (e.g., population and income growth) and more temporal events (e.g., exchange rates, prices, foreign debt, etc.).

Supply Trends

The rate of cropland expansion has slowed throughout the world, with less new land added in each successive decade. Although the primary cause of this phenomenon is certainly increased pressure on the existing land base, another source of the slowdown could be declining real prices for most major crops. Despite the general trend of slower cropland expansion in recent decades, the period following the real price increases of the early 1970s was characterized by more rapid expansion.

Examination of the coefficient of variation from crop production trends evidences increased variation in world production, especially in the most recent decade. Several plausible explanations for this phenomenon are offered, including the effect of the extension of farming on more marginal lands and climatic changes. An additional source of this increased variation could be the shift to more intensive agronomic practices; as newer crop varieties are used and inputs are applied at higher rates, the effects of ideal weather conditions are maximized, as are the effects of adverse conditions. Clearly, the United States has moved from a position of one of many suppliers immediately following World War 2 to the dominant supplier of bulk farm exports in the 1960s, but the paper failed to recognize shifts in the U.S.'s market share since the early 1960s. The U.S. share of all grain exports declined steadily throughout the 1960's—from 50 to 40 percent—and it was only when demand grew rapidly in the 1970s that the U.S. share returned to the 50 percent level. Meanwhile the share of world soybean trade declined steadily as South American exporters expanded their productive capacity. The significance of this point is the distinction between the trend toward the United States becoming the dominant supplier of agricultural exports versus the United States becoming the primary location of excess productive potential. Since 1960 it is likely that we have become more the latter than the former.

Demand Trends

The relative importance of population and income growth in deter mining food demand is presented very effectively in the paper. As much as half the growth in world demand is directly attributable to higher per capita income, especially in the middle-income developing countries. The dietary transition which occurs when average per capita incomes pass a threshold level has been the source of much of the increase in livestock production overseas. Since animals typically require several calories of feed to produce one calorie of product, the conversion of more of the world's population to meat consumption has created an exponential growth in feed demand. Even more encouraging is the fact that many more people are poised to make the dietary transition when world incomes return to their long-term growth path.

World food demand growth has been reinforced by several policies, including export subsidization and low administered prices in some importing countries. Another positive policy for world trade in the 1970s was the decision by central planners in the Soviet bloc to raise per capita meat consumption by expanding their livestock industry. The paper failed to mention that special export credit and food aid have had a positive effect on food demand while other policies have actually lowered food demand. In general, protectionist policies like those in the European Community and Japan have held domestic food prices well above world levels, dampening consumer demand and encouraging domestic production. These policies have worked against international trade and have encouraged food production at comparatively expensive prices.

Postwar Groundwork

The war experience and international institutions which evolved after World War 2 worked to free the fundamental forces of supply and demand in world markets. In addition, the rapid economic growth which occurred in the postwar years allowed importing countries to sacrifice their less competitive food industries by creating employment opportunities in non-agricultural areas. However, this process was not universal—internal policies impeded the exit of inefficient farmers in Western Europe and Japan, and the decline of agriculture resulted in higher unemployment in many of the developing nations. Expanded world trade did allow exporting countries to utilize more of their excess capacity, but it was not without cost in many importing countries.

U.S. Role

Although it was implied that the United States chose the role of residual supplier to world markets to maximize exports, it is not altogether clear that this is how the United States arrived at this position. Many analysts feel that the reliance of the United States on private exporting firms in a world of state trading agencies has contributed to its role as residual supplier. Also, grain embargoes and a strong U.S. dollar have done much to reinforce the residual-supplier role. There is good reason to believe that the policy of minimizing domestic surpluses by maximizing exports has itself caused more investment in U.S. agriculture (in response to higher export levels), which has in turn exacerbated the oversupply problem, only at higher levels. It is clear that expanded world trade allowed exporters and importers to be freer from domestic constraints and served to maximize consumer welfare.

Growing Importance of Trade to the United States

Although higher export levels have often eliminated food surpluses in the United States, they also have encouraged expansion and slowed the exit of inefficient farmers from agriculture. The economies of scale which resulted from higher production levels may have lowered unit costs to consumers and delayed expenditures on farm programs, but competitive market forces might have accomplished the same objectives without higher exports. The farm trade surplus has undoubtedly reduced trade deficits and supported the U.S. dollar, but the costs of a stronger dollar to other export industries must also be considered, especially since farm programs have subsidized farm production (an advantage not shared by other export industries).

The residual supplier role of U.S. agriculture has had positive and negative effects. Increased dependence on export markets has made U.S. agriculture more vulnerable to domestic and international economic events, including world recession, monetary policy and its effect on exchange rates, and recession in the United States. In addition, expandeds production in the United States was accomplished primarily through more intensive use of manufactured inputs. The result of greater reliance on input from outside the farm sector has been increased vulnerability to inflation, higher interest rates, and petroleum price rises. Higher exposure to events outside the farm sector have resulted in more complex trade-offs between farm policy and macroeconomic policies. Not only do the effects of monetary policy on food exports have to be considered, but also the implications of monetary and fiscal policy on producer costs and farm income.

Trade Prospects, 1985-88

Food demand is expected to grow more slowly in the next five years than it did in the 1970s, primarily because of more gradual income growth. World population will increase more gradually than in previous decades, but an older population is expected to result in higher average consumption. Another point to consider is that most of the population growth is expected in the low-income developing countries where average food consumption is lower. More importantly, economic growth is expected to be slower in most of the world and will depend on the U.S. recovery. The only exception is expected to occur in the middle-income developing countries, where strong growth is anticipated after a two to three year hiatus. While these countries have demonstrated economic resilience in the past, there are also reasons to expect a more gradual recovery in the 1980s.

It was assumed that the severe financial difficulties faced by many of the middle-income nations would be mitigated as the demand for their exports rose with world recovery. Implicitly, they would also have to be very successful in executing austerity programs and in obtaining foreign credit to reach this goal. Even if middle-income countries can ameliorate their debt problems, the period of low investment in the early 1980s could still slow economic growth. Also, many middle-income countries are dependent on oil revenues and will not return to the fast-growth track until world supplies tighten.

World food supply is also expected to increase at a slower rate than in the 1970s because of smaller cropland increases and slower yield gains. The paper indicates that there will continue to be cropland expansion in some developing countries because of investments made in the 1970s, but it fails to mention the effect that a strong dollar could have on foreign cropland expansion. If the dollar weakens and crop prices remain low, then the incentive for expansion will be removed; otherwise foreign producers will continue to expand cropland area at the same rate as in recent years. Yield increases are likely to be lower because of higher input costs and lower crop prices.

The supply-demand imbalance expected in the intermediate term is smaller than it was in the 1970s. As a result, U.S. exports are expected to increase more slowly—perhaps at the pace of the 1960s. A weaker U.S. dollar, which augmented food demand in the 1970s, is expected to raise demand in the mid-1980s by lowering food prices and making oil imports less expensive (the income effect). However, a postive factor for food imports in the 1970s was the abundance of investment capital created by the OPEC oil boom. Importers will not have access to as much easy credit in the 1980s unless oil prices rise significantly.

World Trade Policy

Import policies could change world demand prospects in the 1980s, preventing the full impact of basic trends from being realized. Austerity programs in many importing nations will result in restraining food imports as long as foreign exchange is in short supply. There is no guarantee that importing countries will be able to relax import constraints in the near future, and in fact these programs may continue for quite some time. In addition, more countries are expected to adopt protectionist policies to insulate themselves from increased variation in world markets, and, as is pointed out in the paper, there will be fewer participants in world markets who are willing to adjust freely to changing market conditions. Free trade is being threatened by mounting protectionism in both importing and exporting countries, a mood fostered by unwillingness to adjust to adverse market conditions. The result of this trend could be more shifting of the burden of adjustment to the United States, where government stock and supply-control programs are farmers' only protection from foreign disruptions.

Another concern presented in the paper is the potential for pricing low income countries out of world foodmarkets. Unless credit is made available to those nations, the lack of foreign exchange and credit availability is likely to remove them permanently from world markets. Together, more restrictive trade policies and lower market participation could damage international markets for years, preventing realization of long-term trade potential. However, these risks may be overstated since policies often reflect prevailing market conditions. As conditions improve, trade policies will probably be relaxed, and the impediments to food trade will diminish. Participation in world markets will also increase as economic recovery improves low-income countries' financial situation and the availability of credit in world markets increases.

U.S. Farm Policy

U.S. exports are expected to rise by 3 to 4 percent per year, the same rate as in the 1960s. However, devaluation of the U.S. dollar and the ability of the United States quickly to expand exports could result in export increases of 4 to 5 percent per year in the mid-1980s. Regardless of the exact rate of export growth, it is very likely that total food demand in the United States will not expand rapidly enough to utilize the excess productive capacity which has developed in this country. Competition for export markets will be more keen, and, as the residual supplier, the United States will continue to carry the burden of adjustment. Hard choices will need to be made: should supply-control and income-support programs be maintained at considerable cost to taxpayers, or should the free market be allowed to force adjustment through lower land prices and the exit of farmers from agriculture?

Not only will the costs and benefits of farm programs need to be considered, but also the coordination of these programs with U.S. and foreign macroeconomic policy must be reconciled. Previous export policies have focused on surplus disposal or have been small in proportion to the value of farm exports. These policies often failed to reflect the full value of exports to the U.S. economy—the utilization of excess capacity, lower unit costs, and the value of employment in supporting sectors of the economy.

Previous policies have not recognized the trade-offs between maximizing exports and increased market volatility as opposed to a program which promotes sustained exports at lower levels.

Several trade policies were recommended in the paper: increased export promotion, more export credit to change the U.S. residual supplier role, and expansion of the GATT agreement to incorporate food trade and include more countries. Another possibility, which was not considered, is the formation of state trading agencies or some institutionalized representative to allow the United States to compete more effectively in world markets and to enhance our ability to negotiate long-term trade agreements. The paper suggested linkages of domestic and trade components of farm policy to assure that they reinforce one another. To accomplish this, target and loan rates must not be set higher than world price levels, otherwise U.S. farm products will become less competitive on world markets. Also, supply-control programs must not interfere with our ability to maintain adequate export supplies at reasonable prices, or our reputation as a reliable supplier will suffer. Inefficient farmers must be allowed to exit agriculture, and land prices must be allowed to adjust to changing market conditions if the United States expects to maintain its competitive position. Another aspect of farm policy which should be considered is the farm credit program. Farm credit must be managed so that inefficient producers are forced to exit agriculture, otherwise oversupply problems will continue to handicap efficient producers and will erode the U.S. farmer's competitive edge.

Improved coordination between farm programs and other government programs is also essential to the health of U.S. farming. More attention should be paid to the detrimental effects of monetary policy on food exports, with enhancement of trade programs in order to minimize the effects of a strong U.S. dollar. Another possibility is the creation of a more general income-support and occupational retraining scheme for both the farm and non-farm sectors. This would ease the transition for inefficient producers but would not interfere with the operation of world markets the way that the existing price-support and supply-control programs do.

Chapter 2

Prospects for Integrating the Trade Strategies of Agricultural Exporting Nations

John A. Schnittker

At first glance it appears that no agricultural policy action could be more remote than to integrate the export strategies of a number of competing agricultural exporting nations. No one has proposed it seriously for 1984. For many years U.S. policy toward even the highly respectable (in international circles) cooperation arising from institutionalized international commodity agreements has ranged from cool to hostile under both political parties. Informal collaboration among grain exporting countries, which flourished in the 1950s and early 1960s both as a check on U.S. practices under its food aid programs and as a part of the International Wheat Agreement, is long since dead. In addition, integration of agricultural policies as a step toward integration of export policies has been urged by the European Community, virtually making the idea off-limits to serious consideration by the U.S. government.

Further, the United States has lost export market share for grains and soybeans in recent years, and would appear to be in a weak position to discuss integrated export strategies in the next few years, since those strategies might incorporate some degree of cooperation in place of competition. U.S. farm and trade interests almost universally oppose any and all agreements with other exporters.

On the other hand, President Reagan recently joined in the Williamsburg Summit resolutions which included the promise of multilateral coordination of economic performance, which could include agricultural trade. Any such agreement which included even the most elementary language regarding restraint by exporters could doom the United States to an extended period of agricultural excess capacity, in wheat, feed grains, oilseeds, cotton, and rice, given the situation we face in 1984. This would end the dream (or explode the myth) still treasured by farmers and the trade that we will, in this decade, export our way to farm prosperity as in the 1970s, unaided by domestic policies or extensive crop failures.

Every effort made in the past ten years in the United States to redesign our grain marketing system by means of legislation in order to try to make it more useful in wielding market power based on our dominant position in the world grain market, and possibly to make it more compatible with an integrated trade strategy, has failed by a wide margin. More correctly, these measures have never been given the slightest favorable consideration by Congress, by the leading farm organizations, or by grain trade groups, nor has any convincing analysis been developed to show that the changes would meet the objectives of their sponsors.

As listed by Schmitz et al. these efforts included:

1. H.R. 3042 was introduced by Congressman Weaver on March 15, 1979. This bill would amend the Commodity Credit Corporation (CCC) Charter Act to create within the CCC a National Grain Board to provide the highest possible prices in foreign markets for American agricultural producers and to provide price and supply stability in domestic markets. The CCC would become the marketing agent for all export sales of wheat, rice, corn, grain sorghum, barley, oats, rye, and soybeans. It would be authorized to negotiate sales for export of such commodities, barter such commodities for other goods, accept purchase bids from foreign purchasers, and offer selling bids in the world market. A private exporter could still export such commodities at prices, terms, and conditions approved by the Corporation.

2. On May 14, 1979, Congressman Mottl introduced HR 120 which urged the President to establish an international food cartel with Canada, Australia, Argentina, and other major food-exporting countries. It would negotiate with OPEC, using food commodities as a bargaining tool.

3. Senator Bellman introduced S. 356 (the International Wheat Exporting Commission Act of 1979) on February 6, 1979. This bill requested that the President take action to create such a commission to establish a minimum world market price of wheat from member nations, prescribe the share of wheat each one may export, initiate and carry out any actions needed to insure an adequate

supply of wheat, protect purchasers of wheat against wide price fluctuations. The bill followed discussions between U.S. legislators and Canadian Wheat Board officials.

4. The National Farmers Union requested the Congress and the President "to appoint a commission to reach an agreement with Canada, Australia, and Argentina on the world market share of wheat for each country and on a minimum price" (Terpstra 1979).

5. The American Agriculture Movement (AAM) passed a resolution stating that the President "must act to correct the balance of trade deficit and halt inflation by establishing a pricing policy for grain exports equivalent to a bushel of wheat for a barrel of oil" (Terpstra 1979). In addition, the AAM proposed that:

   A National Board of Agricultural Producers be created to devise and approve agricultural production and marketing policy. The United States shall establish its parity level as the export price level in all trade transactions with other countries, and will not bring its price down below that level. The Board must approve the prices, conditions, and terms of all import and export sales (Committee on Agriculture 1978).

6. On May 23, 1979, the Senate considered and approved by a vote of 80 to 15 a resolution offered by Senator Church that asked the President to:

   actively work toward convening a negotiating conference of wheat exporting nations with the intent of reaching a cooperative arrangement to improve wheat trade policy and achieve equitable prices for producers while assuring adequate supplies for consumers.

That listing is far from complete, since Congressman Weaver's bills as described in (1) above, for example, go back to 1975.

There has, however, been strong opposition to the notion of a grain export cartel among certain sectors of the economy. During the hearings before the Senate Committee on Foreign Relations on May 8, 1979, the Western Wheat Associates, U.S.A., Inc., commented:

> We do not believe it is possible to manage an OPEC-type monopoly on world wheat production to raise prices regardless of supply and demand factors. Setting an artificially high price for wheat would

stimulate production in many nations that would not be part of the agreement and in effect, would defeat the purpose of the cartel. Wheat can be produced in more than 100 countries around the world (McCalla and Schmitz 1979).

WHAT KIND OF COOPERATION? WHAT OBJECTIVES?

Two types of cooperation aimed at greater government intervention in agricultural marketing, and one potential approach to cooperation toward reduced governmental action, come to mind at the start. These approaches are distinguished by the type of forum in which they would be negotiated by participants, and by their objectives.

One approach would represent an actual cartel type arrangement, agreed to by the principal grain exporters, probably in meetings which did not include either grain importers of the world or international organizations. (Grains represent the only important U.S. agricultural commodity for which trade agreements have a long history.) Such an arrangement would be designed explicitly to increase international grain prices so as to raise producer incomes in the exporting countries by extracting more money from the governments and consumers in importing countries. The countries organizing the cartel could also establish as important objectives market price stabilization and pressure on grain importers to reduce barriers to increased grain trade; but the price objective would probably be first and foremost.

A second approach to trade cooperation could be negotiated in an international forum such as the International Wheat Council, which has been the administering body for the International Wheat Agreement for some fifty years. In this case three basic negotiations would proceed at the same time: (1) negotiations between exporters as a group and importers as a group; (2) negotiations among importers as to what supply and price guarantees they want to demand from exporting countries and what they would pay by way of increased prices or more stable prices, for a greater assurance of adequate supplies at all times, more credit, etc.; and (3) a negotiation among principal exporting countries designed to establish and maintain a concerted position for their group in the main negotiations between exporters and importers.

This approach would incorporate many aspects of the negotiations and renegotiations of International Wheat Agreements which have been carried on since the 1930s, or of other international commodity agreements.

In the early years of those grain negotiations, the "wheat importer club" included principally developed countries, since they were then the main importers of wheat, but in more recent years the developing countries have dominated that club in view of the important role they now play as world wheat importers.

One could describe an endless array of provisions that would fit under either of these two general approaches. These could range from (1) tight control over at least minimum and maximum prices in world trade; rigid price differentials among different wheats or complex systems for determining appropriate price differentials when market prices approached minimum or maximum agreed prices; relatively fixed shares of markets for exporters; guarantees as to minimum purchases; size of reserve stocks, etc., to (at the other extreme) (2) "best efforts" agreements on the same issues, or some of them, without any rules or procedures for enforcement, or (3) arrangements for information and consultation only.

A third approach to governmental trade cooperation in agricultural trade policy integration was suggested in discussions of the original draft of this paper, and is not developed here in any length. This is to initiate international discussions with the specific objective of achieving a staged reduction in the degree of government intervention in agriculture, aimed at reduced restrictions on trade. In a sense, this is the mission of the GATT, but it has not been seriously pursued, even though the role of domestic farm policies in escalating trade restrictions has been recognized and discussed for over twenty years.

WHAT COULD BE DONE?

One need not dwell at any length on questions of whether or not, in a practical or operating sense, a concerted strategy among exporters alone, or an international agreement arising out of a concerted strategy of both exporters and importers, could be designed. Schmitz and others have demonstrated with considerable authority that the nature of world grain markets, including both exporting and importing countries, the relative concentration of grain exports in a few countries, and the degree of control by most governments over the grain trade, including a high concentration of state trading on both the export and import side, are such that an exporter cartel or a grain agreement could be designed and operated *from a technical standpoint.*

Schmitz points out, for example, that about 95 percent of international wheat transactions involve state traders on at least one side of the transaction, as exporters or importers. About one-third of the trade in wheat takes place between state traders on both sides of the transaction.

Also, more than 40 percent of world feed grain trade involves state trading on at least one side of the transaction. Further, a relatively small number of multinational grain firms account for a large proportion of U.S. and world grain exports, with two privately held firms accounting for half of U.S. and world grain trade in some years.

The concentration of exportable grain supplies in a few countries is also important, with the United States accounting for more than 40 percent of wheat exports in recent years, and the U.S., Canada, Australia, Argentina, and France accounting for some 85 percent of world wheat exports in most years. The United States has roughly 60 percent of world coarse grain exports in most years, and over 90 percent of coarse grain exports are consistently accounted for by five or six countries.

These are not all necessary conditions for increased coordination of agricultural trade either among exporters or between exporters as a group and importers as a group, but they are important factors in simplifying the organization of such an arrangement, whatever its objectives, if it is to be at all rigorous. Obviously, even if these technical and structural conditions could be met in an ideal way, they would not be sufficient to insure the adoption or successful operation of increased coordination of world grain trade arrangements. Custom, tradition, political factors, and domestic price support programs are the overriding considerations in determination of trade arrangements, and they have a lot of momentum.

In this paper I propose to look briefly at a number of the questions that I raised in the opening paragraphs, in order to examine the actions and attitudes that have worked against constructive integration of agricultural trade strategies of exporting nations. The discussion will be primarily in terms of grains.

INTERNATIONAL COMMODITY AGREEMENTS

Attached as Annex A is a listing of U.S. participation in 1980 in international agreements for various agricultural commodities. The attitude that the United States has taken, and the main features of those agreements, are also summarized in the annex (taken from Schmitz).

The U.S. attitude toward participation in the International Wheat Agreement was relatively cooperative until the late 1960s. The United States had been one of the leading organizers and a leading member of the IWA from the 1930s on. The United States, Canada, and Australia were the principal and most active members of the export group in the IWA, while Argentina was a somewhat passive member.

The Wheat Agreement at that time was composed of: (1) a relatively weak but still moderately effective minimum price agreement; (2) consultations periodically through the year under the auspices of the director general of the International Wheat Council; and (3) a food aid program which had been tacked on to the Wheat Agreement during the 1950s. In the early 1960s, when our surpluses were very large and prices were low, the U.S. found that it was being "out-priced" in world markets for certain types of wheat. U.S. adherence to the IWA minimum permitted other countries to set prices below U.S. market prices and claim adherence to the minimum price provisions of the IWA, which were not rigorous. After consultation with exporters, the United States reduced its export prices in 1963 by means of an increased export subsidy (a subsidy was paid at that time on all U.S. wheat exports in order to make the sale). This process of more aggressive pricing continued into the late 1960s.

In 1967 a new International Grains Arrangement was concluded during the Kennedy Round of trade negotiations. The arrangement included a minimum price as before, but it was based on a more complex formula for determining when different countries with different types and qualities of wheat had reached the minimum price, for a food aid program, and for periodic consultations among exporter and importer countries. A comprehensive freezing of support levels in relation to world prices proposed by the EEC was rejected en route to the agreement.

Within a year after completion of this agreement and only after its ratification by the U.S. Senate, a new domestic wheat surplus forced U.S. prices below support levels, and below the minimum prices applicable to U.S. wheats in the new International Grains Arrangement. The United States did not attempt to "protect" the minimum by purchasing surplus wheat or by other means. Canada acted to maintian its prices, and its market share declined.

Another problem arose in the 1960s, as U.S. officials were urged by Europeans and others to broaden the scope of the International Wheat Agreement to cover coarse grains. When early position papers referring to draft provisions of the proposed International Grains Arrangement of 1967 became available to U.S. trade groups, the reaction was swift and stern. U.S. trade groups then and now firmly opposed any expansion of the International Wheat Agreement to cover coarse grains, even to the point of objecting to entering into continuing consultations on coarse grains matters, to renaming the International Wheat Council the International Grains Council, or to maintaining official statistics and research on coarse grains as well as wheat. Persons representing grain trade groups and companies in the United States typically refer to International Grain Agreements as price fixing agreements—a virtual kiss of death as far as support for such agreements is concerned.

Since the mid-1970s all minimum price arrangements in the International Wheat Agreement have been terminated. The International Wheat Council is now largely a consultative and informational body, and nominally the administrator of a series of small national food aid programs, which are coordinated but not controlled by international agencies.

COLLABORATION AMONG GRAIN EXPORTING COUNTRIES

In the 1950s and until about 1963, officials who represented the United States in informal international wheat talks (among exporters, for example), and at the International Wheat Council had developed close professional and personal relationships with persons who performed the same representational functions for Canada, Australia, and to a lesser extent Argentina (which had a high turnover of officials in those days).

With more aggressive U.S. export pricing beginning in 1963, the professional basis for this comfortable relationship among negotiators began to fall apart, since it had been based heavily upon an affirmation by U.S. representatives that considerable restraint would be used in export pricing via the U.S. export subsidy which was set daily by these same officials. Implicitly, there were assurances that the United States would not make any attempts to increase its share of the world's commercial wheat market above some loosely defined "recent period." In fact, the U.S. share had been eroding. Also, by that time, changes in personnel began in a number of countries, with retirements and promotions, and the informal exporter club was never put back together in the form that existed from about 1956 to 1963.

THE U.S. EXPORT MARKET SHARE

Countries tend to consider the highest market share they ever achieved for a particular commodity, in the aggregate or for a country or region, to be their "fair share" of the market in the years ahead. This matter was much debated in informal exporter confrontations in the 1960s, during negotiations leading up to the International Wheat Agreement of 1967, and since that time. There had been long periods when exporter market shares for wheat did not change materially, and other times such as the 1970s when they changed dramatically. The same is true for coarse grains, where trade was not very large until the late 1960s. The United States forged ahead rapidly in regard to tonnage and share of the market once the demand for coarse grains world trade increased sharply, beginning about 1970.

My premise in regard to this point is that the recent and continuing decline in U.S. agriculture exports and especially in the U.S. share of the market for coarse grains and wheat would be a major barrier to U.S. participation in an agreement for integrating trade strategies in any substantial way among grain exporting nations. This would be true whether the objectives of integration required more government intervention or less.

THE DECLINE IN AGRICULTURAL EXPORTS

For coarse grains, the world recession and financial constraints have taken a heavy toll on trade. Between 1970 and 1980 world coarse grain trade rose by 59 mmt or 5.4 mmt per year, while U.S. coarse grain exports increased by 53 mmt or by 4.8 mmt a year. Since 1981 world coarse grain trade declined sharply, with U.S. exports declining by 15 mmt, virtually accounting for all the decline in world trade. U.S. corn exports declined proportionately less than did other coarse grains (figure 1).

Why is the coarse grain trade so sensitive to economic and financial conditions? As consumers' incomes fall, as in the recent world recession, they reduce their consumption of meat and poultry which, in turn, reduces the demand for feed grains. Furthermore, countries like Poland with severe foreign exchange problems use what money they have to import food necessities such as wheat (for bread) in place of feed grains for meat and poultry production. USSR coarse grain imports gained in 1983-84, but in Eastern Europe imports are far below two years earlier.

Given our outlook for slow world economic growth and slow progress toward solving international financial problems, earlier coarse grain trade projections for 1985 now appear overly optimistic. World coarse grain trade will probably not rise to its peak 1980-81 level for 3 to 4 more years. U.S. exports may not return to the record 1980-81 level until about 1988, since the increased production and shipping capability of traditional exporters, and subsidized exports of the European Community, preempt much of world demand. These prospects are an immense disappointment to U.S. producers and a major embarrassment to the government, which as late as mid-1982 ws counting on "an export solution" to our productivity.

Figure 1

U.S. and World Coarse Grain Exports
With Projections to 1985/86

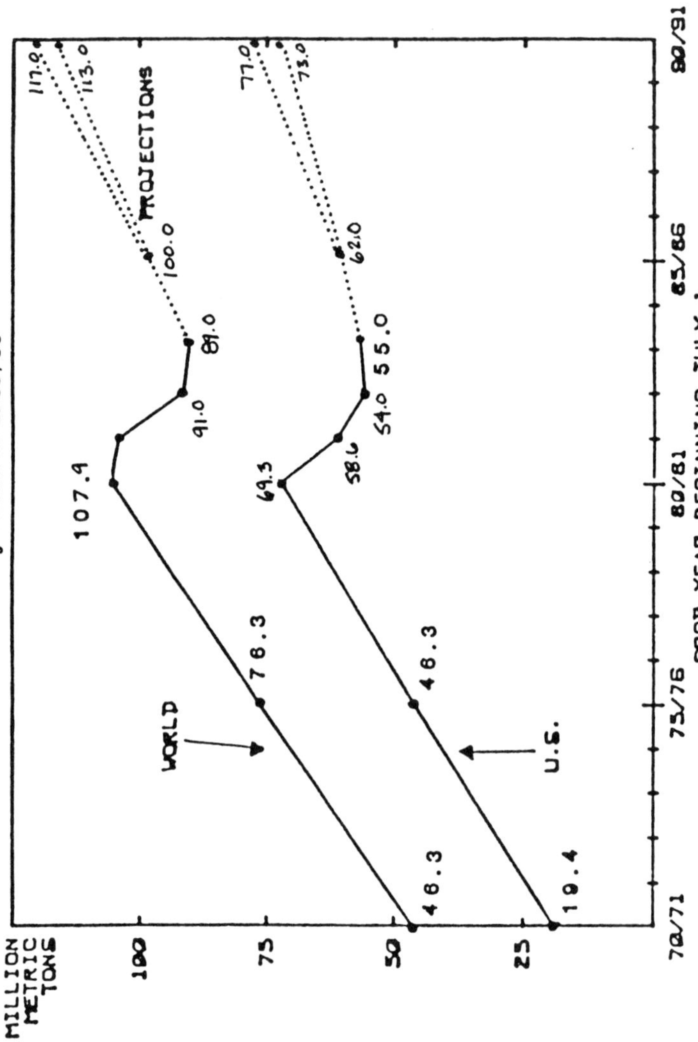

The sharp turn in domestic farm policy, toward massive intervention via the 1983 payment-in-kind program represented a drastic revision in export expectations. It not only represented a new realism about exports, but it raised prices sharply, long before the 1983 drought, seriously reducing exports that season.

WHEAT EXPORTS NOT HIT SO HARD

Not all exports have suffered as badly as coarse grains. World and U.S. wheat exports reached record levels in 1981-82, as shown in figure 2. U.S. exports were well above the trend rate of growth and were 48 percent of world trade. In 1982/83 world wheat exports declined modestly to about trend levels, but U.S. exports fell far below the trend rate of growth, to 41 percent of total trade, and fell further in the 1984/84 season.

The world recession and financial problems appear not to have had a major impact on world wheat trade, although some effect is noticeable. This is to be expected since wheat is a basic food, and its consumption is quite unresponsive to changes in price and income. Clearly, the United States lost out to other wheat exporters in 1982/83 and 1983/84, with U.S. exports declining by about 8 mmt.

On balance it would appear that our recent projection of rising world wheat export remains valid. It may well be 1990, however, before U.S. wheat exports return to the peak level of a few years ago.

U.S. farm and trade interests would almost universally oppose any agreement which involved the possibility of deciding fair shares of world markets for wheat, coarse grains, and other agricultural products at a time when the United States was in this reduced position in regard to shares of exports of our major commodities. Similar situations prevail for cotton, where our exports and our share have declined sharply in recent years, while for soybeans U.S. share has remained rather high and rising despite the resurgence of South American countries in the soybean and soybean product export market. The drought year 1983 followed by the marketing year 1983/84 is of course an exception to this since the United States had sharply reduced supplies and could not sustain its market share because of the drought and heat wave.

Figure 2

U.S. and World Wheat and Flour Exports
With Projections to 1985/86

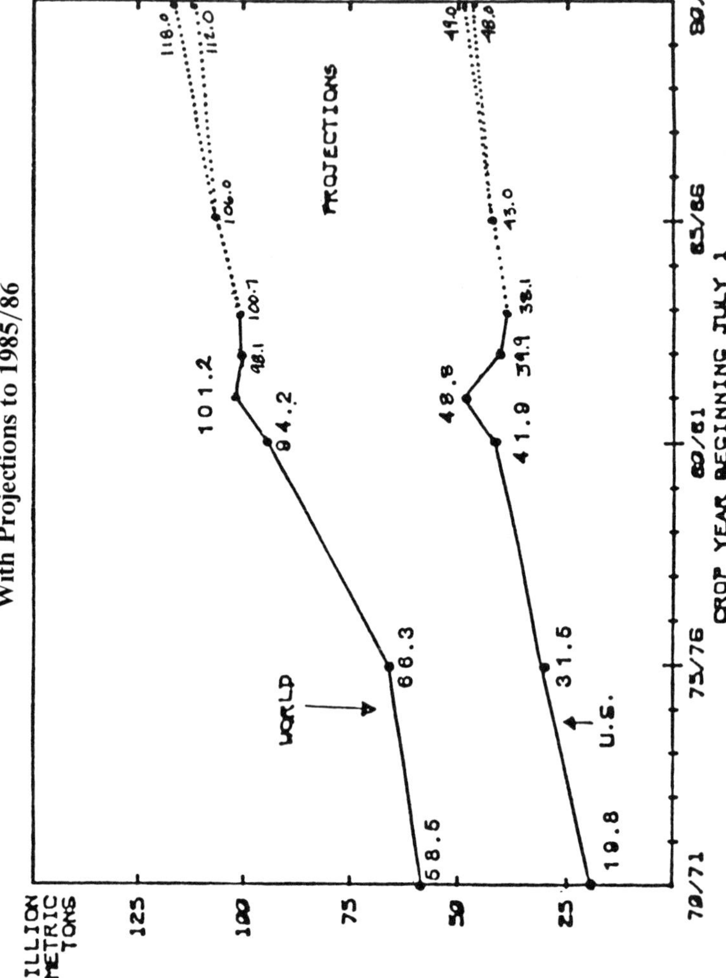

EXCESS CAPACITY IN U.S. AGRICULTURE AS A BARRIER TO U.S. PARTICIPATION IN INTEGRATION OF TRADE STRATEGIES

American agriculture remains the success story of this century, in terms of responsiveness and productivity. In a world market with a rising demand, as in the 1970s, it was the United States that got there first, capturing 90 percent of the growth in feed grain exports, 60 percent of the growth in wheat exports, and most of the growth in soybean exports despite the spurt in Brazilian production and exports.

In a declining market, however, like the world market for grains the past 2 to 3 seasons, U.S. agricultural productivity becomes a problem to farmers because it helps depress prices and incomes, and to government because of our open-ended commitment to support farm prices with massive federal expenditures.

We should not be too smug about our productivity or efficiency. Other countries are efficient too. Brazil has copied U.S. soybean technology; hybrid seed corn and efficient poultry production are everywhere; the Green Revolution raised rice and wheat yields sharply in Asia and other parts of the world 10 to 15 years ago. In fact, overall agricultural production increased more rapidly in the world's poor countries in the 1970s than in the rich countries.

The Size of Excess Production Capacity in U.S. Agriculture

The situation facing USDA planners early in 1983 looked about as follows for late 1983 and 1984:

	Millions of Bushels	
	Wheat	Corn
Total stocks on hand before 1983 harvest	1,600	3,500
Stocks needed as a reserve	1,000	1,200
Surplus component of stocks	600	2,300

In the absence of an acreage reduction program, full production of wheat and corn

in 1983 (assuming average growing conditions and prices around 1983 support levels) would have produced the following annual additions to grain surpluses:	500	1,000

A similar story can be spun for other grains, dairy products, rice, cotton, and tobacco—all the major price-supported crops. Some of the excess capacity for grains also represents excess soybean production potential. Excess capacity; lack of a coherent policy; an administration unwilling to administer the laws vigorously; laws at least obsolescent and not capable of coping with the runaway U.S. agricultural productivity of 1983-84-85 except at very high public costs—these are the distinguishing marks of U.S. policy in 1984.

In my judgment, the 1983 drought and heat wave represent only an incident in an otherwise rather clear prospect of several years of grain, oilseed, cotton, and dairy surpluses in the United States and the world, barring large and continuing droughts in major countries.

EXCESS CAPACITY TO EXPORT AGRICULTURAL PRODUCTS

The record exports of our main food crops (in different years) compared with this season are as follows.

	Record Level	*1983/84 Prospects*
Corn	2,450 mil. bu.	1,850 mil. bu.
Wheat	1,725 mil. bu.	1,400 mil. bu.
Soybeans	900 mil. bu.	740 mil. bu.
Other	500 mil. bu.	400 mil. bu.
Total	5,575	4,390

That looks like about a 20 percent excess capacity. But in fact, as we were shipping the record quantities of various commodities 2 to 3 years ago, our trading companies and cooperatives were gearing up to ship even more. As a result, our capacity to transport, load, and unload bulk commodities for export is now approximately 7 billion bushels, an excess of some 1.4 billion bushels over our record export level and about 2.7 billion bushels above our 1983/84 export prospects.

This is a heavy financial burden on our exporting companies, but it could be a great asset for farmers and for the country if there is a sudden surge in export demand in a few years. Unfortunately for the United States, other countries are expanding their shipping capacity, even as much of ours is idle.

Any arrangement the United States entered into in the mid- to late-1980s that put a cap on our export share at some recent historic average, which may be a necessary condition for getting much cooperation from other exporters for integration of agricultural trade strategies, would make it impossible for the United States to increase its share of world markets materially except under extraordinary shortage conditions. The dream treasured by farmers and the grain trade and related assocations in the United States that we will export our way to farm prosperity would be ended or seriously postponed by such arrangement. It may be a lost dsream in any case for the 1980s, but at least we have not yet, in 1984, negotiated our way to a fixed share of the export share of the export trade for agricultural commodities, a share that might be substantially lower than we had only a few years ago.

MODIFYING THE U.S. GRAIN EXPORT MARKETING SYSTEM BY LEGISLATION

If the United States were to be a party to plan to integrate grain trade strategies to help organize the world grain trade, and if some of the features involving increased governmental intervention referred to in previous sections were incorporated into an agreement designed to implement such a strategy among the exporter countries or the exporter countries in coordination with importing countries, it would be necessary for the U.S. government to play a somewhat larger and probably a more continuous role in grain export marketing. Some have argued that such a course of action would necesarily involve establishment of a U.S. Grain Export Board or Commission, analogous to the Canadian Wheat Board; the approaches summarized in the early pages were of this type. Others have argued that a set of rules and regulations could be designed, possibly requiring some changes in U.S. law, to increase U.S. government involvement somewhat within the framework of the present more or less free enterprise marketing system; this would be adequate if the objectives cited at the start of this paragraph were to be pursued. I support the latter view and have argued it previously.

Congressional efforts toward such an objective chronicled earlier have involved replacing the present export marketing system with a federally controlled and operated Grain Export Board, probably using the private trade as agents. They have never been well planned or well coordinated, and have never had any material and broad support other than the nominal support represented by introduction of Congressman Weaver's (Oregon) bill proposed a number of times by a large number of his colleagues in the House.

I have argued elsewhere that legislative or administrative action of the type embodied in the Weaver bill could come about in the United States in the 1980s or 1990s only under the pressure of successive events demonstrating unambiguous need for such action. That need would be made up of a combination of demonstrated failures of the U.S. grain export marketing system to p ay producers properly, a sharp increase in the United States need to earn more dollars from international trade including higher unit prices for agricultural exports, and/or other crises which generate a broad consensus in the United States among political representatives and trade and farm officials for increased governmental control over exports. None of these conditions is present or even visible today.

INTEGRATING AGRICULTURAL TRADE STRATEGIES VIA INTERNATIONAL COMMODITY AGREEMENTS

Again I will take the grain situation as indicative of the overall situation in this regard, principally because the United States is so dominant in the world grain trade. If we have a chance for successful U.S. leadership to integrate trade strategies in any commodity, it would be in the grains. One could, however, extrapolate these remarks to cover cotton, rice, sugar, oilseeds, tobacco, and some other agricultural commodities.

The most recent example of an actual multilateral negotiation of this type was the effort from about 1975 through 1978 to negotiate an international grain reserves policy as a part of the International Wheat Agreement, under the auspices of the International Wheat Council. The impetus for the discussions and negotiations came from the so-called world food crisis of the mid-1970s, and from the objectives elaborated by various international organizations, especially the FAO and the UNCTAD, of getting the exporting countries to establish reserves against the possibility of future wheat shortages and high prices like those of 1972-75. The World Food Conference of 1975, whose resolutions included a strong statement on the need for world grain reserves, was also instrumental in starting these talks.

The negotiations dragged on for years, with neither the rich nor the poor countries—and neither the importing nor the exporting countries—able to put forward practical and acceptable proposals. This was true even though the negotiation took place under the pressure of a recent experience in which grain supplies had been physically short, grain prices unusually high and unstable, and with the general expectation that this would recur in the 1980s.

The United States in particular took an official "dog in the manger" attitude toward these negotiations. This was evident especially in the U.S. determination in the early stages that any formula for releasing reserves into the world market would be based upon price signals, not on signals arising from limited quantities of grain avilable for use until the next harvest. Other countries, especially UNCTAD members, would not agree to this, and the impasse continued. The International Wheat Council has prepared a chronicle of these negotiations, seeming to indicate that at times the different sides came close to agreement on key points, and that a bit more political will would have yielded a comprehensive new agreement. In fact, the parties were never close to an agreement, and the idea of "an international grain reserve," transformed into the possibility of "nationally owned grain reserves managed under international rules," faded as increased grain supplies developed in the late 1970s. By 1976, when grain supplies were rising, importing countries like Japan lost interest in the idea of cooperation with exporters and with poor countries in the establishment and management of a world grain reserve system.

I have argued elsewhere (*Foreign Policy*, autumn 1975) that the United States should establish a national grain reserve on its own in and for its own interest, apart from what other countries do, and particularly apart from any action by international agencies to negotiate an international grain reserve agreement. This policy was adopted in 1977, first by action of the secretary of agriculture under authority in permanent law, and by recognition of the need for U.S. grain reserves in the Agricultural Acts of 1977 and 1981.

RESERVE NEGOTIATIONS AS A FIRST STEP TOWARD GREATER INTERNATIONAL AGRICULTURAL COOPERATION

If progress is to be made toward integration of agricultural and trade policies, negotiation of an arrangement under which a few key exporting countries including the United States would establish national reserve policies and reach limited agreement on how to use those reserves is probably a first step. But to get to that point, as distinguished from talks designed to lead to (1) a discussion of an exporter cartel, or (2) to a complex and comprehensive agreement organizing the world grain trade, or (3) to the initial steps leading to a staged reduction of government intervention in agriculture in many countries, would require a set of circumstances in world grain markets similar to those of the mid-1970s. It would require a U.S. government that is prepared to lead and is favorable to international cooperation, a more reasonable attitude on the part of Europe and the UNCTAD countries than was evident in the late 1970s, and lots of cooperation and patience by U.S. farm and trade groups.

ANNEX A*

Table 1-4
Principal Features of Formal International Commodity Agreements

Title	Entry into Force	Partici-pating Countries	Price Targets	Formal Export or Production Quotas	Buffer Stocks	Other Policy Measures	Institutional Support
International Wheat Agreement	1971. Preceding agreements 1949, 1953, 1956, 1959, 1962, 1965, 1966, 1967.	Major exporting and importing countries, with exceptions during certain periods.[a]	Not at present. Earlier agreements included a range between max and min. prices	No	No	From 1959 until 1971 importers undertook to buy a min. share of their imports from member countries and exporters to sell the equivalent of their average exports over the preceding 4 years to member countries at prices within the agreed range.[b]	Administered by the International Wheat Council.
International Sugar Agreement	1969. Preceding agreements 1954 and 1959.	All major exporting and importing countries trading on free world market.	Not at present. A range of trigger prices applied from 1969 to 1973, when the economic provisions of the agreement lapsed.	Not at present. Export quotas applied to free market from 1961 to 1973.	Not at present. Min. and max. stocks to be held in producing countries were stipulated from 1969 to 1973.	Not at present. Trigger mechanism linking quota adjustments and stock releases to movements in market prices operated from 1969 to 1973.	Administered by the International Sugar Organization.

ANNEX A*
(Continued)

Table 1-4
Principal Features of Formal International Commodity Agreements

Title	Entry into Force	Partici-pating Countries	Price Targets	Formal Export or Production Quotas	Buffer Stocks	Other Policy Measures	Institutional Support
International Tin Agreement	1976. Preceding agreements 1956, 1961, 1966, 1971, and 1976.	All major producing and importing countries.	Yes. Range between max. and min. prices.	Yes. Export quotas.	Yes. Producing and consuming countries contribute to the buffer stock.		Administered by the International Tin Council.
International Coffee Agreement	1976.[c] Preceding agreements 1962 and 1968.	All major exporting and importing countries.	Yes. Range between min. and max. prices to be established by the ICO.	Yes. Export quotas consisting of a fixed part and a variable part, linked to the price range established by the ICO, or in its absence to average indicator prices for "other milds" and Robusta coffees in 1975.	No.	No.	Administered by the International Coffee Organization

---

REVIEW OF
"Prospects for Integrating the Trade Strategies of Agricultural Exporting Nations"
Joseph Hajda

Among agricultural trade policy alternatives is the proposal for creating a consortium or an association of grain exporting nations to provide for multilateral policy coordination. This league would use multilateral review to achieve convergence of economic performance and promotion of common interests. International agreement would define guidelines for coordinating all the key strategic variables that govern the dynamics of economic performance: identifying markets, producing for those identified markets, and setting world price floors. According to its proponents, multilateral policy review and coordination is one of the alternative solutions to the problems of export market instability and sustained growth. They contend that it would aid producers in all exporting nations and insure adequate supplies for the world's grain buyers.

The obstacles to this proposal are real and genuine. It finds almost no appeal among the governments. This would suggest to a skeptical mind that the idea of multilateral policy review and coordination is illustory. What, then, are the future prospects of such an alternative to the current trade policy strategy?

THE BROAD PICTURE

Focusing on the broad picture of agricultural trade relations, we are struck by the evidence showing the extent to which struggle for national advantage often prevails over international accord. The situation is a reflection of the political dimension which pervades the whole of trade relations among nations. The two issues of how much unilateralism vs. multilateral policy review and coordination, and how much long-term consideration as opposed to short, are appropriate in the exporting countries' dealings with the rest of the world is the ever-present dilemma in trade policy development. But, perceived as the calculated relationship of ends and means, and as a multidimensional process that cannot be entirely divorced from such components of trade competition as political, ideological, and psychological considerations, an articulated trade policy strategy, along with an institution arrangement for agricultural trade, can serve to inhibit international discord but of itself does not assure the mutual trust essential to a long-lasting international consensus.

In the contemporary international trading environment, which imperfectly respects the comparative advantage of various competitors, much depends on the way the competing countries foster attitudes and conduct favorable to the accommodation of trade conflicts. Since trade competition ranges from competitive cooperation to hostile contention among rivals, what emerges from the broad picture of agricultural trade relations is a mosaic that defies the depiction of a simple chart.

Probing the issue, we can envisage a wide spectrum of possibilities. Complete coordination of the trade policy strategies is at one end of the spectrum and complete unilateralism is at the other end. Because dictating outcomes is not within any agricultural trading country's grasp, we do not need to focus on the end of the spectrum designated as complete unilateralism. Instead, we need to consider other kinds of unilateralism, along with pluralistic arrangements for various degrees of multilateral policy review and coordination.

From this perspective, of singular character and importance are the activities of the General Agreement on Tariffs and Trade (GATT), the Organization for Economic Cooperation and Development (OECD), and the UN Conference on Trade and Development (UNCTAD). They facilitate the process of bringing together politically discreet individuals and groups for the purpose of developing coordinated policy strategies. They also facilitate the consideration of measures conducive to more viable patterns of competitive cooperation, cooperative competition, and mutual accommodation. Above all, they provide an opportunity for the diplomatic and political activity defined as consultation. In short, they serve a useful purpose regarding the quest for coordinated policy strategies by means of consultation and/or negotiation.

However, there are many other centers for bringing together professionals seeking to assess alternative trade policy strategies and address the perplexing question of prudence in pursuit of benefits from agricultural trade.

THE TRADITIONAL VIEW vs. THE INTERDEPENDENCE PERSPECTIVE

The issue can be viewed either from the traditional perspective, urging attention to the imperative of national interest, or from an alternative perspective, drawing attention not only to national interest but also to international interdependence.

The traditional view sees agricultural trade relations as if they consisted almost solely of the interaction of nation-states in the pursuit of their respective national interests. From this traditional perspective, there is no reliable mechanism for regulating agricultural trade relations except national "self-help"—emphasizing the reliance on traditional political forms and concerns—and there is no prospect for changing this state of affairs, even though it necessarily stimulates considerable rivalry, much feuding, frequent use of aggressive national mesures, and occasional international confrontations—all of which can be very costly. Agricultural trade strategy, in such an environment, is above all to secure and advance the national interests against those of other countries, and to enhance national power and prestige on the world scene. The most influential political segment plays a key role in determining the road to take in the protection and promotion of national interests.

An alternative view of agricultural trade relations—while not dismissing those traditional concerns—draws attention to the need to perceive interaction with other countries from a different perspective, taking account of the changing face of world political realities. According to this view, most countries have in some measure become in recent decades more interdependent. Two aspects of interdependence are of special importance: (1) increasing economic, political, and other linkages among most countries, primarily through trade and financial flows, and (2) the complex interrelationships among the major forces shaping the world's political economies—such as trade, debt, and interest rates—and including interrelationship between the world's trading and financial systems. An essential ingredient of interdependence consists of linkages through agricultural trade and financial flows as well as interrelationships among the major forces shaping the world's food economies.

From this interdependence perspective, there has been a remarkable internationalization of economic life in most countries since the mid-1960s, and there has been an accelerated internationalization of many food and agricultural economies since the early 1970s. National measures have become more dependent for their success on being harmonized with compatible actions in other nations. The two aspects of interdependence—linkage and interrelationship—demand a substantial degree of cooperation and coordination both among nations and among international organizations—such as the GATT, IMF, and the World Bank—if long-term stability and sustained growth are to be achieved. Given the conditions of intense competition for markets—with all the rivalry, feuding, aggressive national measures, and international confrontations—it is unlikely that the traditional approach will produce the desired stability and growth.

Defined as a condition of mutual sensitivity and mutual vulnerability, and drawing attention to the fact that decisions made in one nation often have important implications and consequences for other nations, the concept of interdependence—with its vision of increasing linkages and complex interrelationships—helps capture the changing nature of political and economic realities of our time. Because the elements of interdependence have grown out of and coexist with elements of the traditional agricultural trade relations, it can be argued that the interdependence perspective offers a more complete image of these changing realities.

THE DOMINANT INFLUENCE

Since custom, tradition, and long-established political factors are among the overriding considerations in determination of most trade arrangements—and they have a lot of momentum—under ordinary circumstances the traditional view is anticipated to remain the dominant influence in the process of trade policy development. Because the dramatic, qualitative changes in the international political economy (and their implications and consequences) are not fully understood, the significance of interdependence—linkages and interrelationships—is not yet fully recognized. Strong traditional, national political beliefs and attitudes work against multilateral, complete coordination of the trade policy strategies among agricultural exporting nations. These beliefs and attitudes can be expected to maintain their momentum in the years to come.

We should not underestimate the role of custom and tradition in shaping the dominant view of political and economic realities. Attempts to assess future evolution of agricultural trade policy strategies are usually related to and colored by the perceptions of the past and the present. The foreseeable future is seen as the continuation of decades of national political history, with national leaders continuing to aim at national adjustment and adaptation to internal and external political demands and expectations. The usual prognosis is that the same socioeconomic and political motives that have historically played a fundamental role in shaping agricultural trade policy strategies for the long haul will continue to do so in future years. Hence, the outlook is clear: the existing national political systems will continue to meet their most important agricultural trade policy imperatives the same way that they have been meeting them in previous years and decades. On the political level, nationalism will continue to show remarkable resilience everywhere. Divergent national political positions will prevent the possibility of a substantial commitment to the multilateral process of mutual adjustment and accommodation. The dominant political mood in international negotiations regarding agricultural trade policy concerns will continue to be unfavorable to an international agreement to create a pluralistic arrangement for coordination. Key individuals and groups advocating the use of aggressive national measures will strongly opt for their nations to take their chances in the struggle for advantage on world markets. In short, there is no need for an American dream plan—or any other agricultural exporting nation's dream plan—in which action to coordinate the trade strategies takes place in the coming years.

Hence, the ends of the long-term export market stability and sustained growth are not likely to be attained in the foreseeable future.

AN ALTERNATIVE APPROACH

The existing dominant political mood favors politics as usual in regard to agricultural trade policy strategies. But it would be unwise to disregards the possibility of different circumstances in the years to come, and to dismiss the judgments of those critics of agricultural trade politics as usual who advocate an alternative approach. In particular, it would be unwise to disregard the voices drawing attention to international interdependence and emphasizing the need to recognize the significance of increasing linkages and complex interrelationships. When the dramatic, qualitative changes in the international political economy and their implications and consequences are better understood, support is likely to grow for an internationally agreed concept of the basic principles of mutual relations fostering the development of a coordinateds trade policy strategy.

It is not inconceivable that the number of voices urging the United States to pursue, in cooperation with other nations, common interests and values in a coordinated fashion will grow under the conditions of a crisis or an emergency. Nor is it inconceivable that the perspective of leadership and strategy can change, and that the strong aversion to coordinating trade policy strategies of agricultural exporting nations can weaken under the conditions of creeping immobility in agricultural trade politics and the search for some device to break the deadlock.

But we do not have to wait for a crisis. Practical steps can be taken immediately to facilitate the long journey toward export market stability and sustained growth. In this respect, of singular importance would be a well-planned round of trade negotiations, under GATT auspices, which could become (1) a comprehensive means to improve the international trading climate, (2) a framework to generate the political will for updating and improving the effectiveness of international rules, norms, procedures, and institutions, and (3) a vehicle to foster mutually beneficial, all-round agricultural trade expansion. Trade expanded in this manner could be the mechanism transmitting growth among countries, enlarging markets, increasing efficiency, and promoting market stability.

Because the United States and other major exporting nations are likely to play key roles in these negotiations, the prerequisites for moving in the desired direction are, first, improvement in their domestic and external policy leadership and, second, application of enlightened self-interest in the negotiations. Each alone would be insufficient: the two types of change need to be combined. The quality of leadership is crucial, and so is enlightened self-interest. While each nation will naturally look out for its own interests, each nation must also look out for the common interest, defined in terms of export market stability and growth.

The two types of change are vital if negotiations are to deal effectively with the realities of agricultural trade: current arrangements are a major source of long-term instability and of constraint on the maintenance of sustained growth. Therefore, the highest priority needs to be assigned to strengthening existing rules, norms, and procedures, as well as to updating existing international institutional structures. But it would be also necessary to take two other simultaneous steps: (1) extend the process of close cooperation, going beyond simple calculations of national interest where each country presses its own ends to the neglect of the common cause, and covering a wider range of national policies; and (2) intensify joint efforts of countries that play a critical part in making the international trading system work.

The main forum for negotiating internationally agreed guidelines to govern the trading practices should be the GATT, but negotiations outside of GATT should be encouraged, especially if the institutional mechanisms of the present GATT fall short of being equal to the task of fashioning and sustaining a diplomatic and political undertaking to move toward the basic ends of stability and growth.

THE ART OF CONSULTATION

Building an enduring, negotiated trading system of this kind will depend on all concerned countries' willingness to practice more completely the art of consultation. We know that some consultation is always taking place, but it has only limited impact on national decision-making processes, seldom constituting an important influence.

As we look at the possible approaches to coordination of the trade policy strategies among agricultural exporting countries, we need to perceive coordination as a process of reacting to disarray, preventing unwanted activities, removing impediments to stability and growth, and managing potential or actual disruptive elements of trading arrangements. The whole process depends to a large extent on the diplomatic activity defined as consultation. We can envisage a spectrum of activity which can be broken down into five levels of consultation, ranging from minimal consultation to systematic consultation, each of which can utilize multiple channels of contact.

First, exchange of points of view or information, with or without analysis. This is a continuous activity in the sphere of agricultural trade relations, and it is undertaken bilaterally or through cooperative discussion in a multilateral institution—such as the GATT, the OECD, or the International Wheat Council. The important question is: how is the feedback used?

Second, communication of actions or decisions which have already been taken by a trading nation or are imminent. This is a near-continuous activity in the sphere of agricultural trade; its bilateral and multilateral dimensions are as in the first level.

Third, advance notice of actions or decisions with a view of receiving the comments of others and/or their endorsement. This level of consultation is utilized from time to time on a bilateral and/or multilateral basis, and involves the review of national agricultural and trady policy goals, means, and methods.

Fourth, discussion with the aim of reaching a consensus on strategies to be adopted or actions to be taken in parallel by everyone concerned. This level of consultation involves a bilateral and/or multilateral coordination to achieve convergence of national agricultural trade systems—requiring convergence of diplomatic, political, and economic performance—and to facilitate a synchronization of policies by calibrating policy stance.

Fifth, systematic consultation—close, comprehensive, and timely consultation—for the purpose of arriving at decisions or actions—whose scope may be limited, but a substantial degree of coordination is produced when a joint regime is established to implement an agreement. A joint regime can be dfined as an institutionalized system of cooperation and mutual accommodation, including a collection of rules, norms, and procedures that the contracting parties support in order to regularize behavior and resolve issues that surface on their common agendas. This should not be confused with an exporters' cartel or a form of political amalgamation.

Without ignoring the fact that some countries practice the last two levels of consultation in a regional context, we can say that current support for the two kinds of consultation is minimal at the global level.

Practical steps toward a stronger common purpose are well within the argricultural exporting nations' means. In the planning stage, a major practical step can be a coordinated strategy concerning the methods for a balanced and gradual reduction of protection for agriculture, and the fuller integration of agriculture into the open, non-discriminatory, multilateral trading system, while taking account of the specific characteristics and role of agriculture. This would involve the consideration of the likely effects of the adjustments which alternative approaches would entail and how best the various objectives of agricultural policies could be achieved in ways compatible with the ends of long-term stability and sustained growth. Taking the current situation as the starting point, bilateral and multilateral consultations would have to proceed on a commodity-by-commodity basis, exploring linkages among nations, to be followed by the joint examination of the interrelationships between the various commodities and the effects of various adjustments. The whole process would have to be so designed as to lead to meaningful negotiations under GATT auspices.

A FRAMEWORK OF PRINCIPLES

Practical steps toward a stronger common purpose will require a cohesive group of key individuals from the agricultural exporting nations who would have the capability to move their countries from agricultural trade politics as usual to a more cooperative approach to the art of consultation—the politics of cooperation. They would have to be capable of communicating and cooperating with each other with a high degree of solidarity so as to reach an accord concerning the basic principles of mutual relations.

A framework of principles covering the major issues of mutual relation would likely consist of the following: the necessity of avoiding aggresive national measures, feuding, conflict, and confrontation; the need of mutual restraint; the expectation of refraining from exploiting opportunities to gain unilateral advantage at the expense of the other trading nations; the need to consult in every possible instance before taking measures; the willingness to build a firm, long-term relationship; and the resolve of all participants to devote themselves to common tasks.

Under such conditions there would be an increase in integrative capabilities among agricultural exporting nations. Their mutual adjustment would affect the different aspects of the process or orientation—the process by which they would decide where they think they are and what they ought to do.

RESPONSIBILITY FOR ENFORCEMENT AND COMPLIANCE

Assuming an increase in cooperative tendencies among agricultural exporting nations, a most fundamental question is where the primary responsibility for rule enforcement and monitoring of compliance should rest. The three leading suggestions are that it remain with each country; that it be moved to the GATT system; or that it become a part of the United Nations system. Another option is to create a new international organization unaffiliated with the GATT and the UN systems.

Each of these options is subject to a major difficulty: the first one, the lack of faith in future self-restraint in regard to self-steering by each country; the second, the distrust of the GATT as a reliable instrument; the third, the great weakness of the UN system in regard to its integrative capabilities—that is, the capabilities to enable different countries to work together effectively—and there is no sign suggesting that the UN system might dispel the reputation for unreliability; the fourth, the considerable resistance to the notion of creating new international organizations.

We can assume that placing the primary responsibility within an updated GATT framework would be more appropriate than the other options.

CONCLUSION

It is possible that, in accordance with the previous history of agricultural trade relations, the many problems will be met by the application of largely unilateral expedients, and that viable international arrangements for effective mutual accommodation through systematic consultation will not be created for some time. This does not mean, however, that we should not attempt to employ diplomacy as the art of judicious persuasion, consultation, negotiation, and pressure, in order to secure more satisfying rewards.

Multilateral policy review and coordination is an aspiration arising from the perceived shortcomings of current agricultural trade arrangements. The need is to improve long-term export market stability and sustained growth. When aspiration and need point clearly in the same direction, multilateral policy review and coordination cannot be lightly regarded as an agricultural trade policy alternative. It is not one which we can afford to judge merely from the short-run point of view.

REVIEW OF
"Prospects for Integrating the Trade Strategies of Agricultural Exporting Nations"
Julius L. Katz

Schnittker states at the outset that "at first glance it appears that no agricultural policy action could be more remote than to integrate the export strategies of a number of competing agricultural exporting nations." Save for a suggestion that negotiations on grain reserves might, under certain circumstances, be a first step toward greater cooperation, the reader is left with scant reason to question this judgment. The paper could as well be ended with the same sentence, substituting "In conclusion" for "At first glance."

Why are the prospects for international cooperation so dismal? Schnittker seems to believe that the obstacles spring largely from attitudes in the United States. U.S. policy for many years has ranged from cool to hostile. U.S. farm and trade interests are opposed to any form of cooperation, especially in current circumstances when the U.S. market share has fallen in recent years for major exported crops. As the final bit of evidence a lack of interest in the United States in efforts to integrate export strategies, he cites the record of failure in the Congress to garner support for legislation to redesign our grain marketing system in the direction of a central marketing authority so as to concentrate market power.

The opposition of U.S. farm and trading interests to integrating export strategies is a fact well documented in congressional testimony, presentations before governmental advisory bodies, and resolutions of farm organizations. It is less clear to me that such opposition extends to informal consultative arrangements. Nonetheless, the obstacles to integration of export strategies are, to my mind, broader and more fundamental than the attitudes of U.S. farm and trade interests or even of U.S. administrations.

On the basis of my own personal experience, over more than a decade, in both the negotiation and functioning of various international commodity arrangements, I find it more than a little misleading to state that "...an exporter cartel or a grain agreement could be designed and operated *from a technical standpoint.*" Such a statement fails to convey the practical difficulties of translating theory to reality. It is not, as Schnittker suggests, that "custom, tradition, political factors, and domestic price support programs are the overriding considerations in determination of trade arrangements. . . ." Rather, the fundamental reason for past failures of commodity agreements and efforts to achieve exporter coordination is the difficulty in finding economically rational means of resolving the conflicting interests and objectives of the participants.

Typically, an effort to organize a market will have stated objectives along the following lines:

1. Maintenance of a level of prices remunerative to producers and fair to consumers
2. Avoidance of excessive fluctuations in prices
3. Maintenance of appropriate stock levels to assure consumers against excessive fluctuations in production and prices
4. Assurance that participants will equitably share in the burdens of adjustment in production and stocks

It will be noted that these objectives are stated so generally and with such balance as to be unexceptionable. In the real world, however, each participant in an international arrangement will bring to the table a different perspective on what is a "fair" or "remunerative" price and what represents an "equitable share of the burden of adjustment."

It will be suggested that all that is required is a will to succeed (or, as it is expressed in international forums, "political will"), that with reasonable give and take solutions can be found, and that most of the issues can be reduced to quantitative expressions and the differences bargained out. There are at least two things wrong with this assumption.

First, since the issues involve real economic costs, it may not, in fact, be possible to find compromises. Exporting nations may prefer to take their chances in the marketplace rather than to concede market share by agreement. Alternatively, nations may find that the obligations they are being asked to undertake are in conflict with domestic policies and programs which are inviolable for domestic political reasons.

A second problem is that where a political compromise is found, the result may be an arrangement which is either economically ineffectual or economically undesirable. The International Cocoa Agreement, for example, may be a triumph of political will, but it is an ineffectual agreement, based upon the defense of an arbitrarily agreed upon price range. The International Tin Agreement succeeded over the course of many years in ratcheting up the price of tin above its probable free market level by means of a buffer stock and tight export controls. But the agreement had the effect of reducing sharply tin's share of the container market by fostering the growth of substitute materials such as aluminum, glass, and plastics.

To illustrate just a few of the many issues likely to be confronted by the participants in a commodity arrangement, I would ask the following:

1. Is it sufficient to deal with a single commodity, or is there a family of commodities that need to be handled simultaneously? Should an arrangement deal with wheat alone, or is it essential that coarse grains be included? In the Tokyo Round negotiations, the EEC insisted that coarse grains be included. The United States, which maintained a major share of the world coarse grain market, would not agree. Most other important participants did not attach as much significance to the issue and could have gone either way. The issue was never fully resolved.

2. How are the price objectives to be established? High-cost producers will seek to achieve prices higher than those existing in the free market. Efficient producers will resist such higher prices, fearing the stimulation of overproduction. Typically, the EEC has sought higher wheat price objectives than those favored by the United States.

3. Is the commodity homogeneous or is it characterized by quality and locational differences leading to price premiums or discounts? Any attempt to represent such price differentials in an agreement will be futile since the differentials will vary in accordance with the demand for and supply of particular qualities and locations. It is in large part because of this "technical" problem that the 1968 Grain Arrangement foundered. It is also the issue on which OPEC nearly fell apart. Only by agreeing to production quotas and by the willingness of Saudi Arabia to accept the largest burden of production cutbacks has OPEC held together.

4. If the arrangement is to be based upon explicit market sharing, i.e., export controls, how are the shares to be allocated? Historically? If so, newer exporters are disadvantaged. If newer exporters are permitted larger than historical shares, they may be gaining shares they could not obtain in the marketplace, this at the expense of traditional exporters.

5. If the arrangement is to encompass an understanding on stocks, how will the burdens be distributed? Who pays for the stocks?

When are they accumulated? When are they released?

6. Finally, there is the general issue of compliance. How can compliance be assured? What are penalties for non-compliance? How are non-members to be treated? Clearly, non-participation by a major exporter or importer may make agreement impossible. For example, the Coffee Agreement could not function without the participation of the United States. The ineffectiveness of the Sugar Agreement can be traced directly to non-participation by the EEC, plus the pursuit of EEC policies directly in conflict with that arrangement. On the other hand, non-participation by the United States in the generally ineffective Cocoa Agreement is of little consequence.

It is not my purpose to argue that it is technically impossible to design an international commodity arrangement to serve a given set of objectives. Experience over the past two decades, however, has left a landscape littered with the remains of failed negotiations and broken down agreements. These failures have not altogether been the result of obstinacy by U.S. administrations aided and abetted by unwilling farmers ands traders. More often the cause has been an inability to overcome conflicts of interest between the major participants. When agreement has been reached, it has at times flowed more from political expediency than from economic rationality.

As will be seen from these remarks, I have no quarrel with Schnittker's conclusion that prospects are poor for institutionalized commodity agreements among agricultural exporters, especially exporters of grain. I, for one, would not encompass within this conclusion the kind of cooperation which might flow from non-binding consultative arrangements. Nor would I be so quick to dismiss the International Wheat Council as a "debating society."

The existence of regular consultative forums, such as the Wheat Council and ad hoc forums occasionally sponsored by the OECD can, in my view, be useful. They provide an opportunity for senior policy makers and ministers of major exporting nations, as well as importers, to examine and discuss each other's policies affecting production, stocks, and trade. The impact of such discussions is indirect, but there is, I am convinced, an impact on national policy. Whatever the impact, it is much less likely to have the kind of economically distorting effects which could follow from arbitrary price or market sharing arrangements resulting from efforts to integrate export trading strategies.

Chapter 3
Domestic Policy Options for the Future of U.S. Agriculture

Bruce Gardner

The policy options to be considered are alternative means of achieving desired objectives for the U.S. agricultural economy. The menu of relevant options, as well as the choice among them, depends on the objectives. Prior agreement on objectives cannot be presumed; consequently, this topic is discussed in the first section of the paper. The menu of relevant options also depends on the impediments that exist to achieving the objectives—domestic production constraints, international competition in commodity markets, political institutions, the beliefs and desires of producers and consumers. These conditions, some of which are also important in politically revealed objectives of past U.S. policy, are discussed in the second and third section. Then the paper turns to a description and evaluation of several policy approaches that should be considered as contenders for future U.S. agricultural policy. The paper does not attempt to defend a particular choice among these options, but does try to identify the factual and analytical information required to make a rational choice, and thus to narrow the issues, so far as possible, to manageable proportions.

OBJECTIVES OF AGRICULTURAL POLICY

The objectives to be discussed are those which can be defended as ends which, if attained, would promote the general well-being of the public in the United States and abroad. These objectives include the efficient provision of food for U.S consumers, an economic environment in which producers of farm products can earn returns comparable to returns elsewhere in the economy, an agricultural production system that does not cause unnecessary environmental or resource costs, and agricultural and food trade policies that permit other countries to follow their comparative advantages in production and which promote the improvement of diets on a worldwide basis. The objectives can be reduced for many purposes to a single goal: to use our agricultural resources as effectively as possible in producing food and fiber products.

Objectives as stated here are not necessarily the objectives that have actually governed the development and administration of past U.S. agricultural policies. These policies are the outcome of a political process which weighs and resolves the interests of various groups in our society. The policy outcomes reflect the strength of various interests and generally can be expected to be most favorble to the most politically powerful groups. In some cases this orientation of policy has worked against the interests of farmers, for example in the embargoes and food price ceilings of the 1970s. But more often in the period since the Great Depression agricultural policy has been implemented to further the economic interests of farmers.

The extent to which policy has been structured to aid farmers has varied considerably from commodity to commodity and in different periods of time. These policies have followed several lines of approach. They have attempted to reduce production when supplies were large, to support prices received by farmers through governmental purchases or deficiency payments when prices were low, they have attempted to increase exports and domestic demand for farm products when markets were weak, they have provided subsidized insurance and credit during periods of economic distress and disaster, and they have attempted to provide farmers with increased bargaining power by exempting marketing cooperatives from antitrust legislation and by establishing marketing orders to increase the effectiveness of these cooperatives (or other producer organizations).

Many of the policies intended to aid farmers as an interest group have produced results inconsistent with public-interest objectives. They have achieved one of the objectives, namely, the support of producers' returns, but at the expense of either higher consumer prices for agricultural products or higher costs to taxpayers to generate the revenue necessary for subsidies to farmers. Because the gains to producers from these programs have tended to exceed the costs to consumers and taxpayers, the farm programs are said to generate a "deadweight loss."

Nonetheless, agricultural policy can promote, and in some instances has promoted, the more general public-interest goals. Policies can do this by correcting market failures, stabilizing otherwise wastefully unstable market conditions, remedying the inefficiencies caused by monopoly power among middlemen, countering the restrictive trade policies of other countries, and attempting to move to a more open world economy. The question is, what policies have the most promise in achieving such desirable results? The appropriate policies depend on exactly what constitute the market failures, sources of instability, market power, and so forth that should be remedied.

There is much disagreement among agricultural economists on many elements of the economics of U.S. agriculture. Consequently, we should not be so ambitious as to expect definitive policy recommendations from this paper or from the deliberations of even the best-intentioned experts. Rather, the purpose here is to put forth several alternatives in the form of policy options, the choice among which will depend on the answers to analytical and factual questions that cannot be definitvely decided at our current state of knowledge. Let us now turn to a consideration of what these factual and analytical issues are, after which we will discuss their implications for policy.

THE U.S. AGRICULTURAL SITUATION TODAY

The farm economy is being heavily influenced in late 1983 by two extraordinary events—the Payment in Kind (PIK) program and the July/August drought. Because of these events, the former the largest acreage control program in history and the latter reducing feed grain yield by about 14 percent, 1983 feed grain production will be reduced by about one-third from last year. Corn and soybean prices at the farm level are up about 35 percent and 25 percent, respectively, from a year ago. The rapid change from the depressed market conditions of a year ago does not change the underlying trends of U.S. agriculture, although it does increase our uncertainty about what those trends are.

Table 1 provides some summary statistics on the financial situation in U.S. agriculture. Income per farm declined in 1982 but still had grown since 1940 or 1960 at a rate faster than income per household in the non-farm population. The real net worth of farms has grown at an even faster rate, leaving the average farm family in a quite healthy net worth position. Note that most of the income growth is from non-farm income sources (off-farm employment primarily), and that about 60 percent of net farm income is from these sources in the 1980s.

The farms that are significantly affected by commodity policy are those with $40,000 or more in sales. They accounted for 29 percent of U.S. farms in 1982, but 83 percent of the gross value of products (table 2). These

TABLE 1

Financial Status of Farms, U.S. Average

	Thousands of 1972 Dollars[a]					
	1940	1960	1980	1981	1982	1983
Income per farm:	4.1	6.7	13.7	15.6	13.1	13.3[b]
from farm sources	2.6	6.1	5.0	6.7	4.7	5.2[b]
from non-farm sources	1.5	2.6	8.7	8.9	8.4	8.1[b]
(percentage from non-farm sources)	(36)	(39)	(64)	(57)	(64)	(61)
Assets and debts per farm, January 1						
Assets	28.7	80.1	233.5	231.3	224.5	208.1
Liabilities	5.4	9.1	38.5	38.6	41.8	42.9
Net Worth	23.3	71.0	195.0	194.2	182.7	165.2
(Debt/Asset ratio)	(18.9)	(11.8)	(16.5)	(16.7)	(18.6)	(20.6)

[a]Nominal values deflated by the GNP deflator.

[b]Midpoint of USDA estimated range.

Sources: Economic Report of the President, 1983; USDA, *Agricultural Outlook,* August 1983.

TABLE 2

Cash Receipts, Net Income, and Farms by Sales Class, 1982

	Thousands	Billions of Dollars (Current, Non-deflated)			
	Farms	Gross Returns	Net Farm Income	Net Family Income Per Farm	Net Worth Per Farm
Farms with annual sales of:					
$500,000 and above	25	45.6	14.3	$597,900	$2,651,000
$200,000-499,999	87	29.5	4.7	67,200	1,322,000
$100,000-199,999	186	30.4	3.7	30,900	866,000
$40,000-99,999	393	31.3	2.1	16.200	521,000
$20,000-39,999	273	10.5	0.1	13.400	324,000
Under $20,000	1,436	16.6	–0.1	18,700	137,000
All farms	2,400	164.0	23.9	26,400	347,000
	Percentage of Total				
$500,000 and above	1.0	27.8	59.9		
$200,000-499,999	3.6	18.0	19.5		
$100,000-199,999	7.7	18.5	15.4		
$40,000-99,999	16.4	19.1	9.1		
$20,000-39,999	11.4	6.4	0.6		
Under $20,000	59.8	10.2	–4.5		
All farms	100.0	100.0	100.0		

Source: USDA, *Economic Indicators of the Farm Sector, 1982.*

commercial farm households, in 1982, had an average net income of $47,600, of which 25 percent came from off-farm sources. Their mean assets were $1,042,000, which with a debt of $250,000 leaves their mean net worth at $792,000 as of January 1, 1983. Thus, U.S. commercial agriculture, as a sector, remains in excellent fundamental economic health. The smaller farms cannot expect to earn an adequate living from agriculture, and about 90 percent of their income is from off-farm sources.

The average farm income and wealth statistics mask a wide variation. At the lower end are a small percentage of farms which are in serious financial trouble. Their number is not known with precision. We can obtain an indication of the most serious problems from figures on bankruptcy and foreclosure. Foreclosure on real estate loans is the typical form of business failure in farming. In 1982 the Farmers' Home Administration foreclosed on 844 loans. Although no data on foreclosures by other lenders has been collected by USDA since 1981, when all foreclosures totaled 2,900, or 1.2 per thousand farms, the rate in 1982/83 is unlikely to have reached the failure rate of non-farm business of 6 per thousand.

A more troubling statistic is the report from FmHA that about one-third of its loans are in arrears. However, the delinquency rate on FmHA loans has been quite high for many years. It reflects the fact that FmHA loan programs have been intended to aid farmers who could not obtain credit elsewhere, and perhaps more importantly, that it maintained liberal collection policies. In addition, a major cause of the FmHA repayment difficulties was the issuance of emergency FmHA credit in the late 1970s. The Farm Credit Act of 1978, part of the congressional response to the American Agriculture Movement, created a $6 billion program of Economic Emergency loans which enabled some economically fragile enterprises to remain in business but not to become solid financially.

My overall view of the financial situation in U.S. agriculture as of 1982/83 is that farmers are being adversely affected by high interest rates and low prices for some commodities, but that this situation does not constitute a general crisis in the commercial farm sector. Thus, discussion of agricultural policy should proceed on the basis of its longer-term relationship to the economics of the U.S. farm sector.

Since the late 1970s concerns have been expressed that U.S. productivity growth, after an outstanding performance in the post-World War 2 period up to 1970, was beginning to taper off. Such trends are difficult to detect in one or a few years because of measurement problems for many farm inputs and because of the random component of agricultural output. Least-squares estimates of the trends in annual rates of growth in figure 1 are:

Figure 1

Output per man-hour
Crop output per acre
output/total inputs
Index, 1967 = 100
1940
1950
1960
1970
1980

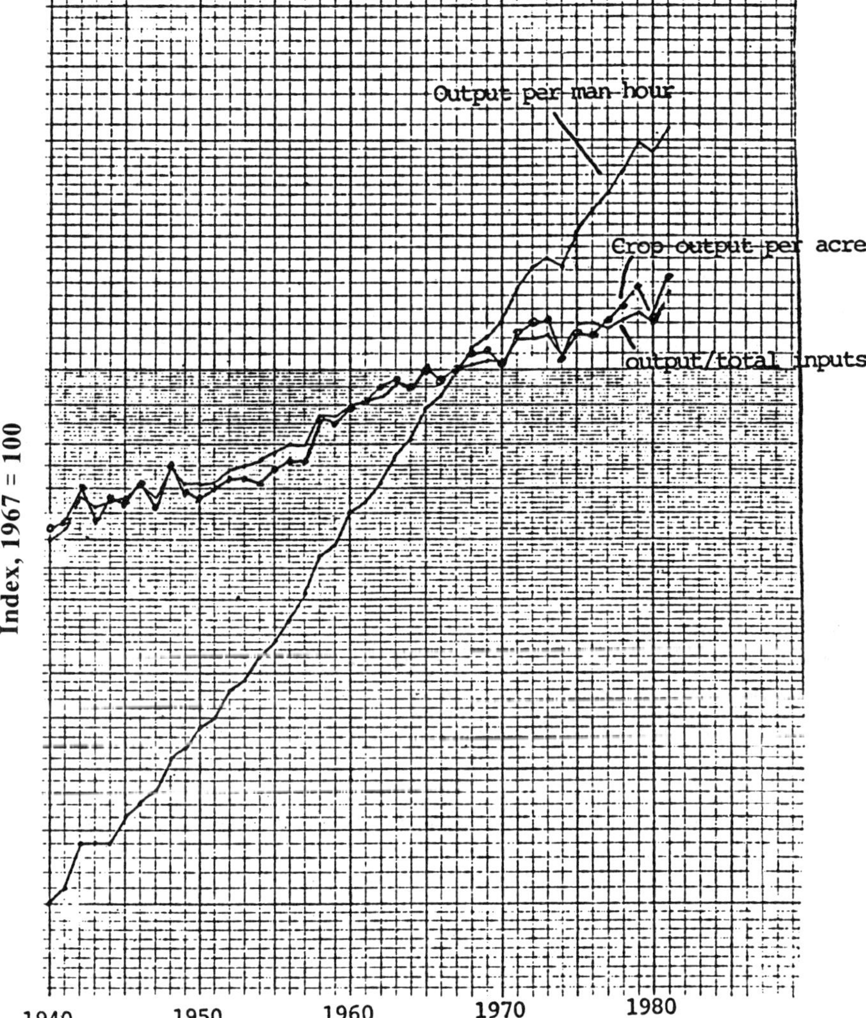

	Output/ total input	Output/ man hour	Crop output/ acre
1940-70	1.7%	5.9%	1.6%
1970-81	1.3%	5.1%	1.7%

The figures suggest a slight decline in the rate of growth of productivity since 1970. The biggest decline is in output per man-hour, usually called labor productivity. However, this is the least meaningful productivity measure. It has risen rapidly in the historical period because labor was being rapidly replaced by capital inputs in U.S. agriculture. But these capital inputs are costly, and their use should be taken into account in calculating productivity. They are not taken into account in output per man-hour. Similar problems arise with crop output per acre but do not cause a large quantitative problem because land use has remained fairly constant over time. Only output per unit of total input, or total factor productivity, is an appropriate indicator of the overall efficiency gains in U.S. agriculture. This indicator does show a slightly (only marginally significant) slower growth in 1970-81.

Generally, agriculture has experienced higher productivity gains than the non-farm mining and manufacturing sector. For 22 mining and manufacturing industries, Gallop and Jorgenson found an average of 1.1 percent annual total factor productivity growth compared to 3.8 percent for agriculture, dsuring 1948-1966.[1] More recent data are available for labor productivity in the non-farm sector, showing an annual rate of productivity growth of 1.3 percent from 1970 to 1981, less than the 5.1 percent for agriculture during this period.

The productivity of U.S. agriculture in another dimension is apparent in our competitiveness in world farm commodity markets and in the low real cost of food in the United States compared to other countries.

The internationalization of farm commodity markets is a key factor in generating a new source of stability as well as new destabilizing stocks. The new source of stability is an increase in the elasticity of demand for U.S. commodities—another outlet for temporarily large supplies, and a set of purchasers who can go elsewhere when U.S. supplies are short. In both instances the price effects of U.S. supply shocks are moderated. On the other hand, the export market is a new source of shocks to the demand for U.S. commodities, tending to increase price variability.

CURRENT ISSUES IN POLICY

Given the general policy objectives and economic state of agriculture, we can be more specific about issues to be resolved in the policy arena as we prepare for the required agricultural legislation of 1985 and for the longer term.

Protecting small farms. They no longer have significance for the supply of commercial farm products; as an industry agriculture could do without them. Should we ignore them in farm policy, or should we try to reestablish small-scale farming as a viable economic enterprise? What should be done about the well-being of persons on small farms, and how can best use be made of the substantial human resources they represent?

Protecting our land base and rural environment. What can be done to insure against undue depletion of our productive capacity through erosion, land conversion, loss or productivity through salinization, etc.? How can external harm to the nation's water and air quality be kept in check? Are there important linkages between commodity policy, particularly grain export policy, and the intensity of land use?

Promoting productivity growth. Past productivity growth has been traced to public investments in research and extension for several commodities. Yet this same technical progress has been blamed for causing economic hardship to small-scale, less skilled farmers and requiring massive labor force adjustments. What directions should research policy take, and how should it be integrated with commodity policy? Similar issues arise for policies that subsidize capital investment in agriculture—income tax preferences, credit subsidies, and irrigation and drainage subsidies.

Protecting commercial farms from financial disaster. Current debate in Congress involves requiring USDA to extend loans in the hope that higher commodity prices in the future could return failing farms to profitability. Another proposal is to allow farmers whose crops have failed to buy crop insurance retroactively, if they agree to buy the insurance for the next several years at the same time. Generally, the approach is to move away from massive commodity-market intervention to focus on aid to the relatively small number of farmers who are in serious financial difficulty because of adverse markets or weather.

Insuring fair returns to commercial agriculture. Even though commercial farmers are earning incomes and rates of return roughly comparable to the non-farm population on an average basis over the past twenty years, nonetheless, producers of some commodities have suffered long stretches of prices too low to cover costs. Therefore, perhaps a "safety net" to hold producers' returns above a minimum cost level is appropriate. An approximation to this objective is accomplished by deficiency payments under the 1981 act. At what level should the target prices that determine these payments be set, what commodities should be covered, should all farm sizes be equally eligible, and what flexibility should there be for the secretary of agriculture to adjust target prices to cope with commodity oversupply or budgetary pressures?

Protecting producers and consumers from extreme price instability. Even if payments to farmers are successful in smoothing their income streams, fluctuations in supply or demand will still create instability in market prices. Indeed, income stabilization may intensify price variability by encouraging farms to keep producing even when prices are low, hence driving down prices further. If this situation leads to unacceptable budget costs, it can cause the implementation of production controls, like the PIK progrm, which may intensify price reactions on the high side. The issue, with or without other policies, is the extent to which the government should intervene in commodity markets to support prices when supplies are plentiful, and to resupply the market in future periods when commodities are scarce. Should this be done with a governmentally owned buffer stock? If so, for which commodities, for what size of stocks, and with what acquisition and release rules? Should the United States organize a buffer stock unilaterally or in conjunction with international commodity agreements? Is it preferable to subsidize the holding of stocks by farmers, as in the Farmer-Owned Reserve (FOR) program? Alternatively, what role can futures markets play in price stabilization?

Insuring the quality and safety of food. Regulation of business practices in food marketing predates farm programs by twenty-five years, going back to the Food and Drug Acts of 1906. Yet regulatory discussions in this area remain controversial. Under what circumstances should products be banned from the marketplace? How far should food quality considerations go in regulating the practices of farmers in feeding livestock and using pesticides or other chemicals? Are labeling and nutritional educational programs appropriate, and what should be their scope?

Promoting the availability of food to consumers, especially the poor, both at home and abroad. Food aid programs should be targeted at the appropriate groups, and attempts to utilize such programs to boost U.S. farm prices should be made compatible with their humanitarian aims. This is an especially difficult problem for foreign food aid under P.L. 480. How can we best use our resources to combat world hunger while not discouraging the development of a healthy food production sector in the recipient countries? Should aid be limited to famine relief? Should aid be tied to technical assistance or to reforms of foreign food policies which underprice the products of indigenous farmers?

Promoting the international competitiveness of U.S. agriculture. What U.S. policies would be most effective in increasing foreign demand? Should they be undertaken even if they increase domestic U.S. food prices relative to foreign food prices (which is the tendency of export subsidies)? What is the proper role of: (a) the Foreign Agriculture Service, (b) U.S. governmental sponsorship of private export-promoting missions, (c) supplying export credit on favorable terms, (d) bilateral trade arrangements between governments, (e) multilateral commodity agreements? Are export restraints or embargoes ever warranted? If so, what steps if any should be taken to shield U.S. farmers from their effects? To what extent do deficiency payments without production controls function as de facto export subsidies?

Reducing budgetary costs. The 1981 act and subsequent legislation placed tobacco on a "no net cost" basis. Yet prices are still supported by means of marketing quotas and acreage allotments. Should a production control approach be tried for other commodities whose budgetary costs appear out of control, notably milk? On the other hand, what would be the consequences of cutting support prices and moving nearer a free-market agriculture? If this were to be done for commodities like tobacco, peanuts, sugar, and milk, how could the existing programs be phased out in such a way as to minimize harm to producers and disruption of the industry?

POLICY OPTIONS, WITH PROS AND CONS

The United States now has fifty years of experimentation to draw on in formulating agricultural commodity policy, and an even longer history in the trade policy, food quality, and research-extension areas. Most of the live options today involve extrapolation from that experience, although there remain a few untested ideas. There are many ways to package policy proposals, and the following suggestions are quite tentative.

A. Production control to manage the commodity markets better

This approach was the operative feature of the first New Deal programs, which involved payments to farmers who agreed to plow up crops, deliver breeding livestock for slaughter, or hold land out of production. It persists in recent years in the set-aside and paid diversion schemes of the late 1970s, the acreage reduction plans of 1981 and 1982, and the PIK program of 1983. It is the basis of our long-standing tobacco programs and the peanut program. These move beyond acreage control to regulate the quantities of output that a farmer may legally sell each year.

Pros

1. Less output increases prices, so farmers are better off.
2. Little or no federal budgetary outlays are required.
3. By producing less we drive up world prices for any commodity in which our share of the world market is large, thus redistributing income from foreign consumers to U.S. producers.
4. Suitable choice of acreage to idle can reduce erosion and other depletion of marginal lands.

Cons

1. Every dollar that crop producers receive in higher prices comes from consumers or livestock producers.
2. A substantial regulatory apparatus is required to determine who is eligible to produce, and how much; to determine the level of compensation for voluntary programs; and to monitor compliance, since there are incentives to produce more than one's entitlement (or hold idle less than agreed).
3. Controls involving allotments or quotas establish property rights in artificially created assets, which may devolve eventually to many non-farm residents (as in tobacco).
4. As product demand becomes more elastic, production controls have less to offer producers; they cause loss of markets, especially for internationally traded commodities where other countries can expand output in response to world price increases that our programs generate. Thus, the main beneficiaries of U.S. wheat production controls would be Canadian, Australian, and South American wheat producers and the EEC taxpayers.
5. Attempts by U.S. farmers to produce more in response to higher prices caused by controls, while keeping acreage limited, leads to economically unwarranted high-intensity use of fertilizer and other inputs to boost yield per acre.
6. Progressive, efficient farmers are prevented or hindered in expanding their operations, while high-cost, marginal producers are protected.
7. Past attempts to use acreage controls in short-term efforts to reduce excess supplies are not encouraging. Small-scale programs have been ineffective while large-scale programs, like PIK, can increase rather than decrease instability.

8. Short-term acreage controls have adverse long-term effects by signaling farmers that in large-stock, low-price periods the markets will be bailed out by these methods. Therefore, producers will tend to make long-term investment decisions without sufficient weight given to down-side price risks, leading to a tendency for excess production capacity. This tendency is intensified when allotments or program acreages are distributed to farmers on the basis of production capacity.

B. Cash payment to farmers

This approach has increased in importance since the mid-1960s. It was first proposed as an overall basis for farm policy in the Brannan Plan of the late 1940s. Currently the wool program and "deficiency payments" for wheat, corn, sorghum, barley, rice, and cotton follow this approach: the government sends checks to farmers making up (part of) the difference between a guaranteed "target" price and some measure of the U.S. average farm price. The payments under the 1981 act are based on normal yield on acreage planted in the past two years, but in the past have been made on the basis of fixed allotments of acreage from a base established many years earlier. Payments are limited to $50,000 per producer.

Pros

1. Economists have long favored cash transfers over in-kind transfers or detailed regulation as causing less induced behavior and lower administrative costs. Deficiency payments can minimize overproduction incentives if they do not increase with current output, i.e., are based on past output.
2. If payments are based on current output, they can be used to increase production, hence decreasing commodity prices for consumers and making U.S. commodities more competitive in international trade. The lower prices also encourage current consumption rather than CCC stock buildups that would occur if loan rates were set too high. In this context, deficiency payments are preferable to market price supports via governmental purchases or production control.
3. Payments can be tailored to fit the program to particular farm sizes and types more readily than other price support approaches, which benefit farmers in proportion to sales (which may mean more than in proportion to profits). In this sense, a direct payments approach is more easily made progressive.

4. Direct payments make it easier to see the cost of a price-support program, and thus foster more intelligent public choice.

Cons

1. Budgetary costs have tended to become unacceptably large, leading to attempts to control output and drive up prices in order to reduce budgetary exposure. Thus, the payments approach has not been a substitute for production controls, but a prelude to them.
2. If payments are made on the basis of past production, they discourage production and the expansion of progressive farmers while maintaining higher-cost producers and over time generating payments to ex-producers. This last feature was a key element in the demise of the historical-base feature of pre-1977 grain and rice payments.
3. Despite limitations at $50,000, payments go predominantly to well-off commercial farmers for whom there is no economic justification for transfer payments.
4. Foreign producers can claim, with some justification, that this approach is a de facto export subsidy, citing pro #2 above. This could lead to retaliatory intervention in trade by these countries and generally worsen the trade environment.

C. Trade-based policy

This is not an integrated policy option, but consists of a set of independent policies all proceeding from the idea that exports are the key to U.S. agricultural prosperity. Some elements of this approach include:

1. A large effort to promote U.S. agricultural products in foreign markets, through the U.S. Department of Agriculture (Foreign Agriculture Service and office of the general sales manager), including government-to-government negotiation of export deals and governmental aid to private agribusiness groups in export-promoting activities

2. Concessional credit for foreign buyers of U.S. agricultural commodities, and occasional explicit export subsidies on sales of governmentally owned commodities at prices below acquisition prices and world market prices (as in our Egyptian flour sale of last year)

3. Binding governmental abjuration of any future embargoes or other activities that would violate export contracts or restrict willing buyers of U.S. products from buying

4. Continued efforts to market surplus U.S. commodities as food aid for poor countries

Pros

1. The export market was the key engine of farm prosperity in the 1970s, ands it may be hoped that such efforts would get it accelerating again.
2. Sending products abroad may be a cheaper way of achieving price support goals than the domestic alternatives.
3. Export subsidies and threats of more have strategic value in persuading the EEC, Japan, and other trade-intervening countries to conduct serious negotiations for world-wide liberalized trade, which would be of great long-term benefit to U.S. agriculture.

Cons

1. Resources spent on export promotion, while our support prices remain above those offered by competitors, are probably ineffective.
2. Concessional credit or other disguised or explicit export subsidies not only cost the taxpayers money but also raise domestic commodity prices relative to the prices of the same commodities in world markets. Thus, for consumers these policies combine the worst features of direct payments and production controls.
3. Abjuration of export controls needlessly hamstrings U.S. foreign policy capability. Past embargoes have probably had little if any net effect on U.S. commodity prices, but even if they did reduce prices, this is not necessarily "shooting ourselves in the foot." All defense and foreign policy involves costs, and embargoes may be a relatively cheap weapon. In any case, we should not preclude our government from choosing this weapon.

D. Less reliance on governmental intervention in commodity markets

The basic idea of this approach is that past farm programs have not been successful, and that we would be better off as a nation to rely more on unregulated markets to determine farm prices and incomes. Yet because of periodic instability in the commodity markets, and consequent periods of low incomes, there is reluctance to rely on completely unregulated markets. Therefore, a limited governmental role in price or income stabilization should be undertaken. The main option to be considered is whether to take the general step of moving away from federal intervention in commodity markets that either raise or lower prices or farmers' incomes averaged over a period of years.

Subsidiary options are alternative approaches to achieving the general goal. One option is the provision of income protection insurance. Farmers would pay a premium to buy this insurance, and would then be eligible for indemnity payments when receipts fall below an insured level. Another option is price stabilization through a buffer-stock program that returns all commodities taken off the market back to the market at a later time, and so does not constitute a price-support program in a long-term context.

These options have been considered in several forms before. The emerging issues that call for their serious consideration today are the budgetary costs of current approaches and the inability of current programs to avoid the problems of overproduction and inefficiencies of acreage controls.

The general approach is predicated on the conclusion that governmental management has proved unsatisfactory and is probably unable to improve on the situation generated by unregulated markets for agricultural commodities. It assumes that there is no chronic tendency toward overproduction or shortage in an unregulated market context, and that commercial farmers can be expected over the long term to earn returns to their labor, management, and investment comparable to returns earned in the nonfarm sector. It abandons the attempt to prop up high-cost producers, which past programs have proved unable to accomplish anyway. However, it is part of this alternative to accept the idea of short-term instability as a market failure, and to view as necessary an augmentation of unregulated markets by governmental action to deal with market instability.

General option: A general move toward less intervention in commodity markets.

Pros

1. Long-run prices different from unregulated commodity market clearing prices result in either surpluses or shortages, either of which is socially costly.
2. Even well-intentioned efforts to correct real inadequacies of markets tend to run afoul of a political environment dominated by narrow interest-group politics.
3. Historical experience with price support policies is chastening in that inefficient and high-cost farmers have not been saved, nor bankruptcies prevented, and benefits have been capitalized into land values.
4. The federal budget would be reduced by non-intervention, freeing scarce federal funds for better purposes, reducing taxes, or reducing

the deficit.

5. With less intervention, U.S. commercial farmers would be in a better position to produce efficiently for the international market, increasing the productivity and competitiveness of U.S. agriculture as a whole.

Cons

1. It is not proved that unregulated markets allocate the nation's agricultural resources well, or provide adequate income for farmers.
2. Our government intervenes with research that drives down prices, and regulatory policies and export embargoes that disrupt markets. Therefore, it should intervene to offset their adverse effects on farmers.
3. There is no free market internationally because of other countries' policies, and therefore our government must intervene in self-defense.
4. There is no competitive market domestically because of middlemen's market power, and therefore government should intervene.
5. Current programs are a response to democratic political forces that should be respected as the will of the majority.

E. Farm Income Protection Insurance

Stabilization of income could be accomplished by a program which made indemnity payments to producers when their incomes were low. The most straightforward scheme of this type would constitute income insurance. However, net income itself is hardly feasible as an insured variable. There is some potential, however, for gross receipts. An insurance policy on gross receipts would pay an indemnity when a producer's revenue fell below, say, 80 percent of a five-year average of market prices times the producer's normal output. This insurance could be sold by the federal government or by private insurance companies. The difficulties, however, are many. The actuarial basis for such insurance would be difficult to establish. The insurance probably would not be purchased by producers unless the premiums were heavily subsidized. The main desirable features are that producers who are concerned about the risks of temporarily low incomes would be able to take individual action to reduce this risk without giving up their freedom to act as they choose in the marketplace and without the governmental costs and potential resource allocation problems that price supports and governmental management of acreage have in the past generated.

An alternative approximation to an insurance program would be to supplement the current all-risk crop insurance program (which already has subsidized premiums) with the development and perhaps subsidization of put options for the main agricultural commodities. By buying crop insurance and buying put options, a producer could essentially insure against either low yield or low prices, by paying a price for the level of coverage desired.

Pros

1. Even if the market works to allocate resources properly over the long term, there remains unacceptable short-term instability.
2. By charging premiums for the insurance, induced output effects or unwarranted redistribution to wealthy farmers can be avoided.
3. Resources will be allocated more efficiently when farmers' risks are reduced.
4. Producers would be able to choose the degree of income protection most suitable to their individual situations and to the extent they are willing to pay.
5. Political pressures for inefficient forms of intervention will be defused by this program.

Cons

1. If farmers wanted income insurance (enough to pay for it), the market would already be providing it.
2. Income insurance is not actuarially or managerially feasible in the near future, and may never be.
3. If any subsidy is placed on the premiums, the program will encourage undue risk taking and resource misallocaition.
4. Unless the program contains subsidies, it has no chance politically.

F. Price Stabilization

The main policy tool for accomplishing this end is governmental management of commodity buffer stocks. Acquisition of stocks is expected to have no long-term distorting effects on commodity markets because these stocks must at some future point be sold. Thus, the effect on long-term expected price will be to a first-order approximation of zero. The drawbacks of buffer stock stabilization schemes involve the historical difficulties that such programs have had in accomplishing stabilization objectives without evolving into long-term price support policies. An alternative mechanism to governmental management of stocks is to have the government simply pay storage subsidies, essentially an FOR program without trigger prices.

Pros

1. Without intervention, price instability causes needless macroeconomic disruption, especially in international markets, even if income insurance stabilizes farm income.
2. The private sector will not accumulate stocks to cope with infrequent but major catastrophes which generate prices so high that political pressures will not permit "speculators" to receive them.
3. Stabilization domestically can increase the joint welfare of risk-averse consumers and producers and thus is a good social investment.
4. Livestock producers can plan more efficient production patterns over time if grain prices are stable.
5. Political pressures from consumer groups for embargoes and price ceilings will be reduced.

Cons

1. It is unlikely that the government's stock-management policy will be conducted any better than speculative storage by private interests.
2. Governmental storage crowds out some private storage.
3. The U.S. would end up with most of the world's grain stocks and thus tend to carry the world's burden of stabilization at U.S. expense.
4. Governmental stocks tend to overhang the market, and over the long term producers may be better off if prices are free to vary.
5. Political pressures may be irresistible to convert any stabilization scheme into a price-support program.

G. Macroeconomic Spending, Tax, and Monetary Policy

Some have argued that these policies are as important to the health of agriculture today as traditional commodity policies. Weak commodity markets in 1981 and 1982 were attributed to high real interest rates and the high value of the dollar relative to the currencies of foreign buyers of U.S.

farm products. The high interest rates also created the cash flow problem for highly leveraged farmers that has driven some of them out of business. Therefore, it may be argued that nothing wuld be better for agriculture than macroeconomic policies that would bring down real interest rates and the value of the dollar. What policies would accomplish this? Tight fiscal policy (reduced deficits) and easier monetary policy are often suggested. But it can be objected that easy monetary policy is what permitted interest rates to rise so far in the first place by creating inflationary expectations. Here we do not have a set of pros and cons for a particular policy approach, but considerations that should be taken into account when assessing the prospects for any of the specifically agricultural policy options.

H. Aid to farmers in trouble

The financial troubles that have led some to speak of a "crisis" in U.S. agriculture apparently only are serious for a small fraction of farmers (whether 1, 5, or 10 percent, or more, is itself a matter which needs more careful attention than it has been given to date by agricultural economists). A natural policy approach to deal with this situation is to abandon the idea of commodity policy and instead channel loans or grants to farmers who, because of natural disaster or low prices, are at risk of losing their farms. This general approach was significantly advanced in the Emergency Agricultural Act of 1978 with its new category of Economic Emergency loans through the Farmers' Home Administration (FmHA). Emergency loans outstanding now total about $10 billion, or just over $4,000 per U.S. farm.

Pros

1. The approach focuses on farmers who are in trouble and does not spend tax dollars aiding financially secure farmers.
2. Genuinely temporary problems due to no fault of the farmers' can be expected to disappear over the longer term, so the program would be largely self-liquidating.
3. Political pressure for escalating support prices would abate.

Cons

1. The program would inevitably keep some farmers in business temporarily who will not ultimately survive, thus only adding to the size of debt when collapse finally occurs.
2. Such a program is incompatible with free-market approaches to risk management such as futures transactions, forward contracting,

or purchase of insurance, because this program is a de facto all-risk business failure insurance policy with no premium.

3. The program will tend to rise the cost of U.S. food production, making us less competitive in foreign markets and raising prices to consumers, because the process of weeding out high-cost or poorly managed enterprises will be hindered.

I. Development of rural human resources

Some have argued that the most helpful elements of governmental policy for farm people have involved programs to improve the schooling, technical skills, information, and managerial capacity of farm people. Additional human capital has not only helped commercial farmers become more efficient but, equally important, has increased the earning power of small-scale farmers in off-farm employment and has improved the job prospects of those who must leave agriculture. This last point is not a minor one in that the farm population has declined from 23 million in 1950 to about 5½ million currently. Further decline seems inevitable, regardless of commodity policy options followed.

Policy here involves a host of issues that must be narrowed further before the pros and cons can be reasonably assessed. The general idea is that the "market failures" that warrant governmental intervention are not to be found in the commodity markets so much as in the labor markets.

J. Political Rcforms

Many approaches have been suggested in the past thirty years, for example: granting the secretary of agriculture more policy discretion vis à vis Congress; creating an independent agency analogous to the Federal Reserve Board to regulate agricultural policy; constitutional restrictions on the price-setting and economic regulatory powers of the federal government; institutional changes within the executive branch to promote a wider-based "food policy" thrust than the current habitual domination by farmers' interests through USDA punctuated by sporadic incursions of consumer or foreign policy interests in periods of high food prices or international unrest. Any of these options requires detailed study before going further with them. Indeed, all have been proposed with seemingly negligible success to date (although this point is arguable).

Perhaps most valuable at this stage is an assessment of what is responsible for the political durability of certain program elements and administrative structures. For example, practically every farm commodity program enacted contains support price levels established within a narrow range by Congress (in contrast to other regulated industries, which have hardly ever involved governmental price setting). Why? Moreover, how is it that farmers, with only a small fraction (about 3 percent) of the electorate, can so consistently dominate the political agenda concerning their interests? Are there any significant realignments of political forces on the horizon?

KEY QUESTIONS TO BE RESOLVED IN WEIGHING PROS AND CONS, AND CHOOSING OPTIONS

In order to achieve the objective of the Agriculture, Stability, and Growth project of "developing a coherent general policy for American agriculture,"[2] it is necessary to come to agreement on which policy option, or combination of options, provides the greatest net advantages for the nation as a whole. A gneral question that pertains to most of the options is: will the governmental action proposed make all the main interest groups—consumers, large farmers, small farmers, crop producers, livestock producers, farm workers, farm supply industry—better off? Or will some gain at the expense of others? A policy that might come close to making all groups better off would be the promotion of agricultural research to increase crop yields and the efficiency of livestock production. It could reduce crop producers' costs, hence reduce livestock producers' feed costs and consumers' food costs. With rates of return as high as estimated for past research, taxpayers (that is, consumers and producers) would be more than compensated for the funds they put up. Yet even such a successful policy would be likely to generate losses for some. Farm workers might see the demand for their services decline, their wages reduced, or unemployment increased. Farmers slow to adopt the new technology, or producing commodities that compete with the improved commodities (e.g., hog producers when chicken production becomes more efficient) might be made worse off.

The various types of commodity market intervention even more clearly involve redistribution among interest groups, as the lists of pros and cons have stated. In such a context is any objective choice possible?

Clearly a choice is possible; this is just what the political process accomplishes. But presumably what we are looking for in this project is a consensus choice—one whose enactment does not turn on raw political clout but which all or most can agree to support. That is, we want to propose farm legislation that, say, 95 percent of informed voters, and their congressional representatives, would support.

It might be argued that if such policies were in the cards, they would already have been proposed and enacted, since they would be sure winners for the politicians who proposed and supported them. I think there is truth in this position, and that the probability that this project will generate new consensus policies is small. Nonetheless, there is opportunity to move in the direction of consensus and improve our policies at the margin.

One of the arts of politics is compromise, and this may help in developing consensus policies. I believe that the weight of evidence adds up to a case that option D, less government intervention, is best for the nation as a whole and that the cons outweigh the pros even for limited interventions as specified in options E, F, and H. Others may disagree, arguing even for one or more of the intervention options A, B, or C. A possible compromise is, say, target prices, but pegged somewhat lower than in the 1981 act in real terms.

A combination of options can constitute more than compromise, and can lead to results preferable to any option alone. For example, option A, production controls, can be combined with B, deficiency payments. If production controls are applied just sufficiently to offset the overproduction incentives created by payments tied to current output, we obtain a blend option preferable to either A or B above.

NOTES

1. Gallop and Jorgenson use quite different methods from USDA. Nonetheless, it is surprising that their estimate of agricultural productivity growth is twice USDA's. See F. Gallop and D. Jorgenson, "U.S. Productivity Growth by Industry," in Vaccara and Vendrick, eds., *New Developments in Productivity Measurement and Analysis,* National Bureau of Economic Research, Studies in Income and Wealth, vol. 44 (Chicago: University of Chicago Press, 1980).
2. Curry Foundation, "Agriculture, Stability, and Growth: Toward A Cooperative Approach," mimeo, July 1983, p. 1.

REVIEW OF
"Domestic Policy Options for the Future of U.S. Agriculture"
Harold F. Breimyer

Two and a half centuries ago the French philosopher Jean-Jacques Rousseau advanced the idea of a "social contract" as explaining the relation of the individual to his government in a democracy. Each citizen, it was said, stands in a contractual relationship to society as a whole.

The term fell into some disrepute, partly because the responsibility placed on the citizen was distasteful but even more because the one-versus-all equation neglected the hierarchical relation that in fact exists between the individual and society.

The notion of a social contract, though not currently in vogue, may help explain government programs for agriculture. However, it is necessary that Rousseau's simple version be corrected by recognizing the successive levels of aggregation that intervene between the individual and all society.

In several respects farm programs as we have known them are a social contract. They represent a contractual relationship between the enterprise unit in agriculture and society as a whole—the latter encapsulated in the office of central government. The relationship is marked by reciprocal obligation and, of course, by quid pro quo.

But the role of intermediate entities is significant. These can be commodity sectors, as all wheat producers, or all dairymen, or agriculture as a whole (as a sub-unit of the total economy). Indeed, one of the most perplexing features of the "political economy of agriculture" lies in the rights and responsibilities of each farmer relative to the aggregative unit to which his welfare is so closely tied.

Irrespective of the hierarchical complication, the social contract principle has an important merit: it facilitates the specification of objectives for the contractual relationship. And, as noted above, it sets forth the reciprocal obligations of parties.

To specify objectives for the social contract in agriculture leads at once to a vivid revelation that those objectives are not confined to enhancing the welfare of farmers. They include also various social goals such as (1) stabilization of the supply of farm products in the interest not just of farmers but of our consumers and the exchange-earning capacity of export trade; (2) protection of the vital resource of the nation's topsoil; and (3) establishing or preserving whatever organizational structure of agriculture may be regarded as in the public interest.

These opening remarks are not inconsistent with the objectives of agricultural policy Bruce Gardner enumerates in the opening paragraph of page 115-116 of his statement, and the topic headings under "Current Issues" listed on pages 123-125. It is good to see, in Professor Gardner's treatment, a note on protection of the land base. Perhaps his double negative—the wish to minimize damage—should be converted to a strong positive. But this is a minor comment. The topic needs attention. Quite possibly, how to incorporate a soil conservation plank will be a major concern in writing a 1985 farm law.

A little more comment is called for regarding considerations of organizational structure in agriculture and the closely associated distributional effects of farm programs. Gardner, in his listing of objectives or issues, confines his attention to a paragraph about small farms, page 123. Perhaps he intends small farms to serve as proxy for the whole organizational-structure/distributional complex. If so, they fall far short of doing so. This is one of the touchiest issues in farm policy. If society accords agriculture, via farm programs, certain benefits it would not otherwise receive, the question will not die: "Who gets them?"

Obviously, the touchiness is a reason the topic is bypassed so often.

Furthermore, Gardner's language must be considered with care because "small" is a notably ambiguous adjective. Worse, it often serves not for a focus on structural/distributional issues but as a diversion therefrom. To many of us (perhaps most) "small" means sub-standard units. The majority of small farms are part-time—though, it should be added instantly, not all are that.

The structural issue in design of farm programs revolves around not small farms but the moderate-sized, full-time, market-related, commercial proprietary farm. Exact definition is not necessary, but this traditional kind of farm combines in the farm family all four factors of production. There can be some farming of rented acres and some hiring of wage labor, but those practices cannot predominate.

Manifestly, this kind of unit is disappearing as agriculture moves toward a dual structure of a few very large units and many small ones. Yet the legislative history of enacting farm programs is replete with preference for the traditional proprietary organizational unit. Moreover, to this day public support for programs is conditioned on preserving the image of the individual farm family business unit. Urban citizens are indignant at any notion that they are benefactors of very large farming operations, or of absentee landlords who buy land for tax shelters, or of any other major departures from traditional agriculture.

Paradoxically, in his preoccupation with income data by size of sales unit, Gardner is implicitly concerned with the distributional aspects of farm programs, yet he abstains from commenting on proprietary status as such. Nor does he mention the closely related matter of which factor is likely to receive the benefits of public spending in farm programs (its "incidence"). Economists have long feared that land idling, for example, has usually drawn all benefit to the land factor.

PUBLIC CONCERN FOR FARMERS

One more comment may be in order about structural/distributional considerations in design of farm programs. Citizens generally are more sensitive to those considerations than are farmers—or than is the established political leadership of agriculture. Farm leadership tends to come from large, securely financed farmers. It is easy to suggest, or even allege, that for this reason it is hard to establish a good balance among objectives of programs, especially among (1) agricultural versus public interests and (2) size and organizational categories of farms.

And again to pick up the thread, citizens individualize the outcome of farm programs—the who-gets-the-benefits issue. Theoretical economists may devise all sorts of abstract concepts. Citizens are more simplistic: they have supported government programs for agriculture for a half-century for the basic reason that *they care* about the welfare of individual farmers, their families, and their communities. For this reason they are willing to grant agriculture both a measure of aid at public cost and a degree of authority for self-aggrandizing activities. The late Karl Brandt, who was an economic adviser to President Eisenhower, once wrote that "the extraordinary good will which the urban public entertains towad farmers should be treated... with utmost respect."[1] Yea, verily, so it should.

ANOTHER VIEW OF FARM PROGRAMS

Government programs for agriculture can be looked at in a sharply different way. In a sense, farm programs protect the public from farmers, farmers from the public, and farmers from each other.

Examples of the first are public measures to preserve the soil base (soil conservation); of the second, demand creation during a business recession;

and of the third, marketing orders (as in milk or citrus) that force farmers to manage marketings in their collective best interest.

This third kind of action raises intriguing questions. How much obligation ought society feel to help farmers help themselves? Yet, contrariwise, of power of group action be granted to farmers, so that they can in fact help themselves, what precaution should be taken against over-exploitation? This is an age-old issue. Repeatedly in history society grants self-aggrandizing power, only to find later that it must act to rescind some of it. The most incisive illustration is the initial granting of the limited-liability privilege to joint stock corporations. After a century of antitrust restrictions, we still do not know how to keep corporate giants operating in the public interest.

Perhaps a fourth item should be added to the three above. Programs protect farmers from nature. Crop insurance is an obvious example.

INCOME TO FARMERS vs. STABILIZATION

One dichotomy has proved useful in thinking about agricultural programs. It is whether they serve mainly to enhance the income of farmers or to achieve some degree of stabilization. Obviously, the first is pro-farmer. The second is just about pro-everybody, or can be that.

Even so, it does not follow that any use of programs to bolster farmers' income automatically or inevitably encounters public antipathy. The paragraphs above should make this clear. In that respect, the inference Professor Gardner draws on page 116 that farm programs have often "produced results inconsistent with public-interest objectives" is, at best, highly questionable. A moderate degree of enhancement of commodity price and income to farmers is not a violation of the public interest, inasmuch as programs were intended to give some income aid.

It is extremely difficult, even hazardous, to try to arrive at a summary judgment about fifty years of farm programs. Probably the record is marked by more diversity than by any generalizable tendency.

It is true, to be sure, that programs have the capacity to violate the public interest, and more than a few have doubtless done so. But one should be cautious about grand labeling.

Gardner's judgment is the more suspect in the light of the opinion held by many economists that programs have been less effective—and in their present form are less well adapted—for increasing the overall income level over time than for moderating the instability that marks agriculture.

My own preference is to emphasize the stabilization feature of programs. I have said that the basic rationale for farm programs from the standpoint of agriculture lies in

> . . . the vulnerability of the proprietary farmer to agriculture's inherent instability, itself explained as variable weather leads to variable crop harvests, which in turn interact with highly inelastic demand for farm products. In the absence of farm programs, variations in supply convert to sharp ups and downs in farmers' prices and to major fluctuations in income also. In addition, demand for farm products is far from stable. Export demand is notoriously undependable but in the last five years domestic demand has not been a bastion of strength either. All this mercurial behavior is a disturbing fact of life for farm business units whose financial reserves are modest at best.[2]

Stabilization as a feature and goal of programs serves not only the intersts of farmers but, as was pointed out earlier, those of consumers too. Also, stabilization can aid export trade. And it helps the agribusiness sector.

Farmers, however, tend to emphasize the income part of program goals. Hence, in a real sense farm programs often are of most value to farmers for reasons that contravene farmers' own wishes.

The income-versus-stabilization dichotomy is useful for the further reason that so many conflicts in program design revolve around it. Most at issue is whether farmers seek a level of income that, if realized via commodity prices, would result in prices so high as to be market-shrinking and therefore would also force farmers to accept tighter restrictions than they are willing to accept.

Furthermore, any repeated or permanent gains in income attributable to higher commodity prices become capitalized in the price of land, creating a windfall for landowners of the time and a barrier to entry by would-be future ones.

These remarks that warn against overemphasizing enhancement of aggregate income as a goal of farm programs applies only to lasting, permanent additions to income. There is good reason to underpin income when demand weakens during the recession phase of a business cycle. But in the dichotomy of income versus stabilization, action for that purpose classifies as stabilizing. It is short-term.

FARM PROGRAM TECHNIQUES

The more difficult part of program making for agriculture lies in specifying program objectives and the broad principles for program techniques. The particulars, the minutiae, of program design are easier to come by. Admittedly, they can present political problems in implementation.

Bruce Gardner addresses program techniques in the context of "policy options." The ten options he lists are not logical equivalents. Production control is not an alternate to trade-based policy; and neither is in the same category as developing rural human resources or achieving political reforms. Moreover, in a practical sense it is difficult to separate techniques as such from the degree of effectiveness that is sought.

Direct Payments

A technique on everyone's list, including Professor Gardner's, is direct payments from the Treasury. These are variously called shortfall, compensatory, or deficiency payments. They are transfer payments; in their pure version they do not remunerate for services rendered. Least of all are they rental payments for idling land.

Direct payments are aimed at compensating for any inadequacy of the income farmers otherwise earn. They often are resorted to as a relatively painless way to improve farmers' income, preferable to imposing the various instruments of supply management.

When relied on heavily, generally, and continuously, they run into the objections raised above to putting too much emphasis on an income objective for farm programs, plus other objections too. In present programs payment rates are expressed in terms of quantity units (as per bushel) and calculated proportionate to the size of a farmer's output, subject only to the limit of $50,000 received by a single farmer. The data Gardner presents on the highly skewed distribution of income in agriculture raise disturbing questions as to whether the deficiency payment scheme now in use is satisfactory, particularly in view of the philosophy circulating just now that government aid should be need-related and not go to people or businesses that already are thriving.

Gardner addresses these issues under the heading of "cash payments to farmers." His denunciation of the lack of "economic justification for transfer payments" to "well-off commercial farmers" is stronger language than mine but highlights the issues (page 128). Moreover, direct payments at incentive levels can lead to increased production, lower prices, and self-escalating payment rates. Gardner properly suggests (page 128) that they can become not "a substitute for production controls, but a prelude to them." On the other hand, payments may be justified during brief periods, notably those of business recession, as noted above. It may be better to supplement incomes in that way than to force sharp cutbacks in production in order to protect price when demand slumps.

But the biggest merit of payments is the one Gardner sets forth, that they "can be tailored to fit particular farm sizes and types..." (page 127). They can be tailored to defend moderate sized proprietary farms, for example.

Direct payments belong in the arsenal of program devices, but astuteness is called for in employing them.

Commodity Supply Management

Commodity management, or supply management, or a combination of those words, has come to be the concept by which supply, distribution, reserve stocks, export trade, price, and income are orchestrated. Often the primary goal is stabilization. The object is to moderate to some extent the wide swings that have long characterized agricultural commodities.

Two basic principles apply. One is that a range of production control techniques is available, to be drawn on as desired, as well as a range of choices in reserve-stock and export policy too. The second is that the several instruments of supply management are interlocked. The management process must be an integrated whole.

Methods for controlling production present a stair-step sequence beginning with the loosest voluntary acreage reduction and ending with tight mandatory quantity marketing quotas. Loosest of all is voluntary acreage idling (acreage reserve), where remuneration is confined to eligibility to receive price support loans and deficiency payments, without a requirement for cross compliance. The big weakness is the contradiction that if the program were to be effective in lifting market prices to the target price level, participating farmers would get no differential reward. In short, slippage and the free rider syndrome doom this program to very limited effectiveness.

To get more farmers to participate, individualized payments must be offered. These are called paid diversion. Payment can be in dollars or in kind. Paid diversion on a scale for major effect on production is exceedingly costly.

There is no escaping the unpleasant fact that truly effective production control can be achieved at moderate cost only by employing some form of compulsion. All-farmer allotments can be sweetened with direct payments, but only a mandatory program can be highly effective without incurring high cost.

Manifestly, how much production control may be sought depends on both the price and income goals that are being pursued and the current state of domestic and export demand. However, with the increasing internationalization of agriculture, the biggest question mark, the source of worst uncertainty, is how to make programs fit with goals for exporting farm products. At issue is not only how sensitive export markets are to commodity prices, but also the effectiveness of several other practices that may be adopted. Gardner touches on these under the topic of "trade-based policy" (pages 128-129). As he says, these are not an "integrated policy option," but they are a major complication in making and carrying out farm programs.

We are hurt just now by the absence of any consensus as to the responsiveness of international trade to not only sales prices but various non-price aspects of the conduct of trade. One should tread lightly and tentatively in addressing this part of policy making.

Separate Policy/Entity for Export Management

At a seminar held in November 1983 on the University of Missouri (Columbia) campus, the idea was advanced that for major export crops, export policy should be partly or fully detached from domestic stabilization programs. The export agency would be able to develop export policies independently (or partially so) of price supports. More than that, the agency could price-discriminate in world trading. The idea seems not to be included in Professor Gardner's paper; it may be worth consideration.[3]

Reserve Stock Programs

Some kind of reserve stock program is a fixture. Within that maxim a wide range of choices can be offered for reserve or buffer stock management.

The principle involved is consistency within the supply management program. It is extremely risky to use commodity reserves as anything other than a relatively free-flowing storehouse. If support and release price levels are too high relative to the tightness of the production control that is engaged in, only one outcome results. It has been the curse of commodity programs ever since 1933. It is excessive accumulation. More often than advertised, the villain is not support level but the accompanying release price. The stocks program works best if the release price be kept down close to the loan rate. This principle virtually militates agains the attractive

Farmer Owned Reserve that has been a feature of programs of recent years.

POTPOURRI

A few random observations will now be made, some with reference to observations by Gardner, others not.

Soil Conservation

The need and the likelihood for folding in provisions for minimum protection of soil was mentioned early in this paper. The topic is repeated here as a reminder. To investigate the several alternative techniques would require a new paper. But a further note will follow later.

Farm Income Protection Insurance

This option is getting a lot of attention, primarily from younger economists who think they have found something new. In reality, it was considered at length during the 1950s. It was dropped then, for the same reasons that will lead to its rejection now. Among other flaws, straight income insurance would not distinguish between inadequacy caused by the market and by the farmer's delinquency; if it is a market-price supplement, other instruments are easier to handle. One interesting angle: if farmers were really to assess themselves for effective production control, they would find it a lot cheaper to apply uniform allotments upon themselves.

Nonetheless, the option deserves consideration and no objection is raised to Professor Gardner's including it. Conceivably, some assessment on farmers could be incorporated with other program methods.

Aid to Financially Pressed Farmers

Gardner devotes a page to this topic (pages 134-135). To this there is one abiding moral: if aid of that kind is to be given, it must be special-program and pinpointed. It cannot be embraced in general commodity management programs. Least of all can price support levels be pitched high enough to bail out younger farmers caught in the asset deflation and high interst rates of the last five years.

The Neglected Tax Subsidy Issue

Why is it that apparently no one other than Harold Breimyer points out the monstrous inconsistency whereby the federal government makes agriculture eligible for tax-deduction devices of a dozen varieties, thereby stimulating production and reducing tax revenue, even as it simultaneously spends tax dollars to restrain production and take products off the market in price support?

A second facet of the policy is that inasmuch as many deductions or shelters are deductions from income subject to tax, they are highly preferential as to beneficiaries. They benefit farmers (including non-farm investors in farming) who are in high tax brackets, and penalize those in low brackets. This may be a separate issue; but the consequence of tax policy explained in the paragraph above is directly related to program making. It needs to be recognized.

A Utopian Ideal

Both Gardner's paper and this one are intended to ventilate ideas and options and not advocate. But there may be license for one more idea or option that represents one person's ideal. It is that farmers be offered contracts that combine production control, any income supplement, soil conservation, and crop insurance. It would be a package offered on a take-or-leave basis. Conceivably, and probably desirably, the farmer would be required to pay a premium covering some part of the total cost (but not a large fraction). It is also conceivable that degrees of protection, including level of price support, could be built into the choices.

The super-ideal version would base the acreage part of the package on good land use. This would replace history. Or, provisionally, historical and land-use criteria could be combined. Farmers with good land that is not subject to erosion would come off well. Those farming erodable hillsides would not. But if viewed against the long-run public interest, would the outcome be bad?

The last comment about this Utopian ideal is that it may constitute the epitome of the social contract between the individual farmer and all society, not only of our time but of generations to come.

But that is not the last word for this paper. The last word in policy-making for agriculture or any sector has to do with the political process. Gardner puts the topic as the last of his options, though it is not truly an option. Questions could be raised about the validity of some of his comments, but not about their relevance. However, the final thought here is a restatement about the place of staging levels between the farmer and society. At times commodity organizations seem almost to be contemptuous of welfare considerations for agriculture as a whole. Insofar as this impression is accurate, the behavioral pattern is an obstacle to making wise policy for agriculture. The social contract is hierarchical; and therein lie many problems in the political process.

NOTES

1. Karl Brandt, "Discussion: Farm Fundamentalism—Past and Future," *Journal of Farm Economics,* December 1962, p. 1232.
2. Harold F. Breimyer, "U.S. Farm Policy in a World Dimension: The Setting in 1983," talk given at seminar, University of Missouri (Columbia), November 10, 1983.
3. V. James Rhodes, "Significance of Trade Policy to U.S. Farm Policy," and Harold F. Breimyer, "U.S. Farm Policy in a World Dimension: The Setting in 1983," *United States Farm Policy in a World Dimension,* University of Missouri (Columbia), Agricultural Experiment Station, Special Report 305, 1983.

REVIEW OF
"Domestic Policy Options for the Future of U.S. Agriculture"
Luther Tweeten

Gardner stresses efficiency objectives, emphasizing "use of our agricultural resources as effectively as possible in producing food and fiber products." The preamble in farm legislation usually states additional objectives not mentioned by Gardner, such as preserving the family farm and providing parity of income to farmers. Although the legislation neither preserved the family farm nor always transferred income from higher income-wealth taxpayers to lower income-wealth crop producers, it is my impression that preserving the family farm and promotion of equity are objectives still desired by many. Other objectives are administrative simplicity and continuity in program framework over time, the latter to provide a more stable planning environment for producers. Combining these additions to Gardner's list, the policy objectives are summarized as follows:

1. Efficient allocation of resources and products
2. Competitive pricing in elastic world markets
3. Reduced U.S. Treasury costs
4. Stability in food and fiber prices, but not to such a degree that price signals fail to induce needed resource and output allocations
5. Legislation simplicity and continuity to provide a predictable planning framework for producers and consumers, but flexibility to respond to system shocks from year to year
6. Preservation of a competitive economic environment in agriculture by maintaining enough family farms to avoid undue concentration of economic power in a few large farms
7. Equitable distribution of program benefits so that transfers do not go from lower income-wealth taxpayers to higher income-wealth producers
8. Conservation (socially optimal) of natural resources so that agriculture is not only efficient but sustainable in the long run

Projections for U.S. agriculture indicate that future demand and supply for farm output are likely (because of productivity gains) to shift forward at somewhat comparable rates, suggesting no strong upward or downward trend in real farm prices or rates of return on farming resources for the next decade or two (Tweeten, March 1983). Much short-term variation is expected around the long-term trend, however. In addition, farmers seem destined to experience cash-flow problems even if long-term prices and rates of return are favorable. Commodity programs can directly address the instability problem but are not effective tools to address the cash-flow problem. The latter requires a sound monetary-fiscal policy to avoid high nominal and real interest rates.

Given this background, the challenge is to devise an agricultural policy that is economically efficient, socially desirable, and politically acceptable. Gardner properly is an agnostic on meeting this challenge in any one program framework; rather, he presents a menu for choice along with a guide to the advantages and disadvantages of each.

ADDITIONAL POLICY ALTERNATIVES

Gardner presents a bland program menu of standard fare. Innovative approaches to food and agricultural policy are rare and often unworkable. But some new recipes are worth identifying and examining in light of policy objectives and farm problems listed above. As a review and not a paper, this discussion cannot list all the advantages and disadvantages of the following innovative approaches in light of the foregoing background, but some of the obvious ramifications are mentioned.

1. End direct price supports and supply control but improve forward contracting opportunities (hedging and put options) by (a) extending the futures contracts for up to three years, (b) making government a speculator of last resorts to deepen the future market, and (c) providing direct technical assistance by government to forward contracting farmers until they become familiar with procedures.

2. Gardner did not list mandatory acreage or supply control as an option. The internationalization of agriculture virtually precludes high rigid price supports achieved through acreage or marketing quotas; supports at 75 percent of 1910-14 parity or higher might lose half our grain markets and seem out of the question politically. But an innovative related alternative proposed by Greig (1983) is worthy of attention. His "oligopolistic self-determination" approach, designed to reduce variability and promote efficient resource use in farming, is as follows:

a. Farmers as individuals would gather in local ASCS offices or other facilities with modern telecommunication equipment. Each producer would state his acreage (or production) plan for next year.

b. The results would be tabulated at some central location such as the Washington ASCS office. Using computer models and professional judgments, the central location would estimate the market price associated with production plans, taking into account carryin stocks and expected utilization.

c. The estimated price would be relayed to producers, who would then be allowed to revise their acreage (or production) plans.

d. This process of submitting production plans followed by price feedback would continue through a fixed number of iterations, until a stable plan evolved, or until the secretary of agriculture ruled that sufficient iterations had occurred. At that point bidding farmers would be locked into their last bid, with acreage or production bids of each producer to be enforced by acreage market quota limitations administered by ASCS for next year's crop.

There would be no price supports, deficiency payments, or acreage diversion payments. As many commodities as desired could be included in the system, perhaps with production decisions made simultaneously. Any farmer desiring to produce any crop would do so, even with no crop history; in fact, any producer of a crop included in the system of allocation would be required to participate.

This approach would entail the onerous administrative problems of mandatory controls. It also would not assure acceptable prices and would probably bring political pressure on the government to maintain at least the final estimated price.

3. Some contend that the U.S. is being exploited in international trade by countries which import our products at low world price levels and sell them at high domestic price levels to their consumers. One alternative would be to differentiate markets, charging the domestic price to consumers in countries supporting prices and charging a lower price in elastic markets of countries not supporting prices. In theory, this could be done by requiring export firms to practice price discrimination, with proceeds above world prices to be paid to our farmers. Countries purchasing our exports at lower prices and selling the commodity to countries with higher prices would be penalized by removing them from the preferred price category. In practice, it would be very difficult to separate markets by avoiding transshipments.

The alternative above, in theory, could be administered through existing export firms without establishing a farm export marketing board similar to that used in other countries. Other options would be possible if we established a monopoly export marketing board. Acting either alone or in a cartel with other major farm commodity exporters, we could charge a high price in all export markets to reap monopoly benefits which would be passed on to our farmers to stabilize prices and raise farm income. Shortcomings of uniform monopoly pricing are numerous, including the possibility that exports would be sufficiently price-elastic to reduce export earnings below free market levels after a few years. Production controls would be necessary to restrain supply in the face of higher prices. Competing exporters included in a cartel have never shown much inclination to control production; member discipline might break down as in OPEC.

4. Another approach to provide some farm income security without supply control or Treasury cost while remaining competitive in world markets would be a two-price plan. The mechanics might be to issue certificates to farmers equal to the domestic portion of their past production. Any commodities sold in the domestic market would have to be attended by certificates requiring purchasers to pay, say, 75 percent of 1910-14 parity. Additional output would be sold for export at the world price. Farmers wishing to compete in export markets could do so. Farmers would not receive a blend price; the lower export price received for marginal output would restrain production both at home and abroad.

Problems with this approach include (a) high outlays for administering and policing a program which would invite abuse by buyers and sellers, (b) high domestic consumer food costs ands inflationary pressures, and (c) charges (and perhaps countervailing action) by foreign countries that we are "dumping" excess supplies on international markets.

None of the proposals above fosters structural objectives such as preserving family farms and targeting benefits to those who need help most. The following two proposals would attempt to do so.

5. One alternative is to terminate supply controls and price supports, replacing the current system with direct payments featuring tight limitations. Limitations would be held to, say, $20,000 per recipient to restrain Treasury cost, reduce incentives for overproduction, reduce chances of transferring funds from lower-income taxpayers to higher-income farmers, and focus payments on small and medium sized family farms most in need of assistance. A major pitfall of the proposal, a tendency for large landowners to break up units "on paper" into sufficient sub-units to gain full payment benefits, could be partly circumvented by making payments only to day-to-day farm operators who share significantly in the returns to

labor, management, and equity of the operating unit. Thus, attempts to divide units would create more family farms—presumably one objective of farm policy.

6. Another alternative which more fully recognizes that small farmers are not necessarily low-income farmers and more fully focuses benefits according to need would be an income maintenance program patterned after the negative income tax. The government would pay farm families some proportion of the difference between a target net income from all sources and actual income. The payment form might also make provision for net worth to avoid transfers to wealthy large farmers who have temporarily low income.

Problems with this proposal include (a) failure to deal with instability of farm prices and food supplies, (b) political reluctance to provide such a program only for farm families, and (c) disincentives to efficient use of labor and other resources. Many town and city residents might move to small acreages to be eligible for benefits.

Proposals 5 and 6 might be accompanied by a reserve stocks policy.

COMMENTS ON SPECIFIC POINTS

Now I turn to a few of the rather specific instances where I take issue with Gardner. He states that "only output per unit of total input, or total factor productivity, is an appropriate indicator of the overall efficiency gains in U.S. agriculture." He is referring to the ERS series on output per unit of production inputs, which omits public research, extension, education, and other non-conventional inputs. Because agriculture in broad terms includes the non-conventional input suppliers, the ERS measure is not "an appropriate indicator of the overall efficiency gains in agriculture"; rather, it is only a partial productivity index, though admittedly the best one currently available.

Gardner asserts that "these [export demand] shocks occur not only because of weather abroad but also because of agricultural and trade policies of other countries." Export shocks frequently arise from our own monetary-fiscal and trade policies, including export embargoes. Seemingly uncontrollable federal deficits drive up real interest rates, creating a demand for dollars abroad to invest in our financial markets and raising the value of the dollar in international exchange. Since January 1981 the wheat trade-weighted dollar has appreciated about 500 percent. This is a major reason why our export share of wheat fell from 48 percent of world wheat exports in 1981 to 40 percent in 1983. Our monetary-fiscal policy played a major role in the current worldwide recession, which accounts for some of the 3 percent falloff in total world wheat imports since 1981.

Gardner asks, "What should be done about the well-being of persons on small farms, and how can best use be made of the substantial human resources they represent?" He does not answer the question, but leaves the impression that small farms are characterized by low income and underemployed human resources. The emergence of part-time farming as a dominant small-farm pattern no longer enables us to characterize small farmers as either low-income or underemployed. Part-time small farmers often earn incomes higher than those of middle sized commercial farmers, and are fully employed as measured by effective use of their considerable human resources.

According to Gardner, "An approximation to this objective [of holding producers' return above a minimum cost level] is accomplished by deficiency payments." To reduce costs of farm programs, the deficiency payment has been made an acreage diversion payment rather than a compensatory payment under the 1981 act. For 1984, for example, Oklahoma enterprise budgets indicate that the 30 percent acreage diversion required to receive program benefits makes participation only marginally attractive. As a result, participation will be low. And if the direct payment feature is not focused on farms most needing assistance, perhaps its demise should not be mourned.

Gardner states that "for consumers these [commercial credit or other export subsidy] policies combine the worst features of direct payment and production controls." Consumers as taxpayers also need to be concerned about cost-effective ways to achieve mandated price objectives for farmers. Export subsidies can be a highly cost-effective means to raise earnings in elastic export markets, provided they are not so large or obvious that they invite retaliation by competing exporters.

He also states that export "embargoes may be a relatively cheap weapon [of foreign policy]. In any case, we should not preclude our government from choosing this weapon." Export embargoes are neither cheap nor effective weapons of foreign policy. They frequently backfire, doing more harm to us than to the intended victim. Perhaps their use cannot be precluded, but a case can be made for adequate compensation to farmers when they are used—in part to discourage use by State Department officials who do not understand the burdens they impose on producers.

Gardner indicates, "There is no free market internationally" and "There is no competitive market domestically because of middlemen's market power, and therefore government should intervene [to support farm markets]." The issue of whether there is workable competition in domestic and foreign markets needs more critical examination. even if his assertions are true, does that cause low returns on farm resources and justify government intervention? Economic theory indicates that imperfect competition in the marketing sector causes resource misallocation but not low relative rates of return on farming resources in the long run (Tweeten, 1979, chapter 5).

He states that "if farmers wanted income insurance (enough to pay for it), the market would already be providing it." One reason farmers forgo forward contracting and crop and income insurance is that the government now provides these services free or concessionally through credit and commodity programs.

Gardner sees merit in the option "to focus aid upon farmers in trouble . . . advanced in the Emergency Agricultural Act of 1978 with its category of 'Economic Emergency' loans through the Farmers' Home Administration." Data (available only for 1979) reveal that 32 to 48 percent of Economic Emergency loan volume went to farmers with farm income in excess of $22,000 and 50 percent went to farmers with net worth in excess of $120,000 (Hughes, et al., 1982). Twenty-one percent went to farmers with net worth in excess of $300,000. These figures provide little optimism that loans can be focused on the truly needy.

Odds favor continuation of current legislation, with modifications in 1985. It would have been helpful if Gardner had appraised opportunities for improvements in current legislation (for such discussion see Tweeten et al., 1983). What are the advantages and disadvantages of modifications to set target prices proportional to a moving average of past market prices, nonland cost of production, or other indicator? of relying on acreage diversion programs without target prices and deficiency payments? or of measures to make voluntary supply control more cost-effective through less slippage?

REFERENCES

Greig, W. Smith. *Oligopolistic Self-Determination as a Solution to the Farm Problem.* Mimeo (Pullman: Department of Agricultural Economics, Washington State University, August 1983).

Hughes, Dean W., Stephen Gabriel, Ronald Meekhof, Michael Boehlje, and George Amols. "Financing the Farm Sector in the 1980s: Aggregate Needs and the Roles of Public and Private Institutions." ERS Staff report no. AGES 820128 (Washington, D.C.: National Economics Division, ERS, U.S. Department of Agriculture, February 1982).

Tweeten, Luther. "Excess Farm Supply: Permanent or Transitory?" Pp. 35-49 in *Proceedings for the National Agricultural Policy Symposium* held

March 27-29, 1983, in Kansas City, Missouri (Columbia: Department of Agricultural Economics, University of Missouri, 1983).

Tweeten, Luther. *Foundations of Farm Policy* (Lincoln: University of Nebraska Press, 1979).

Tweeten, Luther, et al. "The Emerging Economics of Agriculture: Review and Policy Options." Report no. 98 (Ames, Iowa: Council for Agricultural Science and Technology, September 1983).

Chapter 4

U.S. Agriculture and Third World Development: Harmonies or Disharmonies of Interest?

Robert L. Paarlberg

Is Third World agricultural development good or bad for U.S. agriculture? For that matter, is U.S. agricultural abundance good or bad for Third World agricultural development? For agriculturalists in the U.S., these are divisive questions, but questions of considerable significance, since more than two-fifths of U.S. farm exports already go to Third World customers. Development planners in Third World countries are equally concerned and equally divided on the matter. Some have seen U.S. farm production as compatible with their own food needs and development objectives, while others have expressed anxiety about the burdens which U.S. food abundance might place upon Third World agricultural development prospects.

Here we examine these uncertain harmonies and disharmonies of interest between U.S. agriculture and Third World agricultural development. One purpose will be to show that such interests are seldom what they first appear. In some agricultural product markets, where U.S. and Third World interests seem at first glance to be in conflict, the depth of that conflict has too often been exaggerated. In other product markets, despite a superficial appearance of harmony, fundamental conflicts are too often ignored. The greatest potential harmony of interests may in fact lie in farm product markets that are just now beginning to gain significance in U.S.-Third World agricultural trade. Interests and objectives at both ends of the relationship are calling out to be clarified.

Here we undertake a brief review of three quite different agricultural product markets, as one shorthand means to explore these uncertain relationships. We first examine international sugar markets, where U.S. agriculture and Third World agriculture are in an apparent conflict. We then examine international wheat markets, where some have seen a contrasting first appearance of perfect harmony. In both instances, it will be seen, first appearances are deceptive. In a third product market—coarse grains and feedstuffs—an example will finally be offered of how U.S. agricultural prosperity and Third World development can forge a relationship mutually beneficial in substance as well as in appearance.

A CONFLICT OF INTEREST EXAGGERATED: INTERNATIONAL SUGAR MARKETS

Those who embrace the notion that U.S. agriculture is threatened by Third World farm development might well point to international sugar markets, where a long-standing competitive threat from Third World producers has apparently manifested itself recently in heavy losses suffered by U.S. sugar producers. U.S. producers, it might seem, have been driven out of their accustomed markets by Third World competitors enjoying much lower production costs. Third World cane sugar can be produced for as little as 12 to 15 cents a pound, while production costs in the United States remain above 18 cents a pound.[1] Without a tropical climate, and without an abundance of cheap labor, the U.S. sugar industry appears to be at a permanent disadvantage. In Latin America alone twenty different countries are now producing sugar for export, and neither the U.S. domestic sugar market nor the world sugar market has been growing fast enough, in recent years, to accommodate such competition.

Because of lower consumption trends and inroads by artificial sweeteners within the U.S. sugar market, domestic sales opportunities are stagnating. U.S. refined sugar consumption, which averaged more than 10 million short tons during the decade of the 1970s, had declined by 1982 to less than 9 million tons. U.S. consumption is expected to continue to fall in the years ahead, perhaps to less than 8 million tons by 1985.[2] The entry of cheap foreign sugar into this shrinking domestic market places U.S. producers at an obvious risk. Imports grew to supply 51 percent of U.S. consumption by 1981, and helped to drive U.S. prices well below average production costs, threatening some U.S. producers with major losses. In 1981 U.S. sugar producers in Hawaii alone suffered losses estimated at $83.5 million. For Hawaii's 40,000 sugar workers (10 percent of the state's total workforce), Third World competition seemed to pose a direct threat to income and employment security. Markets beyond the United States were offering little relief. The annual increase in gross world sugar imports, since 1973-74, had averaged only 1 percent, and half of this meager growth was being monopolized by sugar exporters from the European Community.[3]

Facing this bleak prospect, the U.S. Congress in December 1981 voted to reinstate a domestic sugar loan program, to provide firmer price supports at home for U.S. producers. Prior to the scheduled implementation of this program, however, U.S. sugar prices fell so low (30 percent below the December 1981 level) as to raise the projected budget cost of sugar support loans to an unacceptable level. In order to save U.S. taxpayers from an estimated $800 million increase in sugar price support payments, President Regan therefore announced in May 1982 that strict import quotas would once again be imposed on foreign sugar producers seeking access to the U.S. market.

It was known at the time that many Third World sugar producers could be hurt by this U.S. decision to reimpose sugar import quotas. The secretary general of the Organization of American States, Alejandro Orfila, calculated that Latin American sugar exporters alone stood to lose about $90 million in 1982 because of the quota decision. Panama would prove to be one case in point. The 73,650 ton quota imposed on Panamanian sugar imports for the 1982/83 season was well below Panama's 92,000 tons sold in the previous year. This tightened quota restriction, in combination with the still lower prices that now prevailed in unrestricted world markets, forced Panama's state sugar corporation in 1983 to halt the cane harvest and shut down its three mills several months earlier than usual. One of the three mills was not expected to reopen.

Do such events illustrate a direct conflict between U.S. agriculture and Third World agricultural development? Sugar is indeed one extreme case in which conflict has developed. But even in such a case, consider that some of the wounds recently suffered by U.S. agriculture have been entirely self-inflicted. And consider as well that an even more significant foreign threat to U.S. sugar producers is traceable not to the developing countries but to expanding sugar production within industrial Europe.

To keep matters in perspective, we should begin by noting that sugar markets are scarcely vital to the larger prosperity of U.S. agriculture. Sugar crops are produced on less than 1 percent of U.S. farmland, and they contribute less than 1 percent to total U.S. farm cash receipts. U.S. sugar producers (farmers and corporations) number fewer than 14,000, and much of the labor force employed by the U.S. sugar industry is only seasonal in nature. Many who work in the U.S. sugar industry are "moonlighters" or migrants, and some are even brought in from abroad.

Beyond the size of the industry, or the character of its labor force, consider also that many who profit from the U.S. sugar industry are not primarily agriculturists. In Hawaii, for example, individual farmers produce only 4 percent of that state's sugar, the rest being produced by large diversified corporations. The biggest of these companies, Amfac, received 94 percent of its total corporate sales in 1981 from hotels and other non-sugar operations.[4] Gulf and Western (an owner of 25 percent of Amfac's stock) is diversified into movie making and zinc production. Not all who profit from the U.S. sugar industry are even Americans. One of the big Hawaiian companies, Theo. H. Davies and Co., Ltd. is a unit of Jardine Matheson and Co., a multinational conglomerate based (until recently) in Hong Kong. Even the U.S. sugar beet industry exhibits some of these same offshore tendencies. One Michigan beet processor was recently taken over by Barlow Rand, Ltd., a large South African industrial concern. In part because of the corporate diversification that already exists in the U.S. sugar industry, plus its small relative size, some further gradual decline within the less productive segments of that industry might well be absorbed at an acceptable cost to U.S. agriculture. Even in Hawaii, where phasing out sugar production would be most difficult because of the size and the restricted mobility of the workforce in that state, replacement crops for sugar (such as macadamia nuts) might eventually become attractive.

Leaving such arguments aside, any further decline that does occur in the U.S. sugar industry must still be understood as much more than an outgrowth of Third World competition. The high domestic sugar prices guaranteed to U.S. producers have now stimulated production of cheaper non-sugar sweeteners at home, such as high fructose corn syrup (HFCS). As late as 1975 HFCS accounted for only 4.2 percent of per capita caloric sweetener consumption in the U.S., but by 1982 (thanks in part to price discounts to sugar as high as 48 percent) HFCS had gained a 21.4 percent U.S. consumption share. Further inroads by corn-based sweeteners are now certain, following the decisions taken in 1983 by both Coca-Cola Company and PepsiCo, Inc., to permit the use of HFCS in their major cola products.[5] U.S. sugar producers have only accelerated this adverse trend by now locking in their high domestic price guarantees with loan rates and import quotas. Following the import quota decision in 1982, U.S. corn sweetener makers were described as "rubbing their hands with glee."[6]

These recent developments should not have been a great surprise. At the time the U.S. sugar lobby secured congressional and White House approval for a renewed sugar loan program, late in 1981, the rapidly falling world price of sugar was already 25 percent below the price support level being written into the U.S. law. It has been the preference of the U.S. sugar industry for these non-competitive domestic prices that has left the industry so "vulnerable" today to so many different competitors, at home and abroad. By using their considerable political influence in such a short-sighted manner—even pricing themselves out of their own protected sweetener market at home—U.S. sugar producers have brought on much of their own distress. The Reagan administration might have fought to resist this self-defeating denial of market forces, but it was too busy, in 1981, courting sugar lobby support in the Congress for its own controversial tax cut initiatives.

Even so, it has not been the availability of cheap Third World cane sugar that has most threatened U.S. producers in world markets lately. Far more serious has been the dramatic increase in beet sugar production, and beet sugar exports, from the European Community (EEC). The EEC, a net importer of sugar as late as 1975, is today the world's second largest exporter. Under the stimulus of high price guarantees (price guarantees that not even the U.S. Congress is willing to match), EEC sugar production increased by 3.3 million tons between 1979 and 1982, accounting for roughly one-third the total increase in world production. Since this EEC beet sugar cannot all be consumed at home, it must be sold abroad under subsidy, flooding markets that Third World producers could otherwise supply. To the degree that U.S. sugar producers do face a major foreign threat, these days, it comes not so much from their equally hard-pressed competitors in the non-industrialized world but from their far more heavily subsidized competitors in Western Europe.

To summarize, even in an unusual and an extreme case such as sugar, the apparent conflict between U.S. agricultural prosperity and Third World agricultural development is less than meets the eye. That apparent conflict is small in relation to larger U.S. agricultural interests, it has been aggravated by unrealistic U.S. domestic agricultural policies, and it has been overtaken in any case by a larger conflict with EEC producers.

A HARMONY OF INTERESTS EXAGGERATED: INTERNATIONAL WHEAT MARKETS

Just as some might point to sugar, in hopes of demonstrating a direct conflict between U.S. agriculture and Third World agricultural development, others might point to wheat to try to prove just the opposite. Here, at first glance, U.S. wheat export potential and Third World food import needs might seem to be in perfect harmony. In world foodgrain markets, however, a more complex relationship between U.S. agriculture and Third

World development deserves to be recognized.

At first appearance, foodgrain markets are bringing U.S. agriculture and Third World development into perfect harmony. Per capita wheat consumption within the Third World has been increasing steadily at a 2 to 3 percent yearly rate, while outside the Third World it has either been steady or falling in recent years. These higher Third World per capita wheat consumption trends, in part a result of income growth and rapid urbanization, then combine with high Third World population growth rates to mark the non-industrial countries as a potentially lucrative wheat export market. The developing countries, including China, now take more than 60 percent of the world's total wheat and wheat flour exports, compared to less than 50 percent of a much smaller export total only two decades ago.[7] U.S. wheat producers, who supply roughly 40 percent of all wheat and wheat flour entering the international market, and who must export more than half of what they grow, have been among those to profit from this developing-country wheat trade expansion.

Most growth in Third World wheat consumption takes place among rapidly growing urban populations, where incomes tend to be rising, and where income elasticities of demand for wheat are especially high. Africa's urban population is now growing at an explosive annual rate of roughly 6 percent, incomes are rising, and among these African urban dwellers the income elasticity of demand for wheat approaches unity. Wheat consumption in Nigeria, responding to rapid urban income growth in part derived from oil, grew over the past 20 years at annual rates well above 10 percent. As one consequence, Nigeria is now importing roughly 1.4 million tons of U.S. wheat (up 30 percent from five years ago). Sub-Saharan Africa, which has no tradition as a wheat-producing region, must satisfy almost all of its demand through imports.

Not all Third World regions are simultaneously experiencing such a rapid increase in wheat import needs. South Asia, for example, which took 26 percent of total Third World wheat imports two decades ago, has more recently fallen to only a 10 percent share, in part because its income growth has been so modest, and in part because of significant wheat production gains of its own at home. In Latin America, meanwhile, maize still ranks ahead of wheat in total cereal production and consumption. Urban wheat consumption is on the rise, however, and more than half of all wheat consumed in Latin America (excluding Argentina) has been imported from abroad. Southeast Asia has also been taking larger imports of wheat in recent years, as urban foodgrain consumers have begun to diversify their diets away from rice.

Of still greater interest to U.S. wheat exporters, in recent years, have been the foodgrain purchases registered by Third World nations in North Africa and the Middle East. These nations, long-standing producers and consumers of wheat, have over the past two decades allowed their total imports to grow at an astonishing annual rate of 7 percent, so that they now account for roughly one-third of total Third World wheat imports. Wheat imports in North Africa and the Middle East now supply roughly 60 percent of all internal wheat consumption—with calories from wheat providing, in turn, about half of total calorie consumption.[8]

It might appear, upon noting such trends, that Third World wheat customers have interests which are perfectly compatible with those of U.S. wheat producers and exporters. But once again the underlying structure of interests, at both ends of the relationship, is somewhat more complex. Larger commercial wheat exports to developing countries are no doubt beneficial to U.S. agriculture. But prospects for continued U.S. domination in world wheat markets in the years ahead are not so strong, considering the more aggressive posture being taken by a number of U.S. export competitors. And from the other end of the relationship, from the vantage point of Third World agricultural development, an ever larger dependence upon commercial wheat imports from the industrial world may not be compatible with a balanced pattern of economic growth.

Consider first the doubtful ability of U.S. wheat producers to hold on to their accustomed share of Third World markets in the years ahead. The U.S. share of those markets became quite large during the decade of the 1970s, as a function of competitive U.S. export pricing. U.S. domestic wheat loan rates were less obtrusive in relation to foreign commercial demand during the 1970s, and U.S. currency exchange rates were attractive to foreign customers, following significant dollar devaluations in both 1971 and 1973. At present neither of these advantageous conditions is available to U.S. wheat exporters. One result has been a 22 percent drop in U.S. wheat exports since 1981.

U.S. commodity loan rates and target prices for wheat, particularly since 1981, were set so far above the level justified by sagging external commercial demand as to make U.S. wheat export prices fundamentally less competitive in the eyes of customers abroad, and especially Third World customers. Not until early 1984, when U.S. wheat target prices were finally reduced by a small margin, did it appear that competitive export pricing would return as an element of U.S. farm policy. Until that time, by choosing to combine high domestic loan rates and target prices with cutbacks in U.S. wheat production (a 14 percent cutback in 1983), in pursuit of purely inward-looking farm policy and budgetary objectives, the U.S. had unwittingly made its wheat exports less competitive in the world market place. Currency exchange rates further aggravated the problem. The sharp appreciation of the dollar, combined with higher U.S. domestic price supports, gave U.S. export competitors an easier price target to shoot at. Australian and Canadian exporters, in 1982/83 alone, enjoyed an effective 15 to 20 percent increase in their own wheat export prices and went forward with plans to expand their own wheat exports.

Foreign competitors do not intend to miss their chance to take advantage of this less competitive U.S. posture in wheat export markets. They responded slowly when wheat prices surged in the early 1970s, but by now they have made the significant institutional reforms and the long overdue investments in port and transport facilities that will enable them to recapture wheat market shares earlier lost to the United States. Canadian railway improvements and freight rate adjustments could double the capacity of that nation's western grain transport system over the next decade. In 1983/84 alone Canadian, Australian, and Argentinian wheat exports were expected to increase to 41 million tons, 11 percent above the record volume of 1982/83. While U.S. wheat acreage has been cut back to support unrealistic domestic price guarantees, wheat planting elsewhere has expanded. Direct export competitors account for roughly 70 percent of all wheat acreage expansion over the past six years. All these factors together have produced a significant fall in U.S. wheat and flour export shares throughout the world, down from 48 percent in 1981/82, to only 41 percent in 1982/83. It is anticipated that U.S. wheat and wheat flour export shares will continue to decline, to as little as 38 percent in 1983/84.

The anticipated growth in Third World wheat imports therefore may not provide the same sized gains for U.S. producers in the future as in the recent past. But this is only half the problem. Apart from the gains that might be available to U.S. agriculture, what are the supposed gains made by Third World countries from the purchase of so much wheat from abroad? Wheat imports may serve the short-run interests of politically powerful urban-dwelling Third World food consumers. But they may at the same time threaten the interests of rural-dwelling Third World food producers. In the developing world today, where low-income farmers so often make up a majority of the needy population, and where low-cost opportunities to increase foodgrain production are so often abundant, the practice of importing wheat from abroad can be wasteful and shortsighted. Many Third World nations pursuing "urban biased" development plans have made themselves more dependent than they ought to be on wheat imports from abroad.[9] Consider, for example, the case of Egypt.

For centuries an exporter of wheat, Egypt has in recent decades become a major wheat importer. Egypt's limited expanse of arable land, alongside its rapid rate of population growth, could indeed justify a modest volume of wheat imports. Egyptian wheat production since 1956 has increased by only about 30 percent, in part because of a shortage of arable land. While Egypt's population has increased roughly two and a half times since the second World War, its land area under cultivation has increased only 13 percent.[10] To satisfy the rapidly growing demand of its urban consumers for cheap bread, Egypt has resorted to importing an ever larger volume of wheat. Wheat imports grew from an average yearly level of 2 million tons during the 1960s, to 4 million tons by 1977, and now to an estimated 5.6 million tons in 1983. Imports are now equal to roughly three times the level of total domestic wheat production.

Importing so much wheat from abroad is costly to Egypt in several ways. It first places a heavy strain on Egypt's limited supply of foreign exchange. Although Egypt gets as much as 40 percent of its imported wheat in the form of PL 480 "food aid" shipments from the United States, its yearly expenditures for imports of both wheat and maize have nonetheless grown, to reach roughly $1.2 billion. With its oil export revenues and its remittances from abroad recently in decline, and with foreign exchange reserves to cover only about one month's worth of total imports, Egypt by 1983 was facing serious balance-of-payment constraints. The Bank of Egypt in 1983 had to borrow $150 million from the Arab International Bank to finance a portion of its 1982/83 wheat import bill.[11]

But Egypt's oversized wheat imports have also been damaging that nation's own prospects for balanced economic and agricultural development. These large wheat imports are symptomatic of economic development policies that pay too much attention to short-run urban consumer demands, and far too little attention to long-run growth opportunities in the countryside, where the less advantaged half of the nation's population continues to reside. In order to cheapen retail food prices for its politically vocal urban consumers, the Egyptian government has for years adopted the expedient of holding down producer prices in the countryside. By one estimate, such low farm-procurement prices represent as much as a 40 to 50 percent tax equivalent on Egyptian agriculture.[12] Egypt's wheat producers have been hit especially hard by these "cheap food" policies, receiving at times a lower price per ton for wheat than for maize, when normally the opposite price relationship should apply. Given such adverse terms of trade allowed to wheat farmers, it is no wonder that Egypt's acreage under wheat, its use of high yielding varieties, its wheat yields, and hence its total domestic wheat production, have all lagged so far behind potential. Given such generous retail price subsidies offered to consumers, it is likewise no wonder that Egypt's total wheat consumption has continued to grow out of control.

Egypt could better afford its expanded volume of costly wheat imports if its larger agricultural production and trade policies were yielding higher returns. It makes commercial sense for Egypt to use its best irrigated lands to produce high-value foreign-exchange-earning export crops. Unfortunately, the growth rate of the Egyptian farm sector overall averaged only 2.7 percent during the decade of the 1970s. Export markets for Egypt's long staple cotton have also contracted of late, what with the growth of synthetic fibers (which blend just as well with less expensive shorter staple cotton). Cotton production has also lagged. Even though procurement prices for cotton have been raised, many Egyptian farmers still find it more profitable to use their best irrigated land to grow fruits and vegetables, not just for export but also for sale (in a relatively free domestic market) to Egypt's minority of more well-to-do urban consumers.

U.S. wheat sales to Egypt are not the cause of this unbalanced pattern of Egyptian agricultural development. Those sales are less a cause than a consequence of Egypt's own "urban biased" development strategy. But there is nonetheless an unfortunate link between the short run availability to Egypt of so much cheap wheat from abroad and the reluctance of that nation's development planners to take better care of and to make better use of thier own rural sector. Retail subsidy costs to the Egyptian government are now so large that the availability of cheap wheat from abroad might conceivably make it easier for that government to *raise* its procurement prices to farmers, while holding its retail prices steady, so a "downward pressure" on prices in Egypt is not the heart of the problem. A larger measure of damage is being done by Egypt's own reduced public investment in agriculture, resulting from the diminished sense of urgency which comes to attend Egyptian agricultural policy so long as cheap wheat imports remain so readily available. Throughout the decade of the 1970s, while wheat imports were dramatically on the rise, Egyptian agriculture actually was given a *lower* share of total public investment than it had enjoyed in the previous decade.[13]

Efforts which have been made by the United States to link its PL 480 wheat deliveries to the funding of various Egyptian rural development projects have met with little success, given the prevailing attitude within Egypt of indifference toward rural development. The rural development projects funded in this fashion have tended to be of the "follow-on" variety, and were adopted with little careful planning, or primarily in response to short-run bureaucratic convenience. Food aid funding for rural projects can even provide the Egyptian government with a new opportunity to divert more of its own budgetary assets *away from* the farm sector. U.S. food aid to Egypt (which was expanded largely for diplomatic reasons in any case, following the 1975 Sinai disengagement and the 1978 Camp David Agreements), has thus reinforced that nation's "worry later" attitude toward its own rural sector requirements.

The most recent drift in U.S. farm trade policy toward Egypt suggests no quick remedy to this problem. Early in 1983, as one part of its escalating farm trade competition with the EEC, the United States negotiated a sale to Egypt of 1 million tons of wheat flour at a heavily subsidized price ($155 a ton, compared to the prevailing world price of $175 a ton). Egypt, already the world's largest wheat flour importer (with total imports running around 1.6 million tons per year), did gain a short-run advantage from such a generous sale. Some Egyptian officials were no doubt hoping that the United States-EEC wheat trade competition would continue to escalate, thus further reducing their import costs. These hopes were then fulfilled in October 1983, when the European Commission announced a 10 percent increase in its own wheat flour export subsidy, and proceeded to grab a portion of the Egyptian market back from the United States.

But the long-run advantage to Egypt is far more dubious. If wheat markets should for any reason suddenly tighten, or if Egypt's access to concessional U.S. wheat exports should suddenly disappear (perhaps following another change in the diplomatic climate), the ability of Egypt's economic and political system to make such a sudden adjustment would be at best uncertain. In January 1977, when the Egyptian government (under pressure from aid donors and the IMF) announced plans to reduce food subsidies, riots broke out in Cairo and Alexandria. More than a hundred people were killed—and Sadat's party headquarters in Alexandria was destroyed—before the government decided to reverse course. Egypt's escalating dependence on inexpensive imported wheat may be in the end as much of a risk for the Egyptian political leadership as it is a burden on Egyptian agricultural development.

U.S. wheat producers do not gain as much as they might imagine from the sort of business they are now doing with customers such as Egypt. PL 480 wheat sales to Egypt, and heavily subsidized sales of U.S. wheat flour, are clearly an imperfect solution to the commercial export needs of U.S. agriculture. This export strategy is sustainable only with the uncertain aquiescence of hard-pressed U.S. taxpayers, who must ultimately pay for the large concessional element contained in such sales. Taxpayers have already begun to show their limited patience with the growing cost of subsidizing U.S. wheat producers at home.

In this regard, the more favored domestic political position of wheat producers within the European Community represents one more reason to question the competitive room that will be available to U.S. producers in world wheat markets. So favored are the interests of wheat producers within the EEC, that there may be no practical limit to the willingness of the community to match the United States, subsidy for subsidy, in Third World wheat and wheat flour markets. Some downward adjustment in U.S. target prices and loan rates for wheat, and in dollar exchange rates, would make wheat export subsidies far more costly for the European Community. But European consumers and taxpayers remain remarkably willing to bear such costs, and without a radical reform of the Common Agricultural Policy U.S. producers may never regain their recently sacrificed export market shares.

A more promising basis for mutually beneficial relations between U.S. agriculture and Third World agricultural development is to be found not in foodgrain markets, where export competition is so keen, and where the interests of Third World importers are sometimes at risk. Markets which supply feed for livestock are a more promising venue for harmonious relations. Such markets tend to grow more often in response to the most desirable kind of balanced Third World development. It is also in such markets, where U.S. producers are uniquely efficient, that export competitors such as the European Community are least likely to intrude.

THIRD WORLD AGRICULTURAL DEVELOPMENT AND FEED IMPORT DEMAND

Most U.S. coarse grain and feedstuff exports still go to markets in West Europe, Japan, the Soviet Union, and East Europe, rather than to the developing nations of the Third World. But it is among the developing nations—especially those that have embarked upon a successful pattern of broad-based economic development—that coarse grain and feedstuff trade has been growing most rapidly of late. It is likewise among these rapidly developing Third World nations that the potential for further growth in feedstuff imports will be largest in the years ahead. Considering trends in coarse grain imports over the past five years, the greatest growth activity is to be found not among those nations already industrialized but among some of the "others" just now beginning to achieve affluence, as shown in table 1.

U.S. wheat exports too often go to Third World countries suffering from sluggish economic growth, or to nations whose narrow-based industrial development plans have been held back by a lagging farm sector, or to nations suddenly awash with oil export revenues, or to nations plagued by

TABLE 1

Coarse Grain Imports (MMT)

	1977/78 (July/June)	1982/83 (October/September)	Net Change
West Europe	25.4	15.3	–10.1
USSR	11.7	11.6	– .1
Japan	17.0	18.0	+ 1.0
East Europe	8.7	3.9	– 4.8
China	.1	2.6	+ 2.5
Others	21.0	37.3	+16.3

Sources: USDA, FG-35-80, Dec. 12, 1980; USDA, FG-28-83, Sept. 15, 1983.

excessive rates of population growth and rural-to-urban migration. These coarse grain and feedstuff sales, by contrast, have been growing in response to a more desirable pattern of broad-based Third World development, usually built in the first instance upon rapid and broadly based development in the rural sector. It is precisely this sort of industrial development, built upon a sound base of agricultural development, that best mobilizes Third World resources, including human resources, which are still disproportionately located in the countryside. It is only from such a broad base of human resource mobilization and income growth that sustained industrial development becomes possible. And it is only with sustained industrial development that demands for dietary enrichment will begin to emerge. Such demands will usually include a desire for increased per capita consumption of meat and livestock products, which will in turn trigger a growing need for commercial coarse grain and other feedstuff imports.

It is important to note that the same broad base of rising affluence that triggers these coarse grain and feedstuff import demands will also make the purchase of such products entirely affordable. Nations becoming rich enough to embark upon a dietary transition are nations rich enough to enter world coarse grain and feedstuff markets as paying customers. Coarse grain and feedstuff imports tend to be arranged, unlike the foodgrain imports of so many poor countries, on a strictly commercial basis, thereby insuring more tangible rewards for the exporting country and thus completing the circle of mutual benefit.

To illustrate the way in which this sort of trade in coarse grains and feedstuffs can provide unambiguous mutual benefits to U.S. agriculture alongside Third World development, consider the evolving farm trade relationship between the United States and South Korea, a Third World nation well on its way to successful industrial development.

Korea enjoyed annual per capita real GNP growth rates averaging above 8 percent during the decade of the 1970s, a remarkable achievement made possible by the hard work of Korea's highly industrious and broadly capable workforce. Korea enjoys a 93 percent national literacy rate, well above the Third World average. South Korean income growth has also been more broadly based than in most other developing countries. The wealthiest 10 percent of all South Korean households have received only a 27.5 percent share of total household income. In nations pursuing less broadly based development strategies (for example, Peru, Kenya, or Brazil), the income share of this richest 10 percent can range from 40 to 50 percent of the total.

The broad base of South Korean economic growth has included, as one of its more significant components, rapid productivity gains from agriculture. In part because of generous U.S. economic assistance to the Korean farm sector, in part because of U.S. insistence upon sweeping land tenure reform, but also in part because of the importance to the Korean military of maintaining its political base in the countryside (from which a significant share of its officers have come), Korea's development planners have seen to it that the nation's significant rural land and labor resources not go to waste. Sufficient support was given to rural infrastructure, credit, and cooperatives during the decade of the 1960s to insure an average annual rate of growth in the farm sector of 4.4 percent. And then, when high yielding rice varieties became available, in the early 1970s, Korean farmers were given an additional incentive—a price incentive—to put those varieties to immediate use. In South Korea the important price ratio of rice to fertilizer was more than twice the average ratio available to farmers elsewhere in East and Southeast Asia. With the use of HYVs, rice yields in Korea nearly doubled, and between 1971 and 1980 Korean food production per capita increased overall by roughly 30 percent.[14] This increase in rural productivity and rural prosperity helped to broaden and to strengthen the base for Korea's even more impressive urban industrial growth.

The point to be made here is that South Korea's own successful agricultural and industrial development did not diminish export opportunities for U.S. agriculture. It brought, instead, a dramatic increase in South Korean agricultural imports, including specifically agricultural imports from the United States. Between 1974 and 1980 the value of U.S. agricultural exports to South Korea more than doubled, to reach $1.8 billion, as South Korea became the fifth largest U.S. farm market in the world. By way of contrast, the total value of U.S. farm exports to three large and underfed Asian nations that had not yet embarked upon a path of broad-based growth—India, Pakistan, and Bangladesh—actually declined.[15]

Not only did the total value of U.S. farm sales to Korea increase as that nation embarked upon rapid economic growth. The composition of those sales also changed, with exports of coarse grins and other feedstuffs emerging quite clearly as the leading edge of growth. While Korean imports of U.S. wheat have scarcely grown at all since the mid-1970s, note that imports of coarse grains for use as animal feed increased several times over, as shown in table 2.

There is every reason to believe that Korea will continue to increase its purchases of feedstuffs (including soybeans as well as sorghum and corn) in the years ahead, as that nation's rapid economic growth continues apace. Korea's 1982-86 five year plan calls for real economic growth to continue at 7.6 percent per year, and in 1983 a growth rate of nearly 9 percent has

TABLE 2

Republic of Korea Grain Imports (July/June, MMT)

	1975/76		1982/83	
	Total	(From U.S.)	Total	(From U.S.)
Wheat	1.4	(1.4)	1.8	(1.7)
Coarse Grains	.7	(.5)	4.4	(4.4)

Sources: USDA, FG-4-81, Jan. 28, 1981; FG-19-83, July 1983.

already been achieved. The resulting personal income growth will trigger additional demands to enlarge the meat component of the Korean diet. Per capita consumption of meat and livestock products tends to grow even faster than income in Korea, and could continue to expand at average annual rates of 8 to 9 percent in the years ahead.[16] Per capita foodgrain consumption, meanwhile, is likely to fall. Since the meat enrichment of the Korean diet is just beginning (Korean consumption of meat and livestock products is even low in relation to Korea's present level of development), Korea's potential as an importer of U.S. feedstuffs in the years ahead remains strong.

Nor is it just in coarse grains and feedstuffs that Korea's rapid and well-balanced economic development can produce direct benefits for U.S. agriculture. Korean industrial growth can also mean larger markets for farm-grown industrial raw materials, such as cotton, leather, and hides. In the aftermath of a U.S. decision in June 1981 to remove restrictions on Korean shoe imports, for example, Korea's purchases of U.S. cattle hides increased by 30 percent.[17] But here a note of caution is in order, given the more recent protectionist drift of U.S. trade policy in some international markets for manufactured products. U.S. agriculturalists should remember that their sales of farm-grown industrial raw materials to Korea will depend in part upon Korea's ability to sell its finished industrial products, free from protectionist trade barriers, to the United States.

The Republic of Korea is by no means the only example of a rapidly growing Third World country purchasing an ever larger volume of U.S. agricultural products. Several other East Asian Third World countries have been following a similar path. Taiwan and Thailand, for example, more than doubled their purchases of U.S. agricultural products between 1974 and 1980, and in Malaysia, where economic growth rates averaged 8 percent during the 1970s, purchases of U.S. foods increased from less than $30 million total in 1976 to nearly $140 million by 1982. These farm purchases have been increasing not because of lagging growth in the farm sector, but because of overall income growth made possible, in the first instance, by rapid agricultural development. Malaysian agriculture grew at annual rates averaging above 5 percent during the decade of the 1970s.

It is worth remembering that Malaysian agricultural development was at one time viewed as a threat to U.S. agriculture, owing to the rapid growth of that nation's palm oil industry, seemingly in competition with U.S. soybean producers. But now, as it turns out, Malaysia's growing need for feedstuffs has brought some offsetting advantages for U.S. soybean growers. Malaysia's infant soybean-crushing industry, begun in 1980, now buys roughly two-thirds of its beans from the U.S. Malaysia's own palm kernel meal, although in abundant supply, is too fibrous and lacks key amino acids to sustain the efficient growth of poultry and swine.[18] Soybeans are now the top U.S. farm export to Malaysia, valued at $36 million in fiscal 1982.

Several adverse developments might yet reduce these gains available to U.S. agriculture from sales of such feed products to rapidly growing Third World nations. First, the U.S. might unwittingly give away its strong competitive edge in feed markets by setting the export price of its own products too high. Some U.S. export pricing advantages could be lost through the adoption of high commodity loan rates at home, which would give less efficient export competitors an easier price target to shoot at. High U.S. currency exchange rates are an even larger problem, since they can nullify even the most competitive U.S. export pricing policies. U.S. soybean exports, for example, should have been highly competitive abroad in 1981/82, given the 30 percent decline then being registered in U.S. domestic soybean prices. Unfortunately, because of adverse trends in currency exchange rates, the cost to foreign customers of purchasing U.S. soybeans ws actually *on the rise* during this period. The trade-weighted measure of the cost of U.S. soybeans to foreign buyers, in terms of foreign currency, increased by 60 percent between 1980 and 1982.[19]

Second, U.S. farm sales to rapidly growing Third World customers might also be adversely affected if U.S. manufactured trade policies toward newly industrializing countries continues to move in a protectionist direction. The ability of newly industrializing countries to buy more farm products from the United States depends in large measure upon their ability to sell more manufactured products abroad, and especially to the United States. If their own exports fail to grow, the income growth that triggers their own consumer demand will stagnate, and the foreign exchange that they must have to purchase U.S. farm products will not be earned. Perhaps nowhere is the natural harmony of interests between U.S. agricultural prosperity and broad-based Third World development more visible—and more visibly threatened—than in the arena of U.S. trade policy in manufactured goods.

Third, the natural harmony of interests between U.S. agriculture and rapid Third World development might also be threatened if the United States were to withdraw its vital support from those multilateral lending and assistance institutions—such as the International Monetary Fund (IMF) and the International Development Association (IDA) of the World Bank—that are presently seeking ways to stimulate rapid growth and to reschedule the oversized foreign debts of some of the most important Third World customers for U.S. farm products. The recent world recession, in combination with higher interest rates and lower inflation rates, makes unserviceable the external debt of numerous Third World countries, including some who were on their way toward just the sort of rapid growth that made them good customers for U.S. farm products. Without access to economic aid and new lines of credit, these nations will have to cut back sharply on their imports of U.S. farm products. In 1981/82, among four of the largest Third World debtor nations (Brazil, Mexico, Argentina, and South Korea), purchases of U.S. agricultural products fell from $6 billion to $3.2 billion.

CONCLUSION

If we prefer to conclude on an optimistic note, we can argue that a natural harmony of interests does exist between U.S. agriclture and Third World agricultural development. Rapid and broad-based Third World development will trigger a dietary transition that will increase commercial demand for precisely those sorts of farm products—especially coarse grains and feedstuffs—which U.S. producers are best suited to provide.

But there is no guarantee that this sort of harmonious relationship will consistently emerge in United States-Third World economic relations. It may fail to emerge, first of all, if Third World policy elites should continue to pursue narrow-based, "urban biased" development plans. Such plans tend to produce Third World consumer demands for the wrong kinds of imported farm products, such as foodgrain products that can often be produced at lower cost domestically to the greater economic benefit of needy indigenous rural dwellers. Such plans will also result in sluggish rates of overall economic growth, which can make the import of farm products from abroad less affordable, except on concessional terms.

Second, we must note that potential harmonies of interest can also be lost at the other end of the relationship, owing to actions taken or not taken by policy elites in the United States. There is first a risk that U.S. farm policy makers will respond too quickly to domestic political pressures to "protect" some relatively less efficient U.S. farm producers—such as U.S. sugar producers—who feel themselves threatened by Third World farm competition. The domestic protection offered to such producers is not only costly to U.S. consumers and taxpayers, prejudicial to Third World development, and damanging to United States-Third World diplomatic relations; on its own terms, it can even fail to provide the promised measure of "protection" to U.S. producers. U.S. producers gaining such protection may only find themselves more threatened, as a consequence, by shrinking demand at home and by competitively priced domestic substitutes, not to mention continued competition from more heavily subsidized and protected non-Third World producers abroad.

Larger risks are also encountered within the U.S. policy arena. Well-constructed U.S. *agricultural* policies will not by themselves be a sufficient U.S. contribution to harmonious economic relations between U.S. agriculture and Third World development. Well-constructed U.S. policies beyond the arena of agriculture—to preserve an open system of United States-Third World trade in manufactured goods, to improve the management of United States-Third World currency exchange rates, and to repair tottering United States-Third World financial structures—are today no less vital to the task. So fundamental are the mutual benefits to be enjoyed by U.S. agriculture alongside rapid Third World development, that the pursuit of these benefits cannot any longer be confined to policy initiatives in just the agricultural policy arena. U.S. agriculturalists, whose interests will be among those most generously served by rapid and broad-based Third World development, should in their own interest become more vocal and more visible advocates, within the U.S. political system, of policy initiatives in manufactured trade, finance, and monetary exchange better designed to support and to sustain agricultural development in the Third World.

NOTES

1. Nicholas Kominus, "A Sweet Deal for America's Sugar Producers," *Business and Society Review* no. 44 (winter 1983): 16.
2. USDA, "Suar and Sweetener Outlook and Situation," June 1983, p. 9.
3. *Journal of Commerce,* August 23, 1983, p. 9A.
4. *Wall Street Journal,* April 5, 1982, p. 25.
5. USDA, "Sugar and Sweetener Outlook," pp. 11-12.
6. *Wall Street Journal,* July 20, 1982, p. 46.
7. Derek Byerlee and Edith Hesse de Polanco, "Wheat in the World Food Economy," *Food Policy* vol. 8: 1 (February 1983): 72.
8. Marvin G. Weinbaum, "Egypt's Adjustment to a Global Market Economy: The Role of U.S. Economic Assistance," unpublished manuscript, presented to 1983 annual meeting of the American Political Science Assocation, Chicago, September 1-4, 1983, p. 5.
9. Michael Lipton, *Why Poor People Stay Poor* (Cambridge: Harvard University Press, 1977).
10. Raymond F. Hopkins, "Food Aid: The Political Economy of International Policy Formation," October 1980, p. 259.

11. Economist Intelligence Unit, *Quarterly Review of Egypt,* 1983, no. 1, p. 9.
12. Weinbaum, p. 16.
13. Weinbaum, p. 12.
14. USDA, Foreign Agriculture Circular, FG-20-79, December 1979.
15. USDA, *Foreign Agriculture,* December 1981, p. 8.
16. USDA, *Foreign Agriculture,* December 1981, p. 18.
17. USDA, Foreign Agriculture Circular, FDLP-6-83, October 1983, p. 5.
18. USDA, *Foreign Agriculture,* April 1983, p. 14.
19. *Soybean Digest,* December 1982, p. 46.

REVIEW OF
"U.S. Agriculture and Third World Development: Harmonies or Disharmonies of Interest?"

Lyle P. Schertz*

**This paper does not reflect the policies of the USDA.*

Paarlberg's paper addresses issues prominent in policy debate since the post-World War 2 period. This attention is well deserved since these issues are of significance to U.S. agriculture and to human welfare in low-income countries. The nature of economic development in low-income countries and U.S. policies to assist these countries are involved. So are the prospects for U.S. farm exports.

I am in general agreement with the main themes of Paarlberg's paper. However, his approach to sugar is not fully consistent with his theme that "interests are seldom what they first appear" to be. To approach individual commodity policy questions as if supplies and demands of other commodities are not affected, as he essentially does with sugar, can foster policy choices that are not optimum for either the U.S. farm sector as a whole or Third World countries.

Instead of overlooking such indirect effects of policies, I argue, in a manner consistent with his general theme, that decisions need to be based on explicit considerations of direct, as well as indirect, effects of specific policy actions. For example, policy deliberations about assistance to oilseed projects in a low-income country should, of course, encompass the effects of the project on oilseed developments, such as U.S. exports of soybeans. In addition, they should encompass the dynamic short-run as well as longer-run effects of the project on exports of other U.S. farm products such as feedgrains and wheat. And, those people with interest in other commodities should be involved in the policy debate.

This paper, first, briefly identifies some of the principal points made by Paarlberg. These points serve as a backdrop for a second section that discusses critical relationships between Third World development and U.S. farm exports and then a review of the evolvement of U.S. policy toward international assistance for agriculture. The paper concludes with a discussion of U.S. sensitivities to argicultural development in low-income countries. In spite of the importance of development of low-income countries to U.S. exports, individual U.S. commodity groups consider many projects to be detrimental to their interest. This concluding section points to the need for a systems approach that deals with income effects, as well as supply and demand substitution effects.

MAIN POINTS OF PAARLBERG'S PAPER

As Paarlberg implies, some of the outcomes of past policy debates may not have been optimal for either U.S. agriculture or low-income countries. I think it reasonable to hypothesize, for example, that the real incomes of people in low-income countries this year would probably be higher and total U.S. farm exports would be larger if U.S. assistance policy in the fifites and early sixties had given greater emphasis to agricultural production in low-income countries and if food aid had been more limited. This hypothesis raises an obvious question with respect to current policies: could U.S. assistance to low-income countries be modified now to have greater positive effects both on U.S. farm exports in the nineties and on the well-being of the poor people in these countries? I do not intend to provide in this paper an unambiguous answer to such a question. I pose the question to emphasize the importance of accepting Paarlberg's concept that "harmonies and disharmonies of interest" are seldom what they first appear to be. It is also important, I feel, to indicatre how I define two terms that are used in the title of this portion of the program and that I use in this paper. First, I use "development" in this paper in the narrow sense to refer to per capita average income levels. The word development can be used to describe other phenomena important to the well-being of people, but this paper does not focus on these other elements. Second, the "interest" of U.S. agriculture is restricted to exports as a proxy for the overall interest of U.S. agriculture. Other issues, such as the effect of production for export on soil erosion or on the distribution of income and wealth among people in the U.S. farm sector are also important. This paper does not, however, encompass these points.

I generally agree with what I understand to be Paarlberg's main points:

1. Relationships between U.S. agriculture and Third World development are very complex. Therefore, casual perceptions about relationships between U.S. agriculture and Third World development may give misleading notions about harmonies or disharmonies. Obvious direct relationships may be overwhelmed, or at least extensively mitigated, by indirect and less obvious relationships.

2. There may be some conflict between low-income countries and the U.S. over sugar. However, there is more to gain by combining forces to fight the European sugar policies than to fight each other over sugar policies.

3. Aggressive U.S. export policies on wheat and the resulting dependence of low-income countries on wheat imports may lead to less than optimum growth of income in these countries, with subsequent adverse longer-term effects on total U.S. farm exports in the future.

4. U.S. agriculture stands to benefit from Third World development that involves rapid increases of income. Benefits from these conditions to U.S. feedgrain and cotton exports are likely to be greater than to other products such as wheat and sugar.

5. Increase in income in Third World countries are likely to be larger if development plans are broadly based and rural-oriented rather than urban-oriented involving low food prices.

IMPORTANCE OF INCOME GROWTH

There is a harmony of interests between U.S. assistance programs that promote income growth in developing countries and U.S. farm policies to maximize U.S. farm exports. Millions of people greatly need better nutrition and clothing. However, their low incomes limit their access to food supplies, unless supplemented by transfers of incomes such as occurs through PL 480. Further, there is general agreement that, as incomes increase, poor people tend to spend a larger proportion of their increased income on food than will higher-income people with the same change of income. Mackie estimates, for example, that for each 1 percent increase in income in the developing countries, agricultural imports from the United States increase by 1.36 percent. In contrast, he estimates that a 1 percent increase of income in developed countries leads to only 0.69 percent increase in imports from the United States.

Poor people are not only poor customers, they are also poor contributors to the production of goods and services demanded by others. Thus, there are two types of losses associated with poor people: they are poor customers for products and services produced by others and they are poor producers of goods and services for others.

The logic is straightforward. Increased incomes in developing countries lead to increased demands for food and fibers. These increases of demand stimulate U.S. farm exports and/or increase commodity prices. And, the increased incomes also stimulate production of goods and services demanded in the lower-income countries and perhaps demanded by farm producers and others in the United States. Consumer well-being, presumably an objective for all economic activity, is enhanced.

The logic above is reinforced by experiences to which Paarlberg refers. U.S. commercial exports to countries with medium incomes such as Korea are significantly greater than they are to countries with low incomes. For example, annual commercial agricultural exports from the United States to South Korea averaged $1.1 billion in the three years 1979-81. To Taiwan they averaged $1.2 billion, and to Brazil $661 million (Mackie).

EVOLVEMENT OF U.S. INTERNATIONAL ASSISTANCE POLICY

The relationships between development and U.S. farm exports leave open the question of how to obtain optimum income growth. For example, Paarlberg points to the rural and agricultural components of development strategies of Korea and Taiwan. These were important contributors to their rapid development. But military assistance to these countries was large and presumably an important contributor to the income growth of these countries as well. Therefore, it is useful to review briefly how stated U.S. government policy on assistance to agriculture of low-income countries has evolved.

Despite the agriculturally oriented economies of most low-income countries and the strong relationship between economic development in these countries and U.S. farm exports, U.S. support of agricultural development assistance has varied over time. U.S. economic assistance in the fifties emphasized industrialization. The large stocks of U.S. farm products seemingly depressed international prices for grains, and the initiation of PL 480 assistance augured well for development policies and programs aimed at the creation of non-farm employment opportunities. Assistance to agriculture was viewed as a stimulant to potential competition for U.S. export sales. The role of increased agricultural production in generating income which, in turn, would generate increased demands for food, was either overlooked or largely ignored. Emphasis on agricultural production was viewed as an import substitution strategy.

More specifically, in the fifties and early sixties there was substantial sensitivity about providing assistance that increased production of certain agricultural products in lower-income countries. Support of cotton, coffee, and tobacco were proscribed, as was support of the production of rice, sugar, wheat, and vegetable oils, if the assistance would lead to "substantially increasing exports" from that developing country (National Research Council, AID).

Inadequate production of food in the mid-sixties, especially in the Indian sub-continent, led to a reevaluation of the emphasis of U.S. assistance on non-agricultural as opposed to agricultural development: larger amounts of U.S. assistance were allocated to agriculture. At the same time, PL 480 was amended to include self-help concepts in providing international food assistance. Before completing individual PL 480 agreements consideration was to be given to the attention the recipient government was giving to food production, and to its commitments for continued efforts in the future.

In the meantime international research centers, inspsired by Americans (but not supported by the U.S. government), demonstrated that crop research focused on conditions in low-income countries could pay large food production dividends. These efforts attracted the attention of the U.S. government, and today USAID support of international research centers approximates $50 million a year.

Self-help provisions have been retained in PL 480 legislation. USAID's stated policy, while modified somewhat from what it was in the 1970s, permits U.S. support of food and feed crop production if the production is to be used domestically.

At the same time sensitivity to specific projects arises from time to time (American Soybean Association and Earl Butz, exchange of correspondence). The question remains, "Why do U.S. farm producer groups continue to mistrust U.S. assistance to agriculture abroad, given the records of exports to countries like Korea and Taiwan?"

REASONS FOR SENSITIVITIES AND POSSIBLE SYSTEMS APPROACH

The longevity of the issues about how support of agricultural development in low-income countries affects U.S. farm exports are, in my judgment, largely associated with five conditions.

First, it is difficult to fully account for direct and indirect effects of agricultural development projects in lower-income countries. It is fairly straightforward to estimate the effect of, say, a coarse-grain development project on coarse grain production. However, the indirect supply effects on production of other crops such as wheat or livestock are more elusive. This is the case also for the effects of such projects on income growth and food consumption and, in turn, on import demand for not only coarse grains, in this case, but also wheat and products like soybean meal. All too often the direct production effects are considered to be the only effects and to have a one-to-one import-substitution effect for the principal commodity, coarse grains, in this example.

Second, political and sometimes analytical activities concentrate on direct effects of U.S.-assisted agricultural projects in low-income countries and often overlook the indirect effects. For example, discussions of tomato, strawberry, or cotton production of other countries often do not encompass consideration of the potential indirect effects on U.S. exports of farm products such as wheat and feed grains.

Third, the future and its uncertainty is discounted heavily. The result is that cost-benefit considerations are often limited to the short term.

Fourth, there remains the latent hope that the incomes and related wealth of poor countries will miraculously increase through industrialization and/or through the repricing of some non-farm resource in a manner akin to what happened to petroleum. In other words, some people hope that Paarlberg's "broad-based" development, focused heavily on agriculture, is not a necessary strategy for realizing income growth that, in turn, will lead to increased U.S. farm exports.

Fifth, U.S. agricultural producer groups anticipate that U.S. taxpayers will continue to provide funds for international food assistance in response to producer groups and institutions that have capitalized on PL 480 programs. If this were not the case, producer groups would be more interested in ways to stimulate economic growth, including aggressive food-production programs in low-income countries. Without economic growth, markets for U.S. farm commodities would not expand.

I conclude that the United States must confront the first three of these conditions if we are to deal effectively with the sensitivities about support of agricultural development in low-income countries. The challenge is, in spite of the difficulty, effectively to anticipate indirect as well as direct effects and long-run as well as short-run effects.

Undoubtedly there are potential disharmonies and harmonies between U.S. agriculture and Third World development. Simple policy prescriptions and proscriptions focused on individual commodities are not likely to identify the opportunities that are harmonious and those that are not.

My reaction to Paarlberg's approach to sugar illustrates what I have in mind. I applaud his notion that Western Europe should be pressed to provide greater access for farm products of developing countries. Eastern Europe and the USSR should be pressed to do the same. But, to limit the sugar issue to sugar overlooks the impact of U.S. sugar policy on income growth in developing countries and in turn on U.S. exports of other U.S. farm products such as wheat, feedgrains, oilseeds, and cotton. It also overlooks the substitution of resources in production of different products.

I visualize the need for a systems approach that consistently considers supply and demand substitutions among products and resources, both in the United States and in lower-income countries. Further, since the trade-offs may be linked to different time periods, the policy debates and the analyses supporting the debates must encompass the long-term as well as the short-term effects.

In summary, focus on individual commodities such as sugar, wheat, or feedgrains with the exclusion of effects on other commodities is not sufficient. Concern for next year's exports without recognition of the implications for the next decade, or beyond, can foster decisions that overlook potential trade-offs between near-term and future benefits. Unless this more eclectic approach is pursued, we run the risk of seeing harmonies when there are disharmonies, and disharmonies when there are harmonies and opportunities that will enhance both U.S. farm exports and the development of low-income countries will be bypassed.

REFERENCES

AID, *The War on Hunger: Guideline for Planning AID Assistance in Agricultural and Related Sectors,* Manual Circular 1612.10, December 6, 1966.

Butz, Earl L., sec. USDA, letter to Ralph T. Jackson, January 20, 1975.

Jackson, Ralph T., executive v. pres. American Soybean Association, letter to Clayton Yeutter, asst. sec. USDA, November 6, 1974.

Mackie, Arthur B., *The U.S. Farmer and World Market Development,* ERS staff report no. AGES830810, Econ. Res. Serv., USDA, 1983.

National Research Council, *Supporting Papers: World Food and Nutrition Study,* vol. 5, National Academy of Sciences, Washington, D.C., 1977.

Chapter 5
Overview: Deliberations Thus Far

Don Paarlberg

Summary of papers and discussions from the Conference on Agricultural Policy held in Washington, D.C., February 21 and 22, 1984, under auspices of the Curry Foundation, prepared for

The National Conference on Agricultural Policy
Kansas City, Missouri, May 21 and 22, 1984

Some of us have been coming to farm policy conferences for fifty years, ever since the commodity programs were first initiated. How does a farm policy conference in 1984 differ from those of earlier years? I list six differences, some of which have come on us abruptly. Others have crept up slowly, so that we are hardly aware of them.

1. Goals are now obscure. When commodity programs were first begun, the goal was clear—to save agriculture from the disaster of the Great Depression which then was threatening farms of all kinds and sizes. Not the situation is not so clear. Some farms are threatened by disaster, but others are in good financial condition. The latest figures on farm foreclosures are for 1981, when foreclosures totaled 1.2 per thousand farms. When it becomes available, the rate for 1982 will probably show an increase but is unlikely to have reached the failure rate for non-farm business, 6 per thousand.

What is it we are trying to do? increase aggregate farm income? stabilize it? help those in greatest trouble? build markets? increase efficiency? safeguard our natural resources? cut program costs? elect our friends? all these things? We seem to be suffering from goal confusion.

Probably the greatest difficulty we had at the Washington conference was our inability to agree on a clear-cut goal.

2. The structure of agriculture has changed. Years ago farms were reasonably similar to one another. Most were of family size, sufficiently alike so that the commodity programs had fairly generaly applicability. But now we have developed a three-sector agriculture, which may be described as follows:

	Percent of Farms	Percent of Production
Large farms (cash receipts in excess of $200,000)	4.6	45.8
"Family farms" (cash receipts from $20,000 to $200,000)	35.6	44.0
Small farms (cash receipts less than $20,000)	59.8	10.2
	100.0	100.0

The commodity programs provide their benefit in accordance with the volume of production. Obviously, they are very important to the 5 percent of our farms that produce almost half our crops and livestock. But they are not very meaningful to the 60 percent of our farmers who produce only 10 percent of what is sold. They may be most helpful to the farmers in the middle range, who lack the high incomes enjoyed by the large farmers and also have less off-farm income than do the small farmers. Certainly, the differential impact of the commodity programs is greater than it formerly was.

3. Off-farm income has increased. Earlier, sales of crops and livestock accounted for almost all the income of farm people, so that commodity programs had great relevance. But by 1981 the off-farm income of farm people was almost twice as large as income from the farm. This varied greatly from one sector to another. For large farms, off-farm income was only about 20 percent of the total. For the small farms it was 90 percent. For farms in the middle range is was something like half. Off-farm income differs enormously from farm to farm, of course.

The commodity programs (corn, wheat, cotton, rice, peanuts, tobacco, sugar, dairy) relate to products that bring in about half the farm income.

Other commodities which lack such programs (beef, pork, poultry, eggs, fruits, vegetables) bring in the other half. When we reckon that half of agriculture is without the commodity programs and two-thirds of the income of farm people is from off-farm sources, it becomes inappropriate to speak of the commodity programs as being basic to all our farm people.

4. International markets have grown. Before World War 2 we exported only 4 percent of our farm output. We could price our products with only limited regard for their competitiveness in international markets. Now exports take from 25 to 30 percent of our output. Price policy, once largely a domestic matter, has come under the discipline of international competition.

5. New people are in the farm policy forum. In earlier times, farmers, almost single-handed, could design the farm programs. In 1985, whether we like it or not, there will be other actors: consumers, taxpayers, environmentalists, agribusiness people, and specialists in foreign trade. This calls not only for new strategies but may bring changes in the programs themselves.

6. Overall economic policy grows in importance. Earlier, agricultural policy was considered as largely self-contained. But experience of recent years shows that if this once had considerable validity, it no longer has.

What are the chief troubles agriculture has now encountered? One can argue convincingly that most of them came from overall economic policies that originated outside of agriculture and were hurtful to farmers:

a. An anti-inflation policy that put on the brakes too hard, throwing some farmers against the windshield
b. Economic policies that increased the exchange rate of the dollar, making it hard to export
c. High interest rates, resulting from our fiscal and monetary policies, greatly troubling to farmers who are deep in debt
d. Trade restrictions on imported industrial goods that angered our trading partners and hurt our agricultural exports
e. Embargoes that caused our overseas buyers to look elsewhere for their supplies
f. Agriculture and trade policies of the EEC, which made for unfair competition with our farm exports

Clearly, it is a new ball game. We will have to think anew and act anew. Any of us who come to this meeting to fire the old artillery at the old enemy run the risk of being off target.

POINTS OF CONSENSUS

Despite disagreement that seemed at times to be overwhelming, we did come up with a general consensus. While it was not unanimous, this consensus appeared to give us a useful framework. I list eight items.

1. Abundance is in prospect. During the last ten years the analysts first predicted tight supplies of food and high prices of farm products. Then the analysis was reversed; the scarcity syndrome disappeared and the surplus scenario replaced it.

What is now the prospect? What is likely to be the overall situation during the life of the 1985 farm bill? We generally agreed that American agriculture would have adequate capacity, perhaps excess capacity, to meet feed, food, and fiber needs at home and abroad. Real prices (that is, prices adjusted for inflation) are expected to be somewhat soft.

But there probably will be some years of poor crops when supplies are scarce and prices are strong. There is no way of foretelling such years. We should not place high confidence in these speculations.

2. Exports are needed. We have become deeply reliant on exports, which now take something like 40 percent of our soybeans, 35 percent of our wheat, and 25 percent of our corn. The domestic market has neither the size nor the growth to make full use of our agricultural plant. Programs for our export crops must provide a bridge to the export market.

3. Cartels hold scant promise. The fond dreams of joint action on the part of the U.S. and other exporters for collaborative pricing, production, and marketing of farm products were dismissed as unworkable. This judgment came from experience with the International Wheat Agreement and from failed efforts to establish an International Grain Reserve.

International cooperation could conceivably proceed along the following five lines, ranged from the most open to the most formal:

a. Exchange of facts and views
b. Communication of actions taken or contemplated
c. Notification of actions to be taken
d. Discussion in an effort to reach consensus on actions to be taken in parallel
e. Consultations on actions to be taken jointly

In general, misgivings arose as the actions increased in formality.

4. There is growing concern about program cost. Cost for the 1983 programs will approximate two-thirds of the net farm income of all agriculture. No one defended this level of costs.

5. ***There was dissatisfaction with present programs.*** No one advocated the extension, in 1985, of the 1981 act. Chief objections were its adverse effect on exports, its deep production cuts, its high cost, and its big farm bias.

6. ***Some trade-off of stability and flexibility is sought.*** Either stability or flexibility can be disastrous in the total absence of the other. Too much stability is the enemy of needed change. Too much flexibility brings undeserved losses. Neither is in keeping with good resource use. In our discussions we groped for some middle ground that would avoid the bad consequences of pursuing either stability or flexibility as a one-dimensional goal.

7. ***Deep production cuts are disliked.*** The PIK program of 1983 received some support as the least harmful remedy for a bad situation. But continued large acreage restriction programs were viewed adversely. They were seen as holding an umbrella for our rival exporters, who increase production and move in to take over the markets from which we withdraw.

8. ***Agricultural developments in the Third World is seen, on balance, as helpful to American farmers.*** We recognized that for particular commodities, and viewed in a narrow sense, agricultural development in the Third World can displace American production. Tomatoes in Mexico and mushrooms in Taiwain are clear examples. But in an overall view, a natural harmony of interests exists between U.S. agricultural and Third World development. Agricultural advance helps general economic growth, which increases the ability to buy U.S. farm products. A case in point is Malaysia. Some years ago American farmers opposed the development of oil palm in that country, from fear that this would hurt U.S. soybean exports. But Malaysia did expand oil palm and did achieve overall economic advance. That country has now built a small soybean crushing industry to supply feed for her growing animal production. Soybeans are now the top U.S. farm export to Malaysia, valued at $36 million in 1982.

We took no votes and we passed no resolutions. But if an inference can be drawn from our deliberations it must be that our commodity programs should be more flexible and less costly, and that pricing arrangements should permit us to be competitive in export markets. The logical but unspecified conclusion from our discussion is that loans and target levels should be reduced, at least relative to the rate of inflation and perhaps absolutely. Greater reliance on the market is implied, and less reliance on government than in the act of 1981.

There were departures from this consensus, both to the right and to the left, in the conventional meaning of those terms. Sharp reductions of loans and targets and minimal limitations on output were recommended by some, but received scant support from the group. On the other hand, an increase in loan levels was recommended but received little backing.

There was a recommendation that target prices be eliminated and that assistance be given only through loans. Advantages seen for this approach were a possible reduction in cost and reduced visibility of benefits going to the big farmers. But there was concern that if targets were eliminated the loans might be correspondingly increased, worsening our competitiveness in the export market. The group reached no consensus on this point.

ALTERNATIVES CONSIDERED

We discussed other approaches which involve greater departures from historic programs. Four that were seriously considered are here summarized.

1. Trade-based policy. This appeared in various forms: different degrees of collaboration with other exporters; limitations on imports; confrontation with the European Common Market; reduction of international agricultural development funds; export subsidies; stockholding; increased export credit; formal two-price plans; an export marketing board; expanded food aid; increased export promotion; and prohibition of export controls. Some of these proposals were viewed with favor. But there was concern that if this road were followed beyond some point it might become "a slippery slope" leading to competitive protectionism in which we, with a large net export blance, stand to lose more than we can gain.

2. Focus on the "family farm." There was concern about the middle group of farmers, generally those with gross incomes between $20,000 and $200,000. These people constitute about one-third of the farmers and produce not quite half the farm products. They do not have the high incomes of the super-large farms, and many do not have the off-farm incomes of the small farmers. While we were unable to agree on a definition for a "family farmer," these people appeared to come closest to our perception of what such a farmer is.

Various ways were considered for diverting a greater proportion of help to these people. Among these were a lowered payment limitation and deficiency payments scaled inversely to size of farm. There was objection that such changes would reduce the effectiveness of acreage control by weakening the inducement for the big farmers to comply. Those who were market-oriented maintained that acreage controls should not be so deep as to require cooperation of super-large farmers. There was some feeling that huge payments to individual farmers were giving the programs a bad image.

It was not possible for the group to come to any agreement on this issue.

3. Soil conservation as an element in farm programs. For years the thought has persisted that we should require certain standards of resource use as a condition for receiving the benefits of farm programs. Thus, we would be buying resource conservation with our program outlays.

The group considered experience with these efforts, and the prospect for such provisions in the act of 1985. There was agreement that better resource use is important. But there was concern that, as in the past, price support and income-enhancement would take priority and better resource use would be honored more in the rhetoric than in the performance.

4. Focus on farmers in trouble. There are no fully satisfactory figures on how many farmers are in serious difficulty and in danger of losing their farms. Estimates made by reputable people range anywhere from 1 to 10 percent. The argument is made that we should scrap programs that provide benefits to those who do not need them and direct our help, with loans and grants, to those who do.

Major problems were seen with this approach. How identify those in need? How maintain an efficient agriculture if success is assureds to those with little managerial capability? How persuade the successful farmers to forgo their benefits so that help can be concentrated on those who are failing? Experience with Economic Emergency loans has not been reassuring.

A number of radical and innovative proposals were laid before the group. We did not deal with these in any detail, in part because we realized that the gestation period for a radical new farm policy proposal is counted in years. There seemed little prospect that these proposals would be seriously considered in the act of 1985. They are listed to reveal the range of our review.

1. End commodity programs altogether. Abandonment of the programs got little support. Despite their obvious shortcomings, the commmodity programs have become so important to many farmers that their abrupt termination would result in disaster. To meet the transition problem a gradual ten-year phase-out was recommended. But it is not clear that if we were to embark on such a course we would stay on it for ten years.

2. Apply mandatory production controls. At the other extreme was a recommendation for mandatory production controls, which would make high prices attainable. But this approach was no more attractive than the one for scrapping the programs. Ever since the wheat farmers voted out mandatory controls in the early 1960s, the conventional wisdom has been that if we are to have controls they must be voluntary.

3. Withdraw tax subsidies. Agriculture is eligible for many tax-deduction devices. These stimulate production, reduce tax revenue, and encourage non-farm people to engage in "tax-loss farming." There was a proposal that these tax subsidies be withdrawn. Whatever might be the overall advantage of such a change, its unattractiveness to individual farmers served to rule it out.

4. Provide income insurance. Farmers could purchase income insurance from the government, pay their premiums, and receive an indemnity payment when their incomes fell below some standard.

But farmers are convinced that they will receive help, without paying premiums, through price support and relief of disaster. And there is no good actuarial basis for insuring price or income.

5. Develop human resources. The farm population has fallen from 23 million in 1950 to 5.5 million. The trend continues. The argument is made that disadvantaged farm people should be given the education and assistance that would help them to succeed in agriculture, or, alternatively, the vocational training that would help them qualify for non-farm jobs. Many of those in poverty or in jeopardy of losing out are on small farms. A substantial series of efforts, called rural development, is underway in their behalf. Such efforts focus on problems quite different from those addressed by the commodity programs.

6. Institute political reform. There was agreement in the group that the commodity programs had become heavily politicized and that the special interests had captured more than their proper share of benefits. Some said the shortcomings of the commodity programs could not be overcome within the present system. Political reforms emanating from several sources were enumerated.

- Granting the secretary of agriculture more policy discretion
- Creating an independent agency analogous to the Federal Reserve Board to regulate agricultural policy
- Constitutional restrictions on the regulatory powers of the federal government
- Institutional changes within the executive branch, intended to broaden the basis of policy making with respect to food and agriculture

The group tended to agree that, for commodity programs, the political processes had not functioned in keeping with the public interest. But there was no enthusiasm for the suggested reforms.

As the Washington conference came to a close, there was general agreement that certain important matters had been neglected. These included the following.

A sharper focus on goals. We were struck by the fact that we were considering remedies for problems that had not been adequately defined. The programs seemed to have taken on lives of their own.

Better information on conditions in agriculture. There was disagreement as to the financial situation of farm people. Some reported crisis conditions. Others cited reassuring overall figures on income and net worth. We could not agree on what proportion of farm people were in trouble. We needed a paper setting forth the facts.

More work on general economic policy. Most of the discussants were impressed with the way in which fiscal, monetary, and trade policy had affected agriculture, often to the disadvantage of farm people. These forces originate largely outside the commodity programs. The governmental machinery for representing agricultural interests is poorly developed. The heavy emphasis on commodity programs has eclipsed interest in these broader matters, which in an earlier day were prominent policy concerns of farm people. The Washington group was quite aware of all this but was not able to recommend a good way of coping.

Need for review of credit programs. Very little time was spent on issues surrounding farm credit: the operating loans and ownership loans of the Farmers' Home Administration, the Economic Emergency loans, Rural Electrification telephone loans, and the loans of the Farm Credit System. This was seen as a gap in our review.

Other matters of farm legislation. The Agricultural Act of 1981 covered a wide range of subject matter. In addition to commmodity legislation these included: research and extension, food programs, rural development, resource use, and various regulatory matters. We focused our discussion on commodity issues, to the neglect of these other matters. This is explained by our limited time and by the concentration of interest on the commodity programs. But these other important matters must receive attention.

This review is intended as a faithful summary of our papers and our discussions. Nevertheless, my opinions may have crept in, unbidden, and colored the content. I therefore summarize my own views, so that the reader can interpret the report in the light thereof.

In my judgment, most of the shortcomings of the commodity programs could be overcome by reducing loan and target levels, providing far more flexibility, and reducing the $50,000 payment limitation. To provide flexibility in loan levels and target prices, some percentage of a moving average of farm prices of recent years, such as now is used for soybeans, is desirable.

I am a bit to the right of the consensus earlier outlined, but sufficiently tractable to endorse it.

Chapter 6
An Overview for Discussion

Howard W. Hjort

This paper is based mainly on the writings and discussion at the Conference on Agricultural Policy which was sponsored by the Curry Foundation and held in Washington, D.C., on February 21 and 22, 1984. It has been prepared to facilitate discussion at the National Conference on Agricultural Policy in Kansas City, Missouri, on May 21 and 22, 1984.

The objectives of the Curry Foundation-sponsored program "Agriculture, Stability, and Growth: Toward a Cooperative Approach" are to focus expert and political attention on the prospects of developing a coherent general policy for American agriculture, and for effectively integrating it with several intimately related concerns.

The simultaneous existence of huge surpluses and inadequate diets is one such concern, and has been for a long time. We are reminded by the sponsor that inadequate diets are in evidence even in many of the richest nations, and in some of the poorest nations very few have enough to eat. Yet we frequently face such huge, price-depressing surpluses that even efficient farmers are placed in jeopardy.

They note that recent developments in international finance have greatly intensified the long existing need for coherent and coordinated Third World development policies, and that recent developments in both American domestic agriculture and world agricultural trade have raised the need for coherent and mutually acceptable agricultural and food export policies among the producer nations.

The Curry Foundation-sponsored program is based on the belief that more coherent and coordinated development, agricultural, and export policies could provide a more stable and conducive climate for turning the immense unsatisfied need for food into effective demand, while allowing producers to meet world demand without impoverishing able and efficient producers.

Four papers were commissioned to initiate the program. One was focused on the world market—longer-term trends, characteristics, recent developments, and implications for the future. Another provided background on U.S. agriculture, and presented agricultural policy options. Prospects for integrating producer nations' agricultural strategies, and relationships between agriculture and Third World development, were the topics of the other two. Each paper was reviewed by two experts. The authors, reviewers, and others discussed these writings and related issues at the February conference in Washington.

Don Paarlberg and I analyzed the prepared papers, reviewer comments, and conference arguments in order to set the stage for the National Conference. Don sent a copy of his paper while I was in Rome, so I had the advantage of his thoughts also. His summary of the papers and discussions is complete, so I decided to focus my paper on the relationships between growth, stability, cooperation, and policies.

I hold the view that greater stability in the domestic and world markets will mean more favorable conditions for cooperation and growth, and that policies are of fundamental importance to stability and growth.

It is easy to be pessimistic about world and U.S. agriculture, especially if one believes that greater stability and more cooperation are essential to sustainable growth. We see neither progress nor growing appreciation of the need for policies that will help promote continuing growth.

The recent recession slowed incomes growth and made debt service much more difficult. A consequence was slower growth in agricultural product consumption and trade. Our share of the world market declined. Our policies became more controversial. Conflicts among trading partners became more pronounced.

Generating foreign exchange to service debt and import agricultural products has become so difficult in some countries that even maintaining per capita food consumption has become impossible. We are told that overcoming the financial crisis may take several years. The gap between need and effective demand for food may continue to narrow, but more slowly than in prior decades when economic and financial conditions were more favorable to incomes growth.

We are told to expect slower growth in world agricultural consumption and trade during the 1980s, with U.S. trade growth perhaps one-third the pace of the 1970s. The world market has become highly volatile, and if the U.S. cuts price support levels it will be even more so. Strong growth in the world market is essential to American agriculture; slow, uncertain, and uneven growth and great volatility are more conducive to conflict and controversy than to cooperation.

The case for more coherent and coordinated Third World development policies among the developed nations was stated, and a way for the United States and the developing countries to benefit outlined. These nations will be the source of most of the growth in the world market, and policies that help them steady and sustain economic growth will stimulate growth in agricultural product consumption and trade.

But the trend toward less adequate financing of development assistance was viewed as an ominous sign. The shift toward protectionism also was identifed as a reason for expecting slower growth in world agriculture. Continued opposition of producer groups to efforts designed to speed growth in Third World food production was feared, another reason for below-potential growth in farm product trade.

Although recent developments in both American domestic agriculture and world agricultural trade have raised the need for coherent and mutually acceptable agriculture and food export policies among the producer nations, the review of the record and recent developments led to the conclusion that coordination or integration of agricultural and food export policies would be essentially impossible to attain. Our shrinking share of world agricultural trade did not make this an opportune time, and recent attacks on the policies of our major buyers are moving us further away instead of closer even to a climate of cooperation, much less coordination or integration.

Inconsistencies in our trade policies are another reason for concern. We favor policies that permit farm products to be sold for less than it cost to produce them, but we prohibit "dumping" of non-farm goods and often protect domestic producers from imports even at prices above cost.

U.S. agriculture policies that will permit even greater instability in the world and domestic agricultural markets were favored by a majority of the participants. Lower loan prices were the favored approach, to "keep us competitive in the world market." Remaining competitive is important, but permitting export prices to be even more volatile also will make our food and farm policies more controversial at home and increase the potential for conflict with our trading partners. Greater volatility also would tend to increase the cost of food and agriculture programs.

For these and other reasons, instead of rapid growth in U.S. agriculture the participants foresee slow growth; instead of greater stability they see great volatility; and instead of a move toward cooperation they see continued conflict and controversy. The task of this paper is to explore reasons for the views of the participants, in the search for policies that promote more rapid growth, greater stability, and more cooperation.

GROWTH

The Past

The world market became very important to American agriculture, and American agriculture became very important to the world market in the 1970s. It was the primary source of growth in the industry. We became the dominant supplier, and continued to be a major importer. More countries came to rely on the world market and the United States for farm products, and most of them increased their dependency on it and us.

O'Brien documents the growth in world agricultural consumption, trade, and production from 1950 to 1982. Production and consumption grew 2.85 percent a year from 1950 to 1972, and 2.35 percent annually from 1972 to 1982. World trade grew more rapidly, 1.7 times faster from 1950 to 1972, and 2.7 times faster from 1972 to 1982.

The developing countries increased imports 9.4 percent a year from 1972 to 1981, compared with only 2.3 percent for the developed countries. The developing countries increased exports only 1.6 percent a year, while the annual increase for the developed countries was 5.5 percent.

North America, Western Europe, and Oceania experienced more rapid growth in exports than in imports from 1972 to 1981, but import growth was in excess of export growth for all the other regions. There were declines in exports from the Asian centrally planned economies, developing Africa, and the Middle East, and very slow growth in exports from the European centrally planned economies. The annual average change in exports ranged from a positive 6.8 percent for North America to a negative 3.5 percent for developing Africa.

Every region experienced growth in imports, but they grew only 0.15 percent a year for Oceania, and 1.0 percent annually for North America. At the other extreme was the Middle East, where the increase in imports averaged 14.3 percent a year.

These sharp regional differences in import and export growth led to a massive increase in the value of world agricultural trade (from $71.3 billion in 1972 to $253.4 billion in 1981 CIF), and major shifts in trade flows.

The world market was the rapid growth market for the United States. From 1950 to 1972 the rate of growth in trade was 2.9 times the rate of growth in domestic consumption; from 1972 to 1982 trade grew 7.4 times faster.

The United States captured a large share of the growth in the world market. Export values rose from $8.24 billion for FY1972 to $43.78 billion for FY1981. Import values also rose, from $4.83 to $17.3 billion, but by less than export values. The net gain from agricultural trade for the ten years was $135.3 billion, and $26.56 billion for FY1981, the peak year.

The demand factors were quite favorable to consumption and trade growth during the 1970s. The increase in world population was the largest ever, even though the rate of growth was slower. The world economy was subjected to severe shocks but, on balance, may have been overstimulated. Inflation became a more serious problem. The accumulation of debt was easy, and debt servicing was also easy as long as economic growth was strong and inflation high. The demand for agricultural products was quite strong under these conditions.

Growth in the world economy has been abnormally slow in the early 1980s. The dollar has been strong relative to other currencies. The real cost of money has been very high, and servicing debt has become extremely difficult. The demand for food and fiber products has been quite weak, and trade growth has slowed markedly, even though in 1982 farm products were available in the world market at the lowest real prices ever.

U.S. exports fell $9.01 billion (20.6 percent) from FY1981 to FY1983, and the net on the agricultural trade account declined $8.16 billion (30.7 percent). Net trade with the centrally planned economies declined the most (62 percent), but there were reductions in net trade with the developing (20 percent) and other developed (25 percent) market economies also.

Most of our agricultural imports come from the developing countries, but most of our agricultural exports go to the other developed countries. In FY1983 the developing countries accounted for 42 percent of U.S. farm exports, 59 percent of the imports, and 26 percent of the net earnings from agricultural trade.

There are 48 countries that usually have a favorable balance of trade in agricultural products with the United States. Of these, 43 are developing countries. Those with the largest favorable balances, in rank order, are Brazil, Australia, Colombia, Indonesia, New Zealand, and the Philippines.

Need vs. Effective Demand

The gap between adequate and inadequate diets has narrowed over the years but more slowly since the supply shortage of the mid-1970s. The growth in per capita consumption was 1.9 times faster from 1950 to 1972 than from 1972 to 1982. Per capita consumption growth has been very slow in recent years.

Growth in per capita consumption was at an annual rate of 0.4 percent from 1972 to 1982 for the United States; it was 6.4 times faster for the rest of the world.

Regional data on per capita caloric intake levels also indicate improved food supplies, and suggest that the gap between the need and effective demand for food narrowed over the years for all the regions. However, the data also suggest that the gap began to widen in some regions in the late 1970s. Since then it has been more difficult to improve diets in many developing nations.

While the general trend has been toward a more adequate diet, the data mask the fact that a substantial number of people actually experienced a decline in per capita food consumption over the past decade. There are large remaining differences in calorie supplies between the developed and developing regions. The potential demand for food is much greater in the latter.

Prospects for Growth

If people everywhere were able to obtain all the agricultural products they wished to consume over the balance of the decade, the percentage gains would be very large for sub-Saharan Africa, South Asia, and Southeast Asia, large for China, North Africa, and the Middle East, substantial for East Asia and Latin America, moderate for the USSR, Eastern Europe, and Oceania, and small for North America and Western Europe.

Population and incomes growth are the major sources of growth in food and fiber consumption and trade. World market prices tend to be of lesser importance except when there are major imbalances between effective demand and supplies. The food policies of most countries are designed to keep domestic prices relatively stable. Population growth is a much more stable source of growth in world agricultural consumption and trade than incomes growth. World market prices are also highly volatile.

Although there is general agreement that the 1980s will be a time of gradually slowing population growth rates, the absolute addition will be the largest ever, and after taking into account the changing age structure, the increase in the "need" for food to maintain per capita consumption will be fully as large as during the 1970s. And, if all the world's peoples were to maintain per capita consumption, instead of some having to consume less, the additional amount they would consume during the 1980s would exceed the increase that was associated with population growth over the past decade.

Most of the increase in world population will take place in the Third World nations. Population growth will be especially rapid in Africa and the Middle East, and quite high in many of the Latin American and South Asian nations. It will be slowest in the developed countries.

Low-income people allocate a much higher share of additional income to food than those with high incomes. Most of the very high-income nations of North America, Western Europe, and Oceania will experience very slow growth in per capita consumption of agricultural products, and with relatively slow growth in population their total requirement will rise slowly.

Farmers in the United States, Canada, the EEC, Australia, New Zealand, and a few other countries will be able to increase production by more than enough to satisfy domestic consumption requirements. The world market for the farm products they export will become more important to them in the future, and their farm products will become more important to the rest of the world.

These nations will continue to be able to increase exports faster than they will wish to increase imports. In most years they are likely to be able to place more on the world market than the importers will be able to buy. They will have to turn increasingly to the developing countries to sell their products.

The Third World will need much more from the world market, more than they will be able to obtain. And with only slow growth in agricultural product imports in the highly developed market economies, the Third World exporters will also have to turn increasingly to other developing countries to market their products.

Most of the future growth in the consumption and trade of agricultural products will come from the Third World. Their development policies will be the key to incomes growth and to growth in agricultural product consumption and trade. Debt service will continue to be the major constraint to economic growth in many of the medium-income countries, especially those in Latin America and Eastern Europe. Increasing aggregate production faster than population will continue to be difficult in the lower-income countries, especially those in Africa.

The development policies of the more highly developed nations will influence the pace at which Third World nations grow. Their macroeconomic, financial, and trade policies will also affect incomes growth in the Third World. On balance, these policies are expected to be less favorable to growth in food and fiber consumption over the rest of the 1980s than they were during the 1970s.

The macroeconomic policies of the highly developed market economies have an important impact on Third World economic growth. Strong growth in the former ususally means stronger growth in the latter. But when the former experience a serious recession, the task of maintaining growth in the Third World nations soon becomes very difficult. Third World export growth slows, or exports decline, and then aggregate production, incomes, and food and fiber consumption growth slows. A higher share of export earnings must be used for debt service, and less is available for imports of essential items. Imports of agricultural products frequently must be slowed by, more than justified by, slower incomes growth, and exports must be accelerated even if doing so reduced per capita food supplies.

A deep or prolonged recession can bring those with relatively high debt to a financial crisis, as the experience of the past three years demonstrates so effectively. Once in a crisis, financial management becomes exceedingly difficult, and the return to favorable economic growth can be postponed for years. These conditions slow growth in the effective demand for agricultural products.

Technology is the primary source of the increase in world agricultural production over time. Essentially, every nation subsidizes the development of technology, in one way or another, and most also subsidize the transfer of technology. The richer nations spend relatively more on technology. Most nations also subsidize the control of pests and diseases, the development and protection of natural resources and credit. Producer prices or incomes are frequently subsidized, and consumer price subsidies are also common. Many of the developing and centrally planned nations subsidize input prices.

Many of the developing and Eastern European nations have been forced to reduce food and agricultural budgets recently, and pressures to do so in most other developed countries have become intense. Expenditures on technology and the control of pests and diseases appear to be under less pressure than those that provide direct subsidies to producers and consumers.

Most of the future growth in production must come from inceasing the productivity of the land already in production instead of bringing additional land into production. It is believed that production will rise fast enough to satisfy effective demand at world market prices that continue to decline in real terms, but this belief rests mainly upon the implicit and explicit assumptions about policies that affect the demand for food and fiber.

The experts believe demand growth will be weaker than during the 1970s, not because of less need but because of the less favorable economic and financial conditions that have obtained and are expected to obtain.

Trade growth is foreseen at two-thirds the postwar pace, and at one-third the 1972 to 1982 pace for the United States. This relatively pessismistic view may be overly influenced by recent events and conditions. There is a tendency to give too much weight to conditions at the time a forecast is being developed, and since the demand factors have been extremely and abnormally unfavorable to growth in agricultural consumption and trade since 1981, this may be a time to be a mild skeptic.

Nevertheless, it is realistic to believe that the general economic, financial, trade, and development policies, traditionally believed to be beyond the scope of agriculturalists, will be the key to how close to capacity American agriculture will operate and to the magnitude of the worldwide gap between adequate and inadequate diets. And the policies of the United States will set the tone for the rest of the world.

If incomes grow slowly, if interest rates remain high, if the dollar stays strong, if trade barriers are raised, and if development assistance is inadequate, then the agricultural sector will remain depressed. Strong but sustainable economic growth, lower real interest rates, a weaker dollar, a move away from protectionism, and more adequate development assistance would mean solid growth in the agricultural sector.

These policies are of fundamental importance to world agriculture. They lead to surges or pauses in world food and fiber consumption and trade, and a relatively small change in world consumption growth means a large change in world trade growth. The task of our food and agricultural policies is to offset the adverse consequence of the pauses and capture the gains associated with the surges.

In spite of the rather pessimistic trade outlook, it is clear that trade growth for U.S. agricultural products will have to exceed growth in the domestic market to keep the agricultural sector from operating at a declining share of capacity. The United States will have to depend even more on the world market, and the rest of the world will have to depend even more on the United States. And most of the growth will have to come from the Third World.

STABILITY

The world market is highly volatile. Prices rise quickly to extreme levels when demand is strong and supplies tight, and fall to below cost of production levels when demand is weak and supplies abundant. The food and agricultural policies of most nations seek to provide greater stability in internal markets than in the world market. But some nations, including the

United States, permit internal prices for their main export commodities to vary with world prices. Consumption, trade, and production are more volatile in these countries.

The world market is a thin market, representing only a small fraction of total world production and consumption. It is a residual market. Amounts in excess of domestic requirements are made available to it, and amounts the importers are willing and able to purchase are taken from it. These amounts are seldom equal. When supplies available to the world market are tight, the price rises sharply, and when they become excessive, the price falls sharply. World price moves are amplified by the policies of nations that maintain relative internal stability.

The supply available to the world market has been very tight at times, but more often supplies have been in excess of effective demand. Tight supplies and very favorable demand conditions collided in the early 1970s, and world commodity prices escalated to previously unbelievable heights in 1973 or 1974. Very unfavorable demand conditions and excessive supplies combined in the early 1980s, and world commodity prices fell to an all-time low in 1982. There have been other times when tight supplies caused commodity prices to rise quickly, and when abundant supplies caused commodity prices to fall sharply, but the extreme and general moves have come when effective demand is strong and supplies tight, or demand is weak and supplies large.

Erratic growth in incomes causes instability in the world agricultural market. In attempting to dampen overheated economies the macroeconomic policies tend to push economies down too far, and in attempting to stimulate depressed economies the policies tend to push them forward too rapidly. Further, the main market economies tend to play follow-the-leader, which moves the world economy in a cyclical manner.

When money is cheap, servicing debt is easy. But easy investment often brings economies too close to capacity, and the upward pressure on prices becomes intense. The inflationary cycle worsens until the fear of runaway inflation causes policies to change. Credit terms harden, and servicing debt becomes more difficult, frequently moving an economy into a recessionary phase. Unemployment rises, and price inflation abates as idle capacity increases. Stimulative policies are adopted, and the cycle begins again.

Fluctuations in interest rates and the relative value of currencies are also sources of volatility in world commodity markets. As previously noted, debt service becomes very difficult when the world economy experiences a severe recession. And the problem becomes even more severe when the main currentcy used to service debt (the dollar) is strong relative to other currencies, and when the cost of that currency remains high in real terms.

These have been and continue to be the circumstances, but they are clear deviations from normal expectations. The U.S. economy led the most recent recession. Relatively high real interest rates were expected when measures were taken to slow the economy, but they should have declined when actions were taken to stimulate the economy. Instead, the massive fiscal deficit prevented their decline and left us with record high rates.

The U.S. economy also led the recovery, and, as expected, the trade deficit has climbed to an all-time high. The dollar should be declining faster than it has, but uncertainties over the strength of the recovery in other countries have kept it high. We are left with record fiscal and trade deficits, record high real interest rates, and an overvalued dollar. Under these circumstances, world and especially U.S. commodity markets can remain depressed until well after the world economy enters a recovery phase. However, moderate growth in the national economy and more rapid growth in the world economy, together with a reduction in our fiscal deficit, real interest rates, and relative value of the dollar, would lead to a surge in the demand for farm products.

World market volatility induced by natural forces or changes in economic and financial policies can be augmented or offset by changes in production agriculture. Weather is the main source of year-to-year variability in production, but prices and policies are also important. Essentially all countries other than the United States use all available resources every year, and use them more intensively each year, to produce agricultural products.

Other than the weather, the United Staes is by far the most important source of year-to-year variability in aggregate world production. Within the last three years the United States has gone from full production to the most massive program to reduce production in the history of the nation. While acreage reduction programs are designed to help stabilize the domestic and world markets, they can be a source of instability.

Bringing new land into production, and using land more intensively, are also sources of volatility in world commodity markets. More land is being brought into agricultural production each year in some countries. The new land is, in general, less productive and more prone to yield volatility than the land already in production. Land used intensively is more vulnerable to production declines caused by drought than is less intensively used land.

Producer and consumer price policies are also sources of volatility in world commodity markets. Some countries permit producer and consumer prices to vary to the extreme; most attempt to keep them relatively stable. The United States is among those which permit highly volatile prices. Those which have a policy of relative price stability force those which permit prices to be highly volatile to make most of the adjustment to world supply/demand imablances.

The world market price for an agricultural export commodity usually is lower than the price or per unit return to the producer, and, therefore, the amount produced is in excess of the amount that would be produced at the world price. In many countries, prices to consumers are lower than producer prices or returns, with the subsidy paid by the government. However, the internal price to consumers usually is higher than the world price for imported commodities.

Many importers, especially the richest and largest, do not permit the world price to cross their borders. Imports frequently are subsidized or taxed to keep them from interfering with domestic prices. Internal prices for imported items are more stable than world prices. The relative stability in internal prices is an important reason for instability in the world price, as the response of producers and consumers to changes in world supply/demand conditions are muted.

Most of the exporters, especially the righest and largest, have policies that protect producers from the extreme volatility in the world price. Some maintain prodsucer prices at relatively high and stable levels irrespective of the world situation, imposing levies or taxes as necessary to keep internal prices stable. Others permit domestic prices to be highly volatile but moderate their impact through the use of deficiency payments when world prices are abnormally low. Some prevent the full return from flowing to producers when world prices are abnormally high. The maintenance of stable producer prices also augments the volatility in world market prices.

Essentially all countries rely on changes in producer prices to induce shifts in production. Relatively small changes in producer prices can induce substantial shifts in resource use, and massive changes induce massive shifts. Producer prices are more volatile when determined mainly by market forces, as in the United States, than when determined by governments, as in the USSR.

When prices are driven mainly by market forces, the normal pattern is for the high-priced commodity in the current year to become the low-priced commodity in the subsequent one. Prices rise or fall more than necessary to encourage or discourage shifts in area and production. At the other extreme, prices too closely controlled fail to send the proper signals to producers, and imbalances among the commodities can persist for years.

For all these reasons, the world market is a highly volatile market. It was more volatile during the 1970s than before, when supplies available to it were in excess of effective demand at prevailing prices. There is general agreement that the world market will continue to be highly volatile during the 1980s. It will be unless effective stabilization policies are embraced.

There is a rich history of fialed international commodity agreements that have stabilization of the world market as an objective. The main reason they fail is that the inherent instability in domestic markets is exported to the world market. That is, they try to stabilize a market that is destabilized by national policies.

There are two broad alternatives to greater world market stability: the many can adopt policies that permit greater internal instability, or the few can adopt policies that will reduce instability. Neither would be effective unless all the major exporters and importers were to cooperate in the effort, and we are told this is extremely unlikely. The other alternative is for the United States to stabilized the world market, in cooperation with as many other countries as is possible.

Because the United States is the only nation that holds land out of production when domestic and world market supplies are large and prices low, and because it is one of the few that permit domestic market prices for the main exported products to vary with the world market price, it is the main shock absorber for the world. The economic, social, and political costs of these policies are high.

Because we are the dominant supplier, we may have to continue to manage supplies, and even more effectively than before, and also to embrace policies that are designed to reduce the volatility in world market prices.

COOPERATION

In addition to being highly volatile and a source of growth, the world market is a source of conflict and controversy. Our food and agricultural policies become more controversial when world market conditions are extreme, as in the early 1970s, when commodity prices set all-time highs, or the early 1980s, when they set all-time lows. Pressures to alleviate the consequences of the imbalance become intense when conditions are extreme, and all too frequently the consequent policy and program changes end up aggravating instead of alleviating the situation.

Great volatility is a source of discontent and disagreement. When supplies are large relative to demand, and the world price abnormally low, the conflicts among the exporters and importers become much more intense. We have attacked our two major customers with renewed vigor over the past three years.

On the other hand, when suplies are tight relative to demand, and prices relatively high, the policies become a matter of deep concern to those who buy the high-priced products, both at home and abroad. Actions taken to ease prices, such as the restrictions on food assistance and the short supply export restraints of the 1970s, become a matter of deep concern to producers and "the trade."

When economic conditions are grim, pressure for import restraints becomes more intense. The case for protection frequently is based on the allegation that import prices are below production costs. Pressures for export subsidies become most intense when world market prices are already below production costs of even efficient producers. Budget outlays for farm programs reach record highs when these condtions exist, just when budget deficits are also breaking records. Funds for development and food assistance become more difficult to obtain. And when world prices are already at a record low, a proposal to reduce our market support prices is given more favorable attention. These and similar actions tend to make the world market even more volatile, and to make our agricultural policies more expensive and controversial.

When world market prices for the products we export in quantity are rising to all-time highs, the pressure for governmental action to moderate the adverse consequences becomes intense. Animal agriculture is subjected to an extreme shock, and subsequently food price inflation becomes an issue. The expenditures for farm programs decline to record lows, but food prices and food assistance program costs rise rapidly. Reserves are favored, but they cannot be obtained. Pressures to restrict exports and relax imports become itense. Agricultural land and input prices rise rapidly and place a new floor under production costs. The fear of a return to below-cost producer prices leads to intense pressure to increase producer income support levels, and those who plead for restraint are ignored.

The farm programs have become more controversial in recent years, and at times have even become a source of greater instability instead of stability in the domestic and world markets. The most frequently mentioned remedy to declining trade shares has been to cut price support levels, an action that would make domestic and world market prices even more volatile in the future. It is virtually certain that more volatility in domestic and world market prices would make the farm programs even more controversial. This would mean more conflict instead of cooperation with our trading partners. On the other hand, greater stability in the domestic and world markets would ease tensions at home and abroad, and create a more favorable climate for growth in U.S. and world agriculture.

POLICIES FOR GROWTH, STABILITY, AND COOPERATION

Over the past decade or so, we have seen the consequences of policies that permit great instability in the world and domestic commodity markets. Nations have lived beyond their means, and later found it impossible to service debts. Incomes have risen rapidly, and have declined. Interest rates have varied to the extreme. The dollar has been weak and strong. We have seen all-time high and low commodity prices, excessive stocks and no stocks, abundant and inadequate food aid supplies, full production and the most massive production control program in history.

Import barriers have been raised and lowered. Exports have been embargoed and subsidized. Reserves have been used and abused. Food price inflation has been high and low. Costs of production have risen rapidly and slowly. Domestic food assistance programs have been expanded and contracted. Landowners have become wealthy, and farmers have been forced to sell to repay land and other debts. Animal agriculture and the agricultural service and supply industry have been subjected to severe shocks. Domestic consumption of food and fiber have surged and declined.

The benefits and the costs of these policies have been high, higher to the United States than to most nations, because we permit more of the volatility in the world market to cross our borders. The controversy over the policies of the nation have led to actions that usually added to the volatility of the world market.

In short, we have policies that keep world market growth below potential, induce greater volatility, and make cooperation difficult. We need policies that encourage more rapids growth in the world market. Greater stability would do so, and greater growth and stability would provide a better climate for cooperation.

Macroeconomic policies that promote steady and sustainable world economic growth will provide a favorable climate for growth in agricultural product consumption and trade. Strong economic growth will also help resolve the financial crisis, a prerequisite to adequate diets in several countries. The fiscal deficit will have to be reduced. Lower and more stable real interest rates, and a weaker and more stable dollar are also essential to strong growth in agricultural product consumption and trade.

Development and development assistance policies should be implemented so that they stimulate incomes growth most when there is weak growth in national production, and least when the national economy is operating close to capacity. A special intermediate credit facility may be needed to help developing countries overcome the financial crisis. The United States should make additional funds available to the International Development Association, so it can go forward with the proposed three-year $12 billion program which will eventually result in increased sales of agricultural products.

Food assistance programs need to be more effectively geared to national development programs. Multi-year commodity agreements are needed, but some funds must also be reserved for unforeseen emergencies. Humanitarian and development objectives should be the dominant ones, not political objectives. The international emergency food reserve should be used when food supplies are tight.

Long-term multi-commodity supply agreements should be widely used to smooth export sales and demonstrate that we intend to be an aggressive seller and a reliable supplier. The agreement should include reserve provisions that provide a hedge against short supplies.

Policies that discourage below-cost export pricing for all commodities and by all countries should be supported, and so should those that encourage trade with developing country exporters. They must be able to earn the foreign exchange they will need to purchase agricultural products from us.

A more comprehensive reserves policy should be embraced, and contracts offered to producers of all the main export commodities, so that we can be a reliable supplier at prices that are fair and reasonable to producers and consumers.

When reserves are adequate, or are likely to be adequate, the secretary should be required to offer a bid diversion or production reduction program, with the contract specifying the reduction in production as well as acreage.

Loan prices should be the main price and income support program. All producers should be eligible for loans on their entire production. Target prices should no longer be used as an income support program. They provide a general subsidy to buyers at home and abroad, mostly to wealthy governments. Instead, the food assistance and special export credit subsidy programs should be used to assist low-income consumers at home and abroad. In addition, the cost of the target price program has become excessive.

The gap between loan and reserve release prices should be narrowed to provide greater price stability in the world and domestic markets. Loan prices for the main export commodities in which we have a comparative advantage, such as corn, should be based on, but slightly below, the actual costs of production on large and super-large farms. The reserve release and the loan prices should be established at levels that will maintain relative stability in real land prices. The prices should be adjusted annually, taking into account productivity trends. The support prices for the other price-supported commodities should be linked to the support price for the comparative-advantage commodities, based on their normal relationship in the market.

Land that cannot stand intensive use should not be eligible for commodity program benefits. Instead, it should be converted to a less intensive use. All the land that is capable of intensive use should be included in the pool of land eligible for commodity progam benefits, and acreage temporarily removed from production through the bid production reduction programs should be taken from this pool. Priority should be given to eligible land that is most prone to erosion. Soil conservation programs should be designed to resolve the most critical land and water problems first.

Farmers with more modest resources and incomes are in need of special assistance to become more efficient, or to depend less on farming. Jobs in rural America are important, and they have been more available over the last decade or two than earlier. Most of those who live on a farm earn more from off-farm sources than from the farm. Rural development policies and programs appear to have been an important force behind the public-private cooperative job creation effort. The return on the investment of taxpayer funds appears to have been relatively high. These programs should be continued, because many now living on farms will have to rely increasingly on off-farm jobs for income.

Special programs to help low and moderate resource and income farmers to become more efficient have been in operation for years also, but they have been limited and appear to have been of questionable effectiveness. The case for an income transfer to those with the potential for growth in agriculture rests both on economic and social welfare grounds. Those who have the potential to increase productivity should be provided special assistance, in the form of either credit, technical assistance, or an income transfer, so that they can augment their resources instead of selling what they own to the large and super-large operators. Community stability will be enhanced if these farmers can remain in farming.

The U.S. farmer generates more income from farming than those in any other country. And those who sell a large and increasing share of all sales have incomes and net worths that are high even by U.S. standards. But the large and super-large operators are also highly specialized, and vulnerable to even relatively modest declines in returns. Extreme volatility in returns can be disastrous. Yet, the case for an income transfer to them is weak. However, the case for market price supports for commodities in highly volatile markets that are based on but modestly below their production costs is strong.

Chapter 7
Future Directions for U.S. Agricultural Policy

Martin Abel and Lynn Daft

INTRODUCTION

The papers in the Curry Foundation study, *Agriculture, Stability, and Growth: Toward a Cooperative Approach,* have focused on the commercial agricultural policy of the United States. This includes domestic price and income support programs for specific commodities (wheat, rice, feed grains, soybeans, cotton, and dairy) as well as export programs (commercial and food aid), all of which are highly interrelated. These programs will be at the center of the policy debate in 1985 as Congress attempts to pass a new Agriculture and Food Act.

There are a number of other food and agricultural policy areas of importance, including domestic food assistance, resource conservation, credit, and research. However, an intensive examination of the commercial aspect of agricultural policy is, in itself, a major undetaking, and the Curry Foundation decided to focus its efforts in 1984 on this area.

In this report, we examine the environment in which agricultural policy will be debated and forged in 1985, some important dimensions of the process whereby agricultural interests will seek to reach a consensus on policy directions for the last half of the 1980s, and a discussion of possible outcomes, including the impact of economic and political forces largely beyond the control of the agricultural sector. This report represents a drawing together of the many threads that have been developed in other papers and an interpretation of their meaning for the future agriculture policy of the U.S. We cite contributions to the Curry Foundation study by noting the author's name in parentheses after citing his argument.

POLICY ENVIRONMENT

Ever since the early 1930's, when government first began to play a major role in agriculture, the development of agricultural policy has been evolutionary. Each successive piece of major legislation has been built on the legislation that preceded it, modified to reflect the changing times and circumstances. Throughout this period, the basic goals and methods of government intervention changed very little.

Will this gradual evolution of policy continue in 1985 and beyond? While no one can answer that question with any authority at this moment, it is clear that we are now at a juncture in U.S. agricultural history where this evolutionary form of policy development cannot be taken for granted as it has been for so long. There are several notable dimensions of the current agricultural policy environment that set it apart from the settings of the past farm bill debates. In many respects, the contrast with the situation that prevailed in the 1973, 1977, and 1981 deliberations could hardly be greater. For example:

— There is widespread dissatisfaction with the results of present policy and a strong sentiment for change. This dissatisfaction is found throughout the industry, including farmers, business leaders, and government policy makers. However, there is little agreement yet over what these changes should be—or even, for that matter, over how much of the needed change is legislative and how much administrative.

— There promises to be far wider participiation in the 1985 deliberations than in those of the past. In part, this is due to the deep dissatisfaction with the current situation and in part to a growing awareness of the potential impact of policy on those industries which service agriculture's input and marketing needs.

— There is also a growing recognition that farm price and income support programs are not the total solution to agriculture's problems. The limitations of these programs in the context of a general economic policy that works against them are becoming particularly evident.

Any debate over public policy is shaped importantly by critical elements of the larger environment within which the policy is being considered. The 1985 farm bill debate will be no exception to this rule.

Thus, an understanding of these elements and their implications for future policy is key to anticipating the direction of that policy. What are the key elements that will influence the farm bill debate? We foresee the following:

- — Production overcapacity;
- — Role of international trade;
- — Federal budget costs;
- — Organization of agriculture;
- — Financial stress in the agricultural sector; and
- — The proliferation of special interest groups with many new participants in the 1985 policy debate.

Production Overcapacity

The U.S. began the 1983-84 crop season with large stocks of wheat, rice, feed grains, and cotton. A combination of the largest acreage reduction program in history and a severe drought in the Midwest took care of the surplus stock problem in short order, except in the case of wheat.

However, the basic overcapacity problem lies in our ability to annually produce more than we can use domestically or export; e.g., about 400-500 million bushels of wheat and about 1.2 billion bushles of corn annually. Thus, in the absence of a miraculous surge in demand, continued poor weather, or effective supply control measures, stocks of price-supported commodities are likely to build rapidly again (Schnittker).

It is generally agreed that surplus production capacity will prevail at least through the remainder of the 1980's, although its magnitude will depend on several factors including agricultural and other policies that affect demand, and exorts in particular. Poor U.S. crops due to unfavorable weather might temporarily alleviate this surplus, but cannot be considered a solution.

Furthermore, the excess capacity problem goes well beyond farming itself. For example:

- — U.S. grain export facilities will operate at only 55-60 percent of capacity in the 1983/84 marketing year;

- — The soybean crushing industry will operate at only 60-65 percent of capacity in 1983/84;

- — Farm equipment sales remain severely depressed, with a large part of the industry's manufacturing capacity idle; and

— Other agricultural supply industries (e.g., fertilizer and chemicals) are facing uncertain markets.

Role of International Trade

Farm exports grew rapidly in the 1970s as a result of rapid economic growth worldwide, rapid growth in international lending, a declining value of the dollar, and the opening of planned economy markets. As a result of these developments, the U.S. expanded its production and export capacity and entered the 1980s heavily dependent on exports. However, the U.S. agricultural trade environment turned decidedly bearish in the early 1980s as a consequence of a deep and prolonged world recession, an appreciating dollar, serious international financial problems for a large number of developing and some Eastern countries, and inflated U.S. support prices.

There appears to be general agreement that U.S. agricultural exports in the 1985-90 period will probably grow at no more than 3-4 percent annually—about the same rate as in the 1960s, but only about one-third the rate of the 1970s. Of course, even with such a slow rate of growth in exports, the U.S. will become increasingly dependent on sales abroad, since growth in domestic consumption of major commodities is unlikely to be much more than 2 percent annually (O'Brien).

The U.S. has a substantial interest in restoring rapid growth in world trade and to maintaining or improving its share of the world market. The developing countries collectively represent the most rapidly growing import market for grains, oilseeds, and oilseed products. Yet, it is this group of countries that now faces serious financial problems and a restricted ability to import. It would be extremely beneficial to U.S. agriculture to return these nations to a rapid economic growth track, and U.S. international economic policies and foreign assistance programs should be directed to that end (Hjort).

History has demonstrated that sustained rapid economic growth and growth in agricultural imports in developing countries requires satisfactory rates of growth in their agricultural sectors. A majority of the population in developing countries lives and works in rural areas and is poor. They depend directly or indirectly on agriculture for their livelihood. When the agricultural sector is growing, rural incomes increase. This increases the demand for non-farm goods and services, stimulating the entire economy. As incomes grow, people want to eat more and better food—i.e., upgrade their diets. In the process, the demand for meat, poultry, eggs, and dairy products increases, as does the demand for feedstuffs to produce these products. Developing countries that have experienced rapid economic growth (e.g., South Korea, Taiwan, Hong Kong, Singapore, Malaysia) have become major markets for U.S. feed grains, soybeans, and soybean meal as well as for other agricultural products. Thus, U.S. agriculture should not fear agricultural development in developing countries. On the contrary, we should welcome it, since it is in the best interest of U.S. agriculture (R. Paarlberg).

Beyond stimulating growth in total world agricultural trade, the U.S. must be prepared to compete in a highly competitive world market. The policy implications of this imperative are the need to develop a comprehensive agricultural trade policy that:

— Identifies U.S. interests and furthers those interests in a competititve marketing environment;

— Links agricultural trade and domestic farm policies in ways that ensures they are consistent and mutually supportive; and

— Recognizes the impact of economic policies on trade through high interest rates and a strong dollar, and is able to offset the adverse effects of these policies (O'Brien).

Maintaining U.S. competitiveness in world markets will almost certainly be a key consideration in the design of the next farm bill.

Policies to get the world economy moving again, especially in the case of developing countries, are generally outside the realm of agricultural policy. However, U.S. agriculture has an important stake in pushing for such policies.

There has been considerable attention devoted in the papers in this study to the prospects for improving trade relations and of integrating trade strategies among exporting nations (Schnittker, Katz, Hajda). Prospects for multilateral agricultural policy coordination are bleak. So, too, are commodity agreements involving cooperation among exporters or among both exporters and importers.

Yet even in a highly competitive world, there are limits to what are considered forms of acceptable competition, and there is a high degree of cooperation among most countries as represented by the workings of the IMF, the World Bank, and the GATT. The first two organizations are playing critically important roles in solving the debt problems of developing countries and trying to get these nations back on a growth path. The GATT has played a major role in trade liberalization, and has a role to play in fighting growing protectionism, improving trade rules, and fostering trade expansion. U.S. agriculture would benefit from a healthier trade climate and it is in the U.S. interest to exercise strong leadership to improve the world trade climate (Katz, Hajda).

Federal Budget Costs

A large and rapidly growing Federal budget deficit and the relationship of this deficit to the health of the general economy has created a climate substantially more conducive to fiscal restraint. Budget deficits since 1970 are shown below to illustrate how they have mushroomed in the past few years. Projections for the next five years point to further growth in deficits unless drastic steps are taken to limit expenditures and to raise revenues.

Fiscal Years	Federal Budget Deficit (billion)
1970	2.8
1975	45.2
1980	59.6
1981	57.9
1982	110.6
1983	185.4
1984	183.7

The budget deficit problem is long term in nature. We need more than a down payment; we need a long-term "installment plan" to reduce the deficit and in turn to bring interest rates and the value of the dollar down. Expenditure cuts on a broad front will be needed, as will tax increases that do not stifle investment incentives (Lawrence).

Agriculture will not, nor should it, escape the budget cutting process. In fact, agriculture stands to benefit greatly from overall deficit reductions since lower interest rates will not only reduce production costs and ease the financial stress problem in agriculture, but also result in a cheaper dollar that would help promote exports.

Farm programs' budget costs are of two principal types:

(1) *Entitlement,* which includes
- — nonrecourse loans
- — deficiency payments
- — gain reserve (interest costs and storage payments)

— commodity (e.g., manufactured dairy product) purchases

(2) *Nonentitlement,* which includes
— credit
— extension
— research
— conservation
— economic and market information

In FY 1983, entitlement programs accounted for nearly 85 percent of the total cost of farm programs ($22.3 billion). Furthermore, although farm program costs are a small share (about 2.8 percent in FY 1983) of the total Federal budget, they grew much faster in FY 1982 and FY 1983 than any other budget category, and could be at high levels in future years unless something is done to hold them in check.

At the same time that commodity program costs were rising, the cost of many other government programs were being held in check. This divergence will not go unnoticed in 1985 if it appears that farm program costs could resume their upward climb from the FY 1984 level.

Also, the Congressional budget process, which is still evolving, introduces a new dimension to the enactment of a farm program. Not only are the program authorities thoroughly debated within the Agriculture Committee, as they have always been, but the budgetary implications of these authorities are now closely examined by the Budget Committees. One cannot rule out circumstances in 1985 resulting in budget considerations that will exert a dominant influence over the policy that is adopted.

Organization of Agriculture

When the forerunners of modern-day commodity programs began in the 1930s, farms were numerous and relatively small in size; there was not much difference between the smallest and largest farms. Farmers were dependent almost entirely on farming for their livelihood. Commodity programs were justified on the grounds that a large and unorganized sector of the economy needed and deserved public assistance.

The structure of U.S. agriculture is much different today. Of the 2.4 million farms in 1982, nearly 60 percent were small scale operations (gross sales of less than $20,000 a year) accounting for only about 10 percent of total production. On balance, these "farms" lost money from farming and were entirely dependent on income from non-farm sources. Such farms are typically owned by people who wish to live in rural settings, but who do not

Agricultural Commodity Price Support and Related Program Costs, FY 1961-87
(millions of dollars)

Fiscal Year	Total Outlays	Total Receipts	Net Cost
1961	5,757	4,427	1,331
1962	6,081	4,029	2,052
1963	6,340	3,223	3,117
1964	6,452	3,276	3,175
1965	6,350	3,702	2,648
1966	5,835	4,299	1,536
1967	5,748	4,058	1,690
1968	5,938	2,735	3,203
1969	7,353	3,233	4,121
1970	7,048	3,271	3,777
1971	7,387	4,565	2,822
1972	7,784	3,800	3,983
1973	7,757	4,202	3,555
1974	4,824	3,820	1,004
1975	2,874	2,299	575
1976	2,689	1,674	1,014
TQ	948	496	452
1977	6,257	2,448	3,809
1978	11,840	6,216	5,623
1979	9,933	6,361	3,572
1980	10,232	7,515	2,717
1981	12,694	8,700	3,994
1982			11,652
1983			18,858
Projected			
1984			6,765
1985			10,962
1986			10,665
1987			10,300

TQ = Transition Quarter

Source: Budget of the United States Government, FY 1985 and History of Budgetary Expenditures of the Commodity Credit Corporation, 1979 and 1982.

depend on agriculture for their livelihood. They also, in the main, do not need and do not participate in commodity programs.

At the other end of the size scale, less than 5 percent of the farms (these with gross sales of $200,000 or more a year) produce over 45 percent of total agricultural output. These farms, on average, had a net family income per farm of $183,954 and a net worth per farm of over $1.6 million in 1982. They are the major beneficiaries of farm programs, but are generally large and efficient enough to survive and prosper without these commodity programs.

In the middle (with gross sales of $20,000 to $200,000) are about 35 percent of all farms accounting for 44 percent of production—farms that more nearly fit the traditional label of "family farms." These are the farmers who most need and benefit from commodity programs; many of them would have a hard time surviving without these benefits (D. Paarlberg and Gardner).

As future farm policy is debated, it will be clear that very small farmers don't need or use commodity programs, and that large farmers, who are well off by almost any measure, reap the lion's share of government program benefits. Equity considerations will therefore loom large in policy discussions when it comes to programs that primarily help large farmers. Furthermore, many of the commodity program benefits are indirect, going beyond cash payments to producers. Thus, there is a growing sentiment to target at least a portion of program benefits to those who need it most: primarily, small to medium size farms with limited resources, and new entrants to farming.

Financial Stress

The expectation that the high farm prices and incomes of the 1970s would persist indefinitely caused farmland values to rise sharply. From 1972 through 1979, real capital gains on farm real estate were $447 billion (in 1983 dollars). However, lower prices and incomes have reversed this trend, resulting in real capital losses in farm real estate of $149 billion from 1980 through 1983, eroding about one-third of the gains made in the 1970s.

For heavily indebted farmers and the banks serving them, reduced cash flow and shrinking asset values pose a significant problem, and the threat of the situation growing worse is very real. Furthermore, the indebtedness problem is concentrated on large farms. Of those farms with sales of $200,000 a year or more:

— 19 percent have a debt-to-asset ratio greater than 70 percent;

— 44 percent have a debt-to-asset ratio greater than 40 percent; and

— farms with debt-to-asset ratios greater than 40 percent account for 71 percent of debt on farms in this sales class but only 36 percent of assets.

Clearly, low farm prices and incomes have intensified the degree of financial stress in agriculture. But there are other characteristics of the financial stress problem that are important (Boehlje):

— Farmers as a group have a much higher debt-to-income ratio now than they did in the past. This measure is relevant to how much cash farmers have to service debt. The overall debt-to-income ratio incresed from less than 1 in 1950, to 2 in 1960, to over 3 in the early 1970s, to 8 in 1980 and to 10 in 1983/84. Today, the average farmer is trying to support ten dollars of debt for every dollar of income.

— Debt today has a much shorter maturity. Maturities on a great deal of real estate debt has moved from 20-25 years in the 1960s and 1970s to 10-15 years or less today, and the annual principal repayment of these loans has increased.

— Farmer assets are very illiquid today. In 1950, the average farmer had 27 percent of his assets in liquid form—financial assets and crop and livestock inventories. Today, on average, farmers have only 11 percent of their assets in liquid form.

— While agriculture has always been risky, there has been a tendency in recent years to shift responsibility for the management of that risk to the private sector; e.g., mooving from government to private crop insurance. And, the management of that risk has been made more difficult by declining asset values.

— With declining asset values, it has become very difficult for farmers to deal with cash flow problems by refinancing debt, as they did in the late 1970s. Therefore, farmers today face a new form of risk—collaterial risk.

— Finally, farmers must manage their debt problems today in an environment of high and unstable interest rates, which presents agriculture with a new form of risk.

Price and income support policies can help farmers deal with financial stress, but only in a small and temporary way. In the main, the financial stress problem will have to be dealt with on its own terms. Furthermore, efforts to deal with agriculture's financial problems through price and income support programs are highly inefficient in that those most in need receive only a small share of the help—i.e., benefits of price and income support programs cannot be effectively targeted on those farms with serious financial problems.

Though Congress has begun to focus on the financial stress problem, it is unlikely that it will enact legislation in 1984.

A Growing List of Participants

The number of participants in the 1985 farm bill debate promises to be much larger than it has been in the past. The depressed state of agriculture together with the dramatic acreage and price swings in 1983 (caused in large measure by the PIK program, but by drought as well) alerted many participants in the food system to the importance of government policies ands programs. These groups have indicated that they intend to be involved in the 1985 debate, although their precise role is unclear at this time.

The potential list of new participants is quite long, including:

— Livestock and poultry producers who are affected by wide swings in feed prices;

— Fertilizer, chemical, and farm machinery manufacturing firms supplying agriculture, whose corporate profitability is dependent upon crop acreage and farm income;

— Food processors and manufacturers, who are the major users of agricultural products;

— Exporters of U.S. farm products, most of which now have substantial excess capacity; and

— Various financial institutions serving agriculture that are confronted with farmers' financial problems.

A larger number of participants will broaden the focus of the farm policy debate by interjecting new concerns that go beyond those of the traditional commodity groups. It may also make the debate less manageable, since more interests are harder to deal with politically than a narrower range.

CONFLICT RESOLUTION

The policy process involves resolving conflicting interests to the satisfaction of a majority of the Congress and the Administration. The conflicts inherent in the 1985 debate are more numerous and more intense than they have been in many years. Furthermore, these conflicts are not limited to the traditional agricultural agenda; they also involve economic policy and budget considerations. Some of the key conflicts are highlighted below.

High on the list will be a clash between the need to reduce budget deficits sharply and the desire on the part of some agricultural interests to improve the economic situation in agriculture by maintaining large government expenditures. One cannot rule out the possibility that budget costs will be found to be of such importance that an expenditure cap is applied to farm programs. This would effectively remove farm programs from their present entitlement status and force the Secretary of Agriculture to determine how best to spend a fixed budget in pursuit of Congressionally mandated objectives.

Another major conflict could be between economic and agricultural policies. If the former continue to result in a strong dollar and high interest rates—both having a highly deleterious effect on the farm economy—agricultural policy will have to adjust to these unfavorable forces. It is unlikely that the tail (agriculture) can move the dog (economic policies).

Some agricultural interests will argue for tight or even mandatory supply controls and high prices, while others will argue for a more market-oriented set of policies that keeps prices low so as to avoid encouraging more production and to improve the U.S. competitive position in world markets. The first approach will reduce export prospects unless offset by large export subsidies, while the latter could bump against budget constraints. The second approach works against a price-income solution to the price and income problems of agriculture, and would restrict future growth in land (asset) value, thereby exacerbating the farm financial problems described above.

Those directly affected by extreme financial stress (farmers and bankers) might argue for a larger government role in dealing with the problems, but if that aproach involves government spending more money it will be confronted by budget realities. Others will argue that the financial stress problems cannot be solved by government and will have to be dealt with primarily by farmers and the financial institutions that serve them.

It is also possible that conflicts among commodity groups could intensify, thereby limiting cooperation among them. In the past, price, income, and export policies have been quite similar for the major crops. These policy similarities resulted from (a) common objectives and problems, and (b) a sense of need to cooperate or, at least, not to oppose others. This situation could change. A seriously restricted budget for price support programs that also limited the entitlement nature of these programs could pit commodity groups against each other in a fight over who gets the most money. Secondly, preferred policy approaches could differ widely among commodity groups, with some favoring more marketed-oriented policies and others prefering greater government control over production and prices.

This list of possible conflicts is not meant to be exhaustive, but to illustrate the difficulties that lie ahead in fashioning a reasonably coherent and workable set of agricultural policies in 1985. The problems involved could, in fact, be even greater than this list implies when one considers other possible conflicts, such as those between funding food assistance and price-income support programs.

MOVING TOWARD A CONSENSUS

The extensive dicussions of agricultural policy based on the papers and two conferences sponsored by the Curry Foundation involved a broad range of views from the agricultural, business, and academic communities. There were areas of consensus as well as areas of disagreement. Don Paarlberg has prepared a good summary of these views, and the highlights of his points are worth repeating.

There was general, though not unanimous, agreement on eight points:

— U.S. agriculture will face a period of abundance and excess capacity for some time, years of poor crops aside.

— Rapid growth in exports will be required for the U.S. to use its production capacity fully.

— Cartels or other formal arrangements to organize world trade or coordinate agricultural policies among nations hold little promise; however, more informal forms of international cooperation and consultation are both desirable and feasible.

— There is a growing concern over high farm program costs.

— There is general dissatisfaction with current programs.

— There is a need for some trade-off between stability and flexibility in policies and programs.

— Deep and sustained cuts in production are disliked.

— Agricultural development in developing countries is, on balance, good for U.S. farmers.

Four approaches representing relatively significant departures from history were seriously considered, although no general agreement was reached on them. These include:

— A trade-based policy that would try to deal in a coherent way with a variety of issues, including: some form of collaboration with other exporters; confrontation of the European Community; funding of international agricultural development; stock holding; export subsidies; expanded food aid; and fighting protectionism in the U.S. and abroad.

— Focus agricultural benefits on the "family farm," defined as farms with annual sales in the $20,000 to $200,000 range.

— Farm programs should be designed to better promote sound soil conservation practices.

— Government programs should be focused more on farms in financial trouble.

A number of radical innovative proposals were presented. They were not dealt with in any great detail because it was felt that they were too extreme to be given serious consideration in 1985. These included:

— Termination of all commodity programs.

— Mandatory production controls.

— Withdrawal of tax subsidies in agriculture.

— A shift away from commodity programs to an income insurance approach.

— Development of human resources to make farm and rural people more employable in the non-farm sector.

— Suggestions for political reform that included: granting the Secretary of Agriculture more discretionary authority over policy; creating an Independent Board to regulate agricultural policy; and changes in the Executive Branch to broaden the base for food and agricultural policy making.

As this summary reveals, the various participants in the agricultural policy process do not yet have a working consensus on agricultural policy, although there are some aspects of policy where a consensus appears feasible. There is still time to develop broad agreement, but reaching such a consensus will be neither easy nor inevitable.

FUTURE POLICY DIRECTIONS

As always, the direction farm policy takes will depend importantly on the economic and policy environment prevailing at the time the next farm bill is debated. As our description of the forces that are likely to be at work in 1985 suggests, it is too early to predict what will happen.

To provide some direction, however, we outline two extreme cases, recognizing that many possibilities lie between. These extreme cases are meant to illustrate how the resolution of the conflicts described above is likely to respond to different political and economic climates. The "extreme case" framework also marks some key indicators of future farm policy direction that can be tracked during the remainder of 1984 and into 1985 as a means of gauging the direction of the outcome.

Best Case Scenario

Under our most optimistic scenario we assume that the following trends are encountered going into 1985, and that there is general agreement then that these trends will continue through the latter part of the 1980s:

— Falling interest rates and a declining value of the dollar;

— Increasing exports;

— Rising farm prices and incomes; and

— Declining farm program budget costs.

In such an environment, there would be little pressure for radical or major changes in farm policy. Most of the focus would be on correcting faults in current legislative authority, in light of the experience of the last few years, and would include:

— Retaining loan rates but making them more flexible, so they can respond to broad movements in market prices;

— Keeping the target price concept but making it more flexible too, and possibly targeting the benefits more to "family farms";

— Retaining but tightening acreage diversion procedures to make them more cost-effective; and

— Providing for multi-year acreage diversion programs on marginal acreage to better meet soil conservation requirements.

In the context of our best case scenario, the farm policy debate and the policy changes that result from it would be in the evolutionary tradition of farm policy. The debate would be intense, but it is also likely to be manageable and produce changes generally acceptable to the broad agricultural community.

Worst Case Scenario

Under this extreme, the economic and political climate in 1985 would be as follows:

— Commodity prices weak;

— Farm income declining or at least showing no immediate prospect of improving;

— Interest rates and the dollar remaining high;

— Export prospects unimproved; and

— Farm program budget costs threatening to rise sharply and remain at high levels.

In this kind of environment, the debate in farm policy would likely be extremely contentious and divisive. And the outcome would be highly uncertain. Changes listed above under the best case scenario will be seriously considered and have a good chance of being made under the worst case situation. But the debate would also focus on a number of difficult dilemmas:

— Providing farm income support while at the same time controlling or reducing budget costs;

— Supporting prices without undermining competitiveness in world markets;

— Allowing assets values to seek an equilibrium with expected earning capacity without major disruption in the farm credit market;

— Limiting government payment benefits while providing an incentive to participate in voluntary supply-control programs; and

— Administrative discretion over farm policy versus providing legislated direction.

Under the worst case scenario, we can see several possible policy directions in 1985, none of which can be predicted at this time:

— The budget crunch precedes and overwhelms the farm policy debate with severe financial constraints providing *de facto* direction to agricultural policy. In its extreme form, a new farm bill would be highly desirable but not necessary, since one could live with the permanent, high price-support authority (1949 Act); there would not be enough money to enforce the higher price supports provided in permanent authority effectively.

— Agricultural interests would be bludgeoned into accepting major reforms in farm legislation—i.e., they would be forced to settle for whatever they could get.

— Necessity could produce creativity, and some new and workable approaches to farm programs might result.

Which of these extremes or the many other outcomes that lie between them are we likely to encounter in 1985? We don't know, and neither does anyone else. At the time this is written, the best case scenario sounds unrealistically optimistic. Interest rates are rising, the value of the dollar remains high and shows no signs of declining soon, and the financial problems facing a number of developing nations remains serious. Farm program budget costs should be significantly lower in FY 1984, though the relief could be temporary; this is especially true if 1984 crops are large, which can not yet be forecast with any accuracy. And while commodity program costs are expected to be sharply lower, the overall Federal deficit remains very large.

At the same time, we do not expect these conditions to prevail indefinitely. Eventually, the Administration and the Congress must face up to the task of bringing the Federal budget more nearly under control. (Perhaps the 1984 election will provide such a mandate.) When they do, we expect an easing of interest rates and a gradual decline in the value of the dollar. Though this will not in itself return exports to the rapid growth of the 1970s, it will at least begin to restore U.S. competitiveness and reverse the present down-trend. Likewise, crop shortfalls in the U.S. or major producing areas abroad are always possible. Thus, a move toward the best case scenario is plausible.

What we are most likely to encounter, of course, is a condition somewhere between the two extremes we have described, with some favorable and some unfavorable trends.

Appendix One
Comments at Conference

Robert Z. Lawrence
Brookings Institution

It is indeed true that today, more than ever before, agriculture and the risk of the macro-economy are highly interdependent. Therefore it is appropriate, I believe, that we begin this conference by examining the general macro-economic context within which agricultural policies have to be implemented.

Agriculture is clearly important for the general economy. It is an important source of exports. Commodity prices have had a major effect both on the inflationary spiral in the 1970s and in the disinflation in the 1980s. Also, the agricultural sector involves considerable government spending and therefore affects our current budgetary situation. However, the feedback from the economy in general onto the agricultural sector is even more powerful. We have only to think of the impact of interest rates, exchange rates, of the growth in protectionism and indeed of the general budgetary situation, to realize the constraints the general economy places on the scope for agricultural policy.

Our current economic situation is really the predictable result, I would argue, of the policies that the United States has pursued over the last few years. Therefore I would like to begin by addressing the way in which Reaganomics has operated in general, and draw out some of its implications for the agricultural sector.

When President Reagan came to office, the U.S. economy was faced with a number of problems: high interest rates and extremely high inflation rates, several years of slow economic growth and low productivity.

The Reagan strategy involved a two-pronged attack. The Administration supported the actions by the Federal Reserve to constrain monetary growth in an effort to bring down the rate of inflation. And growth was stimulated by an extensive program of tax cuts. Thus, we would simultaneously achieve low inflation rates and sustained economic growth. It didn't quite work out that way. Firstly, the policies were implemented in a stepwide way rather than simultaneously. Monetary policy became extremely contractionary in 1980 and 1981 and as yet the expansionary tax cuts had not taken effect. Therefore, a recession ensued, accompanied by high interest rates. Toward the middle of 1982, however, the Federal Reserve reversed its economic policies and relaxed monetary growth, and at the same time the second installment of the tax cuts came on board. By 1983 we had a robust recovery in place, and indeed today we find an economy that from a short-range perspective is doing exceedingly well. Inflation has come down. The consumer price index, which ran at about 12.6 percent in 1980, registered a 3.3 percent rise in 1983. It appears that the Administration has met the objective of controlling inflation and reducing the inflation rate.

But this has not been a miracle. It has been a difficult accomplishment. And the results are the predictable results of three years of recession. There is no surprise on the inflation front. We applied the well-known inflation remedy of restrictive monetary policy and we got the expected results. At the same time we have had strong economic growth and have decreased the unemployment rate to the mid-7 range which had been in effect when President Reagan took office.

The prospects for the immediate future also look rather good. Forecasters see real Gross National Product rising somewhere in the order of 4, 4½, 5 percent, and the economy in the first quarter of the year has been even stronger. The inflation rate as yet does not appear to be moving much more rapdily than one would have expected given the degree of recovery. I believe that we will confront major economic difficulty in the future. Unlike the problems of the 1970s—for example, the oil shocks, the crop failures, the acts of God and others—our economic difficulties today, in my judgment, are attributable to our own policies and can therefore be remedied by our own policies. The recovery has been unusual, and indeed the profile of our economic recession has been unusual. Partly this reflects the mix of policies which we have used. Tight monetary policies which raise interest rates combined with large fiscal deficits to send the government into capital market to borrow and further raise interest rates, thereby giving us extraordinarily high real interest rates. Hence the recovery has a somewhat different profile from normal.

Industries which are highly sensitive to interest rates were particularly affected in the course of the recession. Among those are, of course, the agricultural sector, the durable goods sector, the automobile industry, investment, and housing. In the course of the recovery we have seen some of these sectors come back and others unable to do so. It is quite remarkable if we look at how the manufacturing sector has fared during the recovery. Despite the high real interest rate, the manufacturing sector appears to have been able to enjoy a relatively normal recovery. In the first year of a typical postwar recovery, the manufacturing sector in the U.S. economy has grown at a rate which averages 14 percent. Over the first year of this recovery the manufacturing sector grew at 16.3 percent. The increase in employment in manufacturing of 5 percent in this recovery is typical of growth in the average postwar recovery. The performance in manufacturing is quite remarkable considering that the rise in the exchange rate has eroded the price competitiveness of American manufactured goods. However, I believe that the manufacturing sector's strength comes from two sources. Firstly, from the high defense expenditures, which have provided an offset to the impact of the high interest rates and the strong exchange rates. Secondly, and more recently, there has been an apparent increase in investment, particularly in equipment, which I think is attributable to tax policies.

But American agriculture has not had the offsetting sources of strength, and indseed has uniquely felt the effects of the high real interest rates and the strong exchange rate. These factors have led to the depressed commodity price picture in general. There are supply side stories in agriculture's problems, but the demand side is playing an extremely important role.

Another unusual feature of the recession was its global nature. We have had recessions in the past in which a depressed American economy was lifted to some degree by the strong world economy. That is not the situation today. The U.S. economy leads the recovery and other nations lag behind. In particular, the developing economies—partly through their own policies, but primarily, I would suggest, because of the global economic environments—have found themselves constrained in their ability to service their debts. They now face rising interest rates, which bring their debt situation into the headlines and present and additional constraint for making government policy.

We do have a deficit problem, yet today the situation is different because the deficit is structural. It is not simply due to the fact that we have a weak economy. We had relatively large deficits in the past, but with somewhat over-optimistic forecasting, we could at least convince ourselves that with recovery the deficits would return to somewhat sustainable levels. Our best current estimates suggest that deficits will persist (even if the economy reaches levels of full employment by 1987) at a level of approximately 5 percent of Gross National Product.

So what? Why can't we just allow the deficit to sustain the recovery? Indeed, I think that some of the problems facing us stem from the fact that we have perhaps exaggerated or mis-specified the nature of the problems presented by the fiscal deficit. I don't believe in the short run that the strength of the economy and the size of the deficit would lead to interest rates so high that they would in turn choke off the recovery. I think that the deficit itself is a major stimulus to the economy.

However, high interest rates mean that certain sectors in the economy will be smaller than they would otherwise be. Those dependent upon the long-range investment, the housing industry, and (I would add) the tradeable goods sector, all American industry and farms that compete in international trade, will tend to be smaller and have a smaller share in the recovery than if it were a more balanced once. The size of the deficit is such that the federal government will be taking almost two-thirds of the net national savings of this economy. Therefore, we will have to cut back on capital formation in the economy with a consequent impact on productivity, or we will have to borrow the money from foreigners to use for investment. Both will entail a decline in living standards.

The high real interest rates create problems for the developing countries, the agricultural markets, the other major exporters in the economy, and the banking system. On that score alone, I believe it is important for the United States, the wealthiest country in the world, to become a source rather than a drain on savings to the rest of the world.

A second major problem caused by the deficit, and one that I think has not been sufficiently appreciated, is that we have no effectively lost fiscal policy as a tool of economic stabilization. In 1980 supply siders and monetarists implemented Reaganomics and clearly demonstrated how well Kenyesian policy works. For the first time tax cuts were used to take the economy out of the recession; we witnessed the powerful stimulus of fiscal policy. If, however, we think about our current situation, with deficits of the magnitude that we now have, let's ask ourselves what happens if perchance the U.S. economy should go into another recession in a year or two. The deficits are forecasteds to be about $2 hundred billion under scenarios of strong growth. If we moved into a typical postwar recession with about 2-2½ points of unemployment, we would see the deficit increase to $400 billion. Now we have to ask: what will get us out of this recession? Could a Congress move to increase government spending or to reduce taxes in the face of the already staggering size of the deficit? I believe not. During the postwar period we have been able to apply fiscal stimulus, albeit sometimes poorly timed, because it has been in the context of a declining share of government debts in Gross National Product. The current forecasts, however, are for a rising share of government debts to government expenditures of extraordinary magnitude. The government debt was $716 billion in 1980. It is moving to 1½ trillion this year, and by the end of the decade it will stand at 2.8 trillion. In this context I think we no longer have fiscal policy as a stabilization tool. Therefore, our ability to move the economy out of the next recession will depend entirely on Federal Reserve monetary policy. I believe that the Federal Reserve will not be prepared to rescue the economy willingly. So I see, then, an imperative to act on the deficit problem. I will not go into great detail in describing where those deficits come from, but will limit myself to a few points.

First, contrary to popular perceptions, the Social Security system, Medicare and Social Security itself, are not a major source of the deficit over the next few years. Spending has increased in those systems, but taxes have been raised to pay for them. Looking at the rest of the budget we find two major sources of the deficit. The first stems from the fact that revenues are down. Of the 3.3 percent of GNP that the deficit will rise, receipts will be down by 2.3 percent.

The second place in the budget is on the expenditure side. It is quite surprising that we haven't reduced our spending at all. We have changed the mix of spending. We have cut non-defense expenditures of the government, and we have offset that by a rise in Defense expenditures. Thus, expenditures are not by this view a major source of the deficit (although that doesn't mean they can't be part of the solution). Rather, on the expenditure side, interest payments remain the second major source of the deficit. We have a growing deficit because we have such a large deficit. Each year we delay and run a $200 billion deficit financed at a 10 percent interest rate, we add $20 billion to the burden of debt, at least to the interest burden, in perpetuity.

There's been a lot of talk this year about a down payment plan on the deficit, but I would suggest that is the wrong way to go about confronting the problem. We don't need a down payment; we need an installment plan, because a deficit is a long-range problem. The fact that the Congress and the Administration can agree to reduce it by a small fraction of its ultimate size does nothing to convince the markets and investors that we have made a long-range commitment. Therefore, I think it is imperative that we act as soon as possible. We need to reduce spending on Defense and in other areas without inflicting further hardship on the poor. If reducing the deficit requires tax increases, we can try to do them in a way that does not stifle incentives.

Let me say that, as we look out into the 1980s, I think the economy has the ability to enjoy a period of unusual prosperity, provided that we use appropriate policies. We have taken hard knocks. We have brought down the rate of inflation. It does not appear as if commodity markets will provide the same problems for the general macro-economy as they did during the 1970s. Our demographic situation has improved. We have absorbed a huge proportion of the baby boom generation in the labor market. I believe that our problems are of our own making, and so too are the solutions. It is important then that in your deliberation your bear in mind the crucial importance of the deficit problem. In the agricultural policies to be implemented over the next few years, there is going to be very little room for maneuvering. Agriculture will have to make its contribution to reducing the deficit as well.

Appendix Two

Agricultural Policy and Financial Stress: Further Comments

Michael Boehlje
Iowa State University

Many farmers are currently facing severe financial stress resulting in asset liquidations, problems in obtaining credit, and even bankruptcy. An important question in policy analysis is the applicability of traditional farm policy approaches to the problem of financial stress in agriculture. This is a particularly relevant question, for the 1983 PIK program was one of the most expensive and largest government transfer programs for agriculture in recent history (by some estimates approximately $12,000 of income transferred per farm), and yet many farmers are still facing severe financial stress.

To evaluate the relevance of farm income and price support programs to the current financial problems in agriculture, it is important to understand the broader dimensions of today's "farm problem." Clearly, farm incomes are lower than they were during a large part of the 1970s, but similar income levels were encountered in prior years without the severity of the financial pressures currently being felt. In fact, there are six additional characteristics of the current financial stress in agriculture, and some of them will feel only the indirect impact of price and income support programs.

In addition to lower incomes, farmers have a much higher debt-to-income ratio than in prior years. For the average farm, the debt-to-income ratio was less than 1 in 1950; it rose to 2 in 1960, to approximately 3 in 1970, and now stands at almost 10 to 1. This means that farmers are attempting to carry a much larger debt load per dollar of debt servicing capacity (i.e., income), which adds to their financial pressure. In fact, to obtain a debt-to-income ratio representative of the mid-1970s would require incomes almost to triple—not a realistic possibility in the near future. Furthermore, the maturity structure on debt has shortened; farmers with lower incomes and higher debt loads are being required to repay that debt more rapidly. Institutional lenders such as banks and PCA's have shortened maturities to reduce their interest rate risk exposure. Although Federal Land Banks and other long-term institutional lenders have not adjusted terms significantly, land contracts, which comprise a substantial portion of farm real estate debt, have become shorter in maturity in recent years.

Another balance sheet adjustment that has occurred on many farms is reduced liquidity. In 1950 approximately 27 percent of the asset base on the typical farm firm was liquid (i.e., financial assets or crop and livestock inventories); in 1980 only only 11 percent was liquid. In the past liquidity provided a safety valve for that farmer who did not generate sufficient income to meet the debt servicing requirement; he or she could sell part of the liquid asset base without sacrificing part of the productive plant—the land, machinery or breeding stock. Today, liquidity is gone—forcing some farmers to consider selling part of the fixed asset base to service their indebtedness.

In reality, farmers dramatically restructured their balance sheets during the 1970s, increasing the amount of fixed assets compared to inventories and other assets easily converted to cash in times of financial stress. They also increased the amount of current liabilities compared to longer term obligations, and thus added to the current debt servicing requirements. Improved farm incomes will help reduce the financial stress in agriculture, but will only eliminate this mismatching of assets and liabilities if farmers use the additional income to either pay down debt or increase liquidity, rather than to purchase fixed assets. Even if farmers use their improved incomes to restructure their balance sheets, the process will be slow—thus suggesting that financial stress will be a long-run problem for the agricultural sector.

An additional characteristic of the current financial stress in agriculture is the increased income and collateral risk faced by most farmers. A significant change in government policy in the 1980s resulted in a reduced safety net for agriculture and a movement to gradually transfer the responsibility for managing risk from the government to the individual farmer. This change in philosophy is reflected in the substitution of crop insurance for disaster programs, the changing role of the Farmers Home Administration, and the approach to government farm programs that provides incentives for participation but is not structured necessarily to benefit those who do not participate and pay the "insurance premium."

Although the income risk in agriculture may not be significantly larger this decade than last, the responsibility for managing that risk is being transferred from the public to the private sector. Some farmers still have not accepted this concept.

In addition to income risk, farmers are now facing collateral risk as well. During the three decades from 1950 to 1980, even when farm incomes turned down, the lending community was willing to extend credit to the agricultural sector because collateral values were stable or rising. A key reason lenders have turned conservative during the last four years is that in addition to income risk, they are facing reduced collateral values and deteriorating security positions. With reason, the borrower who has financial losses combined with declining collateral is perceived to be less credit-worthy than one who has financial losses but stable or rising collateral values.

A further consequence of declining collateral values is that the traditional safety valve of the 1970s for farmers who could not meet the cash flow—that of refinancing—is either no longer available, or is quite costly because of higher interest rates. In reality, the agricultural sector no longer has a financial safety valve; adjustments on the liability side of the balance sheet to reduce financial pressure by extending the terms on the debt are no longer possible for many operators, and liquidity is nonexistent in many cases. Thus, a significant number of farmers are having to consider asset liquidations as a means of reducing or eliminating the financial pressures they are facing.

One of the really critical agricultural policy issues today is whether the public should play a role in asset liquidations, by regulating, monitoring, or facilitating the process. Legitimate concerns have been expressed about the attitudes of some lenders who are encouraging cash sales of assets without recognition of the implications for the producer or the asset markets. Collateral values are declining, in part because of forced sales of assets for cash into an environment where there is no cash. We need to be much more innovative in the liquidation process, and we need to evaluate whether there is something that should be done in the public policy arena (asset and debt restructuring, asset buy-backs by lenders, etc.) to assist in this financial stress environment.

A seventh characteristic of today's financial stress in agriculture is that of higher and more volatile interest rates. When queried as to what is the fundamental reason they have encountered financial difficulties, many farmers responded that they did not anticipate the dramatic rise in interest rates that occurred from the mid-1970s to 1980. A shift from relatively low real and nominal interest rates to relatively high rates is particularly devastating for an industry like agriculture that has a large proportion of its total debt used to finance fixed assets on a variable rate. In other industries with a larger proportion of the debt used in inventory financing, it is easier to adjust debt utilization to rising interest rates. Because of the dominance of fixed assets in the asset base of the agricultural sector, and the necessity to finance those fixed assets with longer-term financial obligations, it has been much more difficult for the farm sector to adjust to rising rates than for other sectors of our economy.

When one views the current financial crisis in agriculture in a broader perspective, it is clear that farm income and price support policy will not alone solve the problem. An income-oriented policy, a policy that focuses on price and income supports, will have fairly minor impacts on financial stress. We do need to have improved incomes for a healthy agricultural sector, but the problem in agriculture is much more complex. In fact an income policy focusing on surpluses and supply control may not only miss the target vis-a-vis the problem, but also—because most of the support will go to larger farms, whereas farms of all sizes are exhibiting financial stress—such a program may miss the target audience as well. A broader set of policies and a broader perspective on the problem are essential to develop an adequate solution to today's financial stress in agriculture.